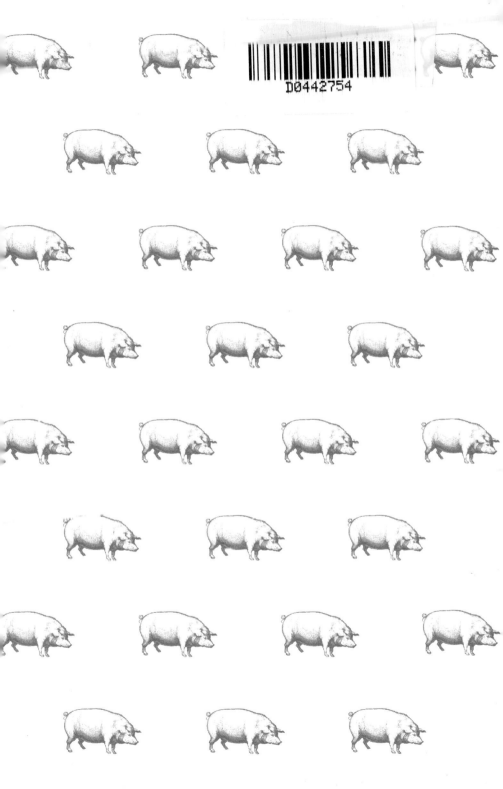

PIG PERFECT

ALSO BY
PETER KAMINSKY

The Moon Pulled Up an Acre of Bass:
A Flyrodder's Odyssey at Montauk Point

The Elements of Taste,
by Gray Kunz and Peter Kaminsky

PIG PERFECT

ENCOUNTERS WITH
REMARKABLE SWINE AND
SOME GREAT WAYS
TO COOK THEM

PETER KAMINSKY

HYPERION   NEW YORK

Library of Congress Cataloging-in-Publication Data

Kaminsky, Peter.
    Pig perfect : encounters with remarkable swine and some great ways to cook them / Peter Kaminsky.
        p. cm.
    ISBN 1-4013-0036-7
    1. Barbecue cookery   2. Cookery (Pork)   I. Title.

    TX840.B3K345 2005
    641.6'64—dc22

                                                                    2004054342

Hyperion books are available for special promotions and premiums. For details contact Michael Rentas, Assistant Director, Inventory Operations, Hyperion, 77 West 66th Street, 11th floor, New York, New York 10023, or call 212-456-0133.

FIRST EDITION

Designed by Lorelle Graffeo

10   9   8   7   6   5   4   3   2   1

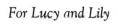

For Lucy and Lily

CONTENTS

ACKNOWLEDGMENTS

IN ADDITION TO THE SCHOLARS, farmers, chefs, friends, relatives, and environmentalists mentioned in this book, I would like to express my debt and my appreciation to my research colleague, Courtney Knapp. Also to my perceptive yet always gentle editor, Gretchen Young, and, equally, my agent/friend/editor, Lisa Queen at IMG, along with Ann Torrego and Sofia Seidner. Also Zareen Jaffery at Hyperion.

Josh Feigenbaum for his company on the road. Likewise Jon and Maggie Taplin. Richard Belzer and Harlee McBride for their friendship and the hospitality of their home in France. Special thanks to Amitav Ghosh, for his encouragement and his counsel. Tom Akstens, Martin Andersen, Jonathan Hayes, Bob Kaminsky, Sean Kelly, Harold McGee, Byran Miller, Richard Redding, Jorge Ruiz, and Frans Vera for their comments, but chiefly to a careful and patient reader, my wife, Melinda.

Finally, to all the pigs who gave their last full measure in the service of gastronomy.

PART ONE

A PASSION FOR PORK

ONE

A PIG'S PROGRESS

So this guy is driving down the highway and passes an orchard. He sees this farmer holding up a pig so that it can gobble apples right off the tree. The pig is going crazy eating apples.

"That's the craziest thing I ever saw," the guy tells himself and he pulls over to the side of the road, gets out of the car, and goes up to the farmer.

"Hey, I couldn't help noticing what you were doing. Does your pig like apples?"

The farmer says, "My pig loves apples."

"Well, if you don't mind my saying so, if you took a stick and knocked the apples on the ground instead of lifting the pig up, you would save lots of time."

And the farmer answers, "What's time to a pig?"

—As told by
Paul Willis, farmer

* * *

AMONG THE THINGS I HAD HOPED to accomplish in my life, chauffeuring twenty-three pigs from Missouri to North Carolina was not one of them. But here we are, three men and a load of hogs barreling down the interstate that runs east out of Missouri into Tennessee. It is late afternoon in late summer, the prettiest light at the prettiest time of year.

Until this morning, our pigs resided in Missouri, at a research facility of the National Institutes of Health. They are part of the U.S. mainland's largest herd of rare Ossabaw Island hogs. About five hundred years ago, the ancestors of these pigs made the transatlantic crossing from the west of Spain to Ossabaw Island, off the coast of Georgia. The Spaniards, descendants of Visigothic boar hunters and swine herders, took pigs along on their voyages of conquest because they loved pork above all other meats. However, no conquistador ever found a good reason to come back to mosquito-ridden Ossabaw. The pigs they left behind, and the generations that followed, rooted around the island all year round.

My partner on the trip from Missouri is Chuck Talbott, a professor of swine husbandry at North Carolina A&T. Along with him is James DeLoach, of the same school. Chuck believes, as I do, that how people keep animals reveals how they think about the land. If animals are merely, and exclusively, expendable things, then so is land.

We have a dream for our pigs. They are going to live outside, eat hickory nuts and acorns, and graze on alfalfa and peanut hay, late-summer greens. They will, I hope, taste better than any other pork in America. And here's the great thing—because of diet and exercise, they should be absolutely loaded with delicious, tenderizing fat that will be nearly as healthful as olive oil! Of course, in the end, just like their less fortunate cousins in the agribusiness hog factories, they will be slaughtered, it is true, but compared with the average pig, they will live longer, free to move about, in natural surroundings, in community with their fellow pigs.

How, you might ask, did a Brooklyn food and flyfishing writer end up raising heirloom pigs in the Carolinas?

The short story is that a trip to Europe brought me my first taste of the supernal *ibérico* hogs of Spain. As it turned out, if I wanted to eat such pork in America, I would have to raise it myself (with some help from my friends). The long version of the story starts, as it does with many obessions, in childhood.

I have eaten and enjoyed pork my whole life. When I was a small boy, my grandma Lena would bring me baseball cards, Tastykakes, bologna, and boiled ham from her grocery store in Kearny, New Jersey. Between my love for her, for Mickey Mantle, for cream-filled chocolate cupcakes, and for cold cuts, my heart was won by anything with pork in it. I loved it, but took it for granted. I became conscious of my soul-to-soul pork connection in one of those moments of clarity that comes when you look back over your life and see a pattern of behavior that repeats time and again. With me, it was the realization that wherever my travels have taken me, I end up seeing if anyone in the neighborhood makes a good ham.

Like a baseball player who recalls every pitch that he hit for a home run, I can recall every time I have tasted great ham. My agent calls me a professional "hamthropologist."

There was the ham I bought in Ste. Genevieve, Missouri, while on a fishing trip for smallmouth bass and staying at a house that was inhabited for many years by a widow with the unforgettable name of Tarsilla Greasehopper. I purchased that ham at a country store a few doors down from the site of John Audubon's flour mill. I noted then that had that enterprise not failed, Audubon might never have taken up his lifelong project of painting America's birds.

As good as that Ozark ham was, the ham that seduced me for life was served earlier in Dahlonega, Georgia, at the Smith House, an Old South restaurant built twenty years after Sherman sacked Atlanta. Amid courses of fried okra, candied yams, crisp and salty Southern-fried chicken, summer squash, collard greens and fatback, roast beef, dumplings, sweet-potato pie, pecan pie, homemade peach ice cream, and iced tea so sweet it made your teeth vibrate, I had what I have since come to recognize as a country-ham epiphany: For a pork lover, the ineffable smoky, salty, funky, meaty mix of flavor from the long-cured hindquarters of a peanut-fed hog is the dining experience against which one measures all others.

You may eat white truffles in Tuscany in October, or their black cousins in Provence in January. You may sip the world's most sublime Burgundy in the aristocratic château of Romanée-Conti, or you may bite into a freshly killed piece of Argentinean beef, grilled over a wood fire on some Andean slope, but I was convinced at that moment, as I remain to this day, that there is nothing more sensorially overloading than a silky, smoky, shiny, paper-thin slice of long-cured ham.

I pursue pork like a detective on the trail of an artful thief. I ask questions of everyone—cops, cabbies, and truckers being notably knowledgeable. Likewise, the guy on the highway crew with the gut that quivers like jelly on a plate as he operates a jackhammer is always a trustworthy authority. When I am on the road in small towns and cities, as I was for years when I wrote for *Field & Stream* and *Sports Afield*, I will often seek guidance from the nationwide fraternity (and sorority) of ham lovers. They are, it seems, everywhere.

In contrast, I have known very few steak lovers to drive across state lines to seek out a particular porterhouse; for a good slice of pizza, you might walk, at most, five or six blocks; homemade chocolate, though pleasantly addictive, does not cause whole construction teams to down tools and wait in line in the hot sun for a plate of bonbons. For some reason, though, good pork has a way of enticing its aficionados that borders on a mystical spell, with long-aged ham exercising an especially potent attraction. Aging endows hams with great character, which can only be acquired over time. Harold McGee, in his classic *On Food and Cooking*, explains the attraction thusly: "Rotten grapes (wine), moldy milk (cheese) and ripened meat (ham) make our lives much more interesting."

I agree thoroughly. In our culture of flash-frozen, vacuum-packed freshness, it is a delightful oddity that it is through corruption—albeit controlled corruption—that food reaches its highest flavor potential. As Jorge Ruiz, an enthusiastic meat scientist I met in the west of Spain, observed, ". . . a great ham, over the year or two of its development, will break down from a simple piece of meat, smelling of salt and blood and little else, into the most complex and satisfying piece of flesh."

Time, and with it, heat, salting, smoking, and cold will produce hundreds of flavor compounds—too many for the layperson to keep straight: amines, ketones, aldehydes, alcanes, aldols, melanoids, and scores of their subsets. Each influences the progression of flavors that begins with the insistent and decadent bouquet that is released into the air when a slice of ham is cut. As the ham comes in contact with your tongue, the punch of salt pushes forward wave after wave of subtler notes—smoky, floral, fruity. Finally, as your teeth come together and you breathe out, you smell the return, only deeper, of that initial aroma of flesh and sweet decay. You would think this last might be off-putting, but in the right balance, it is a heady perfume, just this side of rancidness. Most mammals recognize it as a turn-on. The cosmetics industry may have the consumerist part of your brain believing that flowers and fruit are the odors we find most arousing, but biology tells us that what we really crave is this odor. It is the heavy, pungent scent of another warm-blooded animal, usually of the opposite sex.

A real country ham acquires such character only through aging. Ham, like wine, cheese, whiskey, and good tobacco, needs time to evolve into the hundreds of flavor components that produce the most nuanced and, to my way of thinking, irresistible tastes. To serve a ham before its time is to confuse nouveau Beaujolais with, say, a Corton '59.

A great ham is artisanal as opposed to industrial. It bears a personal style, just like vintage wine or farmstead cheese. It is not just a commodity, but rather something, in its producing, about which someone gave a damn. You can almost taste the caring and the time. They are not merely gifts of nature. They require someone who loves to make them just as much as they require someone who prizes them as food.

A hog must be raised for at least a year rather than the five or six months after which it is rushed to market under the factory-farm system. Only after a year can it develop the skeleton to support the muscle mass needed to integrate the fat, which, taken in sum, makes up texture and flavor. Any younger and you have a piggy veal chop. Pork with character needs to grow up and put on some weight.

Nor, in the case of barbecue, can you rush a great rack of spareribs. You must cook it slowly so that the heat gently permeates the flesh, breaking it down, bathing each fiber in melting fat, absorbing salt, and smoke. True, you can slather on some bottled sauce, toss the ribs on the grill, and have something edible in a half hour, but sublime takes time, at least half a day.

A whole hog, roasted in a pit over peach or hickory or cherry logs, needs a day and a night for the meat to achieve a nirvanic state of juicy smokiness so that the flesh pulls away easily in moist, steamy, bite-size hunks. When you eat such pork, you are consuming a piece of time.

As for pork chops or pork roasts, sadly, these simple preparations are a problem—not because pork is inherently tough and dry, but because modern factory methods and the misguidedly high value placed on lean meat has rushed an insipid product to the table rather than letting the hog mature at a natural pace.

For years, I beat myself up for not being able to fry a pork chop. No matter what I did, I wound up with a piece of dry meat that nearly bounced when it hit the plate. I have since learned that the problem is with the hog producer and not the cook. If you raise a hog properly, you will have succulent, flavorful chops.

My first purchase of a serious ham, one that I would keep for months to use in every recipe as a flavor enhancer, occurred the day after the memorable meal at the Smith House. I was in the pleasant town of Thomasville, Georgia, where my guide, outdoor journalist Aaron Pass, initiated me into the Southern custom of salted peanuts dropped into a bottle of cola, a favorite snack. The old grocery store had a fire-engine-red Coca-Cola machine, the kind where you put your coins in and then slide the bottle out using a mechanism of the same type that nowadays releases luggage carts at the airport. Aaron spied some hams hanging from the rafters. They were wrapped in butcher's paper that was stained by the fat that seeped out of the meat. The wrapped ham was nestled in a burlap bag with big lettering, like you'd find on old flour sacks. Even before tasting the ham, which proved to be spectacular, its wrappers spoke to me. No franchiser, no shrink-wrapper, no portion controller, I thought then, could execute such a homespun presentation. It seemed to cry out, "Here is the real article."

That ham lived up to its promise. For months, I would fry slices of it and then deglaze the pan with black coffee to make the redeye gravy that I would pour over the ham, on a fresh biscuit. Or I would crisp a few slices, dice them, and cook them down with onions, fresh tomatoes, and hot peppers for an *amatriciana* sauce spooned over linguine. Or a few strips thrown in with string beans turned a pedestrian green vegetable into a helping of pleasing soul food.

As I traveled, I found that hams, like fishing holes, roadside diners, and painless dentists, are most dependable when they are accompanied by a trustworthy personal endorsement.

Happily, such testimonials are not hard to come by because I have found two things about ham (also barbecue) to be nearly universally true. First, anyone who has ever tried it loves it. I think it's a species thing; the combination of wood, smoke, salt, and fire always plucks a compelling chord in our recently Cro-Magnon DNA. I say this with the knowledge that there is a lot of humanity that has never, and will never, taste pork. It is forbidden to Muslims and Jews, which makes it all the more remarkable that even though pork gives up a billion-person handicap, "Humans eat more pork than any other meat," according to John McGlone, a professor at Texas Tech who is widely regarded as one of the nation's leading authorities on pork production.

Love of pork among the dining community leads to the second truth that I have found helpful in researching this book. Pork lovers are like people who have had back problems: In the latter instance, every sufferer knows "a really great doctor/massage therapist/chiropractor/yoga instructor." This gifted healer is not only good, he or she is invariably the best. Similarly, whenever I tell someone that I am searching for great pork products, without fail I am advised that a certain smokehouse, barbecue stand, or gas station/convenience store is culinary ground zero in the pork department. Numero uno, no doubt about it.

"No, really, it's the best, here, let me give you their website," they say. These pork lovers have assisted me in the pursuit of a perfect ham, which led me inevitably to the quest for a perfect pig. Notice that I didn't say *the* perfect pig. There are millions of pigs, no doubt many of them lovely, that I will never meet in China or Poland or the Philippines. Given time, and sufficient appetite, I could love them all, but this journey is about how I found the pig that I would spot as my heart's desire, kind of like Tony when he first sees Maria in the dance scene in *West Side Story*.

To maintain a love of pork, however, requires deep faith in our era of dry-as-dust meat whose only flavor attribute is no taste at all and whose sales slogan—"the other white meat"—might just as well be "the other Kleenex."

Thankfully, this exercise of American marketing muscle, which foists upon us the product of factory farms—grim killing establishments that remind one of nothing so much as a concentration camp for quadrupeds—has summoned forth a gastronomic counterreaction. In backyards and stadium tailgate parties, in makeshift smokehouses and storage sheds, in four-star restaurants and truckers' cafes, American chefs and home cooks have sought to resurrect what food traditionalist Ed Behr has lamented as "the lost taste of pork."

Because I love ham so much, and because I love to travel, I set out on a journey in search of heavenly ham. Eight years ago, I tasted one in a small town in Kentucky. As I think back on it, that encounter really started me on my quest, transforming me from a casual ham tourist into a pork pilgrim. Proust had his madeleine. I had Newsom's country ham.

TWO

THE HAM MAKER'S
DAUGHTER

I like pork chops and country ham,
creamed potatoes, stuff like that.
Redeye gravy. It comes from ham,
bacon too, stuff like that.

—Elvis Presley

* * *

I WAS IN LOUISVILLE, KENTUCKY, WITH time on my
hands. Out of boredom, I picked up the city guide that the Marriott
Hotel chain had considerately left for me. My attention was drawn to
a picture of a *fin de siècle* dining room—all oak paneling and Tiffany
fixtures—at the Hotel Seelbach. The chef, Jim Gerhardt, had, according to the caption, cooked at the James Beard House in New York.

Beard was, literally, a giant of modern American gastronomy. He
stood six feet seven and weighed three hundred pounds. He lived on
West Twelfth Street in Greenwich Village. Since his death in 1985,
his home has served as a dining club–cum–food shrine. When a chef

is invited to cook there, it amounts to a culinary *Good Housekeeping* seal of approval.

I telephoned the Seelbach.

Gerhardt wasn't available, but his second-in-command, Mike Cunha, took my call.

I introduced myself: "I'm a food writer from New York and I love country ham. I saw that you had cooked at the James Beard House, so I figured you were the guys who could tell me where I might find one."

"I have two in the refrigerator, so I suppose I could sell you one. Why don't you meet me at the hotel?"

"How much?" I inquired.

"How does fifty dollars sound?"

"Sold," I said, reflecting momentarily that to anyone listening in, my ham purchase was going down like a dope deal. But the ham, Colonel Bill Newsom's country ham, turned out to be so good that a few slices served in the editor's office at *Food & Wine* magazine got me an assignment to visit Princeton, Kentucky, where the Newsom family make their hams, and where the current ham maker in chief, Nancy Newsom, has a country store, the kind where you can buy sausage, fruit, brooms, candy sticks, and laundry soap.

I had no idea where Princeton, Kentucky, was, but I assumed it was near Louisville. Gerhardt met me at the airport, and informed me that Princeton was two hundred and some miles down the road. "Not far from Paducah," he added by way of clarification, which would have cleared things up had I known where Paducah was.

"If you're going to build a menu based on the specialties of this region, which is what we are trying to do," Gerhardt observed on the drive, "you can't find anything more basic or special than a traditional country ham."

As a fellow ham idolater, I understood his enthusiasm. A country ham, full of the complex flavors developed in the course of aging, is one of the glories of American cuisine. Actually, "faded glories" would be more accurate, because the days of the small farmer or service-station owner having a few home-cured hams to sell are pretty much gone. So are the "real" Smithfield hams that once upon a time were fattened on peanuts and left to hang for a year. Today, by Virginia statute, "Genuine Smithfield hams are hereby defined to be hams processed, treated, smoked, aged, cured by the long-cure, dry salt method of cure and aged for a minimum period of six months; such six-month period to commence when the green pork cut is first introduced to dry salt, all such salting, processing, treating, smoking, curing and aging to be done within the corporate limits of the town of Smithfield, Virginia." Six months, in my opinion, is barely—actually not even close to—enough time to make a great ham.

Also gone, it would seem, are all the hog farmers in eastern North Carolina who used to hog down their peanut fields (i.e., let their pigs out in the fields to finish the harvest of nuts and greens). A hundred phone calls had turned up exactly zero farmers who fed their pigs the old-fashioned way.

Nearly seventy years ago, Rex Stout wrote *Too Many Cooks*, a murder mystery in the course of which his hero, detective/gourmet/orchid fancier Nero Wolfe, delivers an address to a convocation of chefs. His subject: the contribution of the Americas to haute cuisine. Country ham tops his list:

> The indescribable flavor of the finest of Georgia hams, the quality of which places them in my opinion definitely above the best to be found in Europe, is not due to the post-mortem treatment of the flesh at all. Expert knowledge and tender care in curing are indeed essential. They are found in Czestochowa and Westphalia more frequently than in Georgia. Poles and

Westphalians have the pigs, the scholarship, and the skill; what they do not have is peanuts. A pig whose diet is 50 to 70 percent peanut grows a ham of incredibly sweet and delicate succulence, which well-cured, well-kept, well-cooked will take precedence over any other ham in the world.

You would have thought, with the dining revolution in America, that such country hams would have become a high-ticket gourmet item in the way that Spanish *serrano* and Italian Parma hams have. Despite the fact that all three are made from, at best, feed-lot pigs, and more often the inmates of confinement operations, long-cured domestic hams are less available in the American market than are their foreign counterparts. The peanut crop, once the prime source of pig nutrition, is now destined for human or beef-cattle consumption.

But even more significant than the change in the pig's diet, Americans associate ham with fat, so I think the psychological calculus runs as follows: "If I am going to sin and eat a pork product, it might as well be European because that effete and decadent continent is more likely to produce a really sinful sin." In other words, if Americans are going to eat pork, their premium hams will come from abroad but their day-to-day pork will be the conventional lean pork—i.e., as dry as bones—that the industry has put forward to counter the unjustified, bad-cholesterol rap of pork. I say unjustified because where the fat of grain-fed beef is rarely more than 40 percent heart-healthy monounsaturated fat, free-range pork, finished on a diet of acorns and grasses, can have up to 55 percent monounsaturated fat. Such fats, also found in olive oil, help raise the HDL (good cholesterol) and lower the LDL (bad cholesterol).

The American food writer James Villas wrote a piece in *Esquire* in the mid-seventies ("Cry, the Beloved Country Ham") that first piqued my interest in learning more about long-cured country ham. In that article, he sounded an alarm that proved to be false in one aspect but true in its overall perspective. It was his feeling that American country hams were so good (they were) that the FDA and the big meat companies would find a way to put the small producers out of business and appropriate the name "country ham" for a high-priced, third-rate product.

The description he gave of ham making in that article tells the story of the way things were for this spectacular regional product.

In the old days the diet of most hogs included plenty of milk and if possible peanuts for soft texture, and lots of table scraps for flavor, hence the expression "slopping the hogs." Depending on locations and temperatures, animals are generally butchered during the first cold spell, around November and never before. Once processed the huge hams are hung bone side down for at least 24 hours, to allow the meat to drain and cool. If the weather remains cold fine, if not the shanks are wrapped in brown paper for protection against flies or spoilage-causing skippers (insect eggs).

After this initial procedure, the hams are taken down, packed in a salt cure, which might have included other ingredients such as sugar, black pepper or mustard, and left for about a month at temperatures ranging from 28 to 40 degrees Fahrenheit. Then they are soaked in water, hung up again to dry, rubbed in pepper or wrapped to ensure further protection against vermin and insects, and smoked 4 or 5 days over slow burning hickory chips, before being left to hang in a barn or storage room to age under natural or atmospheric conditions for not less than a year.

Country-ham makers still follow the same steps but with a more compressed narrative. They start with leaner pigs, usually from a factory farm. The green ham (fresh and uncured) has less fat than an old-fashioned porker, which means it cannot age as long as ham did in the old days; it will dry out before the flavors mature. As for the danger that Villas foresaw of the big players in meatpacking horning in on the gourmet market, this never happened. Long-cured ham is something the accelerated factory-to-supermarket system cannot afford time-wise. Filling the vacuum left by the lack of country ham, prosciutto, and, more recently, *serrano* hams have captured the premium-ham niche quite effectively.

There are fewer American ham makers now than there were in 1974 when Villas wrote, and their hams are rarely aged as long as they used to be. Smithfield, a name that once meant hams made from pigs raised on peanuts and hung for a year and a day, now means neither of those things, and the fine old Smithfield Company has the biggest operation in the country of environmentally ruinous hog factories.

Newsom's and a few other traditionalists who have found their way into the gourmet back eddies of food culture still exist, but barely so. We Americans have not been raised to treasure ham as the elite food that the Spaniards feel it to be. Where a first-rate *jamón ibérico de puro bellota* (Iberian ham from acorn-fed pigs) might fetch $300 from a public of educated and passionate consumers in Spain, hams such as Newsom's will fetch, at most, $59.95. Iberian ham, as of this writing, cannot be imported into the United States because the immaculate and hygienic Spanish slaughterhouses that I visited were not built according to USDA standards. That Newsom's makes its ham without adding nitrates, a preservative that the USDA requires unless the maker can meet very stringent conditions, and the fact that their hams can age so long, make them both remarkable and delectable, which is how the Hotel Seelbach chef, Jim Gerhardt, came upon them.

"We were tasting as many Kentucky hams as we could. Newsom's flavor profile knocked me out [it is cured only with salt, sugar, and hickory smoke—no pepper, no added nitrites]," Jim remembered. "I called Nancy Newsom and she said, 'You know we have always sold a lot of our hams in New York and California, but we don't get as much call for them in Kentucky.'"

"Why is that?" Gerhardt asked.

"Twenty years ago, a chef came from New York on a ham-tasting tour. He said ours was the best he'd ever tasted and he began to order them and so did his friends."

"What was his name?"

"Beard . . . James Beard," Newsom replied. It was a sufficient second opinion for Gerhardt.

When we arrived at Newsom's store in the pretty little town of Princeton, Nancy, a beautiful dark-haired woman with a quick laugh and a friendly drawl, ushered us in and led us behind the meat counter and into the back room for "a vertical ham tasting." Assisted by Eddie Thompson, who had boned and sliced the store's hams for thirty-seven years, we tried hams that had been aged ten, fourteen, eighteen, and twenty-two months. I had never eaten such old hams; in fact, I had been told that they were impossible to produce because the meat would become too dry and hard. But the Newsom ham house sits near swampy low ground, which accounts for a providential amount of humidity that keeps the hams moist for longer periods of time. All of the hams Nancy offered us were good, but the oldest ham had a complexity of flavor that stood out from the rest.

Having whetted our appetites, we piled into Nancy's pickup and drove to a shady street where lunch awaited at her parents' home. Her mom, Jane, welcomed us in the soft, lilting accent of her native Mississippi. Her dad, Colonel Bill (do something noteworthy in Kentucky and they make you a colonel), was in the kitchen frying up the ham and making redeye gravy.

"You fry the ham steaks till the fat is clear," the tall and lanky old man explained. His chiseled features reminded me of the New Hampshire cliff known as "the Old Man of the Mountain." "Then you add coffee and flour for thickening to make the redeye."

Though simple in the making, in its taste, redeye gravy (so named for the "eyes" of fat that form when dark coffee is added to the pan drippings) is a very sophisticated sauce. The burnt bitterness of the coffee exactly counterbalances the saltiness and fattiness of the meat. It probably doesn't need thickening, but in the South, thickening sauces with flour is an article of faith.

When Colonel Bill had finished his preparations, we adjourned to the dining room, where lunch was laid out on a serving table in a sun-filled nook. The light was diffused through sheer white curtains; the full bowls and platters steamed; the blue of the china plates stood out against the lace tablecloth. Along with the ham and redeye gravy, we ate crisp and tart fried green tomatoes, Sevin top turnip greens (a local variety), sliced sweet onions, and buttermilk biscuits covered with spoonfuls of sweet and flowery-smelling sorghum molasses.

"I suppose you'll want to see the ham house," Colonel Bill said by way of signaling the end of the meal. We followed him through the backyard to what Nancy referred to as his ham "treasury," a building the size of a large garage.

"I was in France during the war," he said to me as we walked. "Saw Europe. Best time of my life." I took his confidential tone to mean that he had raised some hell back then. It was the first of three opportunities he took to share this information. He must have had a really nice time.

We entered the smokehouse. From floor to ceiling, the dimly lit, ghostly room—as still as a choir loft in an abandoned church—was filled with hams, two thousand of them. Like the foam on rows of beer steins filled to overflowing, golden-white and blue molds clung to the hams. The cascade of molds reminded me of a limestone cave, cool and silent, full of stalactites. You find such chambers all through the valleys of the Midwest. Tom Sawyer and Becky Thatcher lost their way in one.

Colonel Bill spoke, not so much breaking the spell as carrying it forward as he explained his ham-making process. In late winter, he said, the hogs are slaughtered and the fresh hams are cured in salt. They are smoked in the spring. The critical steps in their maturation come with "the July sweats," when, during the hot months, the flesh of the ham expands into the outer covering of mold. In the winter, the meat contracts, drawing with it taste-enhancing enzymes.

Interestingly, the other jewel of the Kentucky table, bourbon, relies in similar fashion on the seasons of hot and cold. In the summer, the maturing bourbon mingles with the charred inner layer of the oak aging barrels. Then, in the winter, liquid is drawn back through the charcoal, carrying notes of woodiness and a smooth smokiness.

Gerhardt and I took a ham from the rack and inhaled deeply, almost reverently. Colonel Bill stepped forward, as did Nancy. We smiled at the camera that Mike pointed at us. I still have the picture. The rows of moldy hams, fading off into misty blackness; the smoky wisps from the dying hickory fire; the gaunt old man—it looked like a waiting room for the afterlife.

That was eight years ago. Nancy, now the only woman colonel in the ham business, has divorced and goes by Nancy Newsom Mahaffey. Colonel Bill has since passed on. Eddie Thompson too. As Nancy put it, "I was with him to give him a kiss good-bye when he went to meet the angels." She comes up with these sayings as her natural way of speaking. Old-fashioned, of the country, personal. As for her hams, to this day, they set the bar for America. In Spain, her hams would be a million-dollar business. Here she just gets by.

I get the sense with Nancy and her hams, as with so many artisanal producers, that if the traditionalists can stay afloat and hang on for a few years, the growing movement for quality food will stabilize their businesses. In much the same way, the top restaurants in France have helped the smallest and oldest cheese makers manage to remain afloat.

If the Nancy Newsoms of the world go under, in five or ten years, some true ham believer who has just graduated from culinary school is going to set up his or her own business, painstakingly regathering the knowledge that the Newsoms have had for generations.

We are at a point in culinary history where the promise of a return to the old ways needs to be preserved. Soon the old masters will be gone and, like students of a dead language, we will have to reacquire their knowledge all over again.

Perhaps you cannot see such tradition, but you can surely taste it and feel it. During a meal late last year with my friend Pascal Vittu, an expert in traditional French cheese making, I served him a few slices of Newsom's ham. With it, we savored an Epoisses cheese that smelled like old socks. With fresh-baked crusty bread and a chilled *albariño*, we were adrift in a haze of well-fed well-being.

"My teacher Bernard knows where we can get spectacular ham in France," he said. "There's this cheese maker near Burgundy . . ."

I had heard enough. The promise of great ham, French cheese, and Burgundy on its home turf: I couldn't think of three better reasons for a trip. I did not know it at the time, but it was Pascal's invitation that marked the beginning of a yearlong pork pilgrimage.

COUNTRY HAM BRAISED IN
CIDER AND MOLASSES

I have already expressed my gratitude to Jim Villas for writing the *Esquire* magazine piece that made me a country-ham addict. I am further in his debt for the following story and recipe:

Wilkes County, located high in the mountains of North Carolina, is moonshine territory, although nobody has seen a still in years. Nope, nobody. The county also produces some of the greatest country hams in the entire South, and without question the best country hams are in Clayton Long's ham house at Glendale Springs about ten miles from West Jefferson. Over thirty years ago, I bought hams from Clayton's father ("Mr. G"), and seeing a huge, ferocious dog chained at the entrance in those days, I used to suspect that if you arrived as a customer, the dog was kept chained, whereas if you showed up as a state ham inspector or tax collector, the beast was let loose. Today, there's no longer a "Beware of Dogs" sign.

Clayton Long, like his daddy, is a maverick who would no more compromise the quality of his exquisite hams to streamline and increase the production than he'd neglect the acres of Christmas trees he grows while the hundreds of hams are slowly curing under natural weather conditions in the ham house. Unlike most producers, he cures his with only salt and brown sugar; he uses no preservatives or coloring agents; he wouldn't dream of aging a ham less than nine months; and he refuses to ship across the state line since this would require subjecting his hams to ludicrous federal regulations that might alter quality. If you want a Long ham, you have no alternative but to make a special detour as hundreds of loyal customers do every fall. The reward is not only the finest but least expensive country ham to be found anywhere (about $30 compared with $75 elsewhere for a 16-pound country ham).

I've cooked Clayton's ham every way imaginable (besides simply frying it with red-eye gravy for breakfast), but perhaps the most unforgettable method is this braise using apple cider and molasses. Any fine uncooked cured country ham can be simmered in this manner.

One 14- to 16-pound cured country ham
1 cup molasses
1 cup firmly packed light brown sugar
1 gallon apple cider
3 medium onions, chopped
3 medium carrots, scraped and chopped
2 cups dry bread crumbs mixed with 2 cups firmly
    packed light brown sugar

1. Scrub the ham well with a stiff kitchen brush under running water, then position it in a large, deep, oval pan. Add cool water and let the ham soak for 12 hours at room temperature, changing the water twice.

2. Remove the ham from the pan, rinse the pan well, return the ham to the pan, and add enough water to come halfway up the sides. Add the molasses and brown sugar to the

water, stir as well as possible, then add enough cider to just cover the ham. Add the onions and carrots and bring the liquid to a very low simmer. Cover partially and simmer slowly for 3 hours. Let the ham cool completely in the liquid.

3. Preheat the oven to 425°F.

4. Place the ham on a work surface, remove the skin and all but ¼ inch of the fat, and score the fat in diamonds with a sharp knife. Rinse the roasting pan well after discarding the contents, then place the ham in the pan on a rack fat-side up and coat with bread crumb and brown sugar mixture, pressing down with your fingers. Bake, uncovered, till the crumbs are browned, 20 to 30 minutes.

5. To serve, position the ham on a large, heavy, wooden or ceramic platter and carve into thin slices with an electric or serrated knife.

Serves at least 8 with plenty of leftovers for ham biscuits and other dishes.

* * *

PART TWO

A PORK PILGRIMAGE

THREE

THE BLESSINGS OF ROT

PASCAL VITTU'S MENTOR IS BERNARD ANTHONY. He is known as one of the world's greatest *affineurs,* or cheese agers. I didn't know such people existed, but with the French and food, all things are possible. With a complexion as luminously white as summer milk and a permanent twinkle in his eye, he looks downright cherubic, if there are any cherubs who are sixty years old and who wear rimless bifocals. His art entails taking young cheeses from farmers and other local producers and aging them under optimum conditions—washing them, turning them, sometimes covering them with ashes, and providing whatever additional care and attention they need until they are at the peak of ripeness. Bernard's network of cheese makers also includes some wonderful ham makers.

In the course of an interview with Bernard for a *Food & Wine* piece I was researching, he observed that many cheese makers maintain small farms and use the whey that is left over from the cheese-making process to feed their pigs. They also feed them leftover fruits, grains, vegetables, and dairy products. In the fall of the year, the hogs are butchered at a grand party known as the *cochonnaille.*

Local friends and families come and help with the killing, the bleeding, the breaking down of the carcass, the stuffing of sausages. They
pause for a huge lunch with lots of wine, followed by a washup and a
nap. The day ends with a supper of fresh pork, blood sausages, and
even more wine.

Bernard's friend Pierre Moines is such a cheese maker, and his
cochonnaille takes place on his farm in the little Burgundian village
of Pont Pannis, outside Beaune, where the finest Burgundies are
brought to market. Through an invitation procured by Bernard, Pascal and I flew to Paris, hopped into a rent-a-car, and raced down to
the *cochonnaille*. The pig killing was set for one o'clock. A cold autumn rain pelted the windshield. Nevertheless, Pascal lead-footed us
to Burgundy in record time.

We drove, or, more properly, slid into the slush of Pierre's barnyard. The mud was deep and unavoidable, the kind that gets over
your ankles no matter where you step. We arrived in plenty of time
for the one o'clock pig killing, but there had been a communication
snafu. The pig had been killed at eight that morning, so by the time
we arrived, the friends and neighbors who had pitched in were already fortifying themselves against the autumn damp with lots of
red wine.

In the ancient outbuilding that serves as Pierre's cheese
shop/dining room, a fire blazed inside a hearth big enough to park a
car. Meat and beans and vegetables bubbled in huge black cauldrons.
A foie gras sizzled in the pan, sending up puffs of steaming fat like
tracer bullets kicking up dust. The air smelled of hay, rain, animals,
blood, tobacco, burning oak, the heavy wetness of damp stone, the
grapey fragrance of red wine.

We were fifteen people ranged around a refectory table. Dizzy
with hunger and jet lag, I dug into a plate of roast lamb with a side

of beans, fatback, and tomatoes. The fresh pork would come later, at the evening's feast.

"This room dates from 1629. The Cluniac monks built it," Pierre held forth. With his silver hair and silver glasses, he looked sufficiently professorial to deliver a history lesson. From the neck down, though, he was all farmer, about seventy years old, vigorous and powerfully built.

"The monks were not so monkish," he continued. "They hunted a lot and carried on with the local girls before they were driven out in the revolution."

I am always interested to be in the presence of history, doubly so when the history is one of pleasure, but somewhere between Pierre's discussion of the remains of early Roman settlements on the farm, and his surmises on the hedonistic friars, I began to nod out, so I excused myself and made my way to my bedroom for a two-hour nap.

When I awoke, all was quiet as the rest of the household rested from the combination of labor and lunch. I puttered around the living room. Like all farmhouses in Europe, the room was cold and slightly musty. The bric-a-brac included a number of spears from Africa and a wall of heads, among them a brown bear, greater kudu, Cape buffalo, wild boar, and stag. Scattered about the room were old vinegar bottles from all over France, as well as a number of historical monographs, books, and a beautifully tooled shotgun. I put on a heavy sweater and walked through the fields to what Pierre had described to me as a Gallo-Roman cemetery.

The countryside, its aspect softened by the rain and mist, appeared to be swathed in deep green velour. No doubt the limestone soil accounted for the healthy color, reminiscent of Kentucky, which is likewise favored with limestone geology. As a fisherman, I have noted that limestone streams always support a rich food chain, with trophy smallmouth bass or trout at the apex. Agriculturally, limestone makes for bumper crops, thoroughbred horses with strong bones, and, in the case of Burgundy, splendid Pinot Noir and Chardonnay grapes. On the autumnal hillsides, the golden leaves of aspen trembled in the misting wind.

Back at the farmhouse, Pascal was refreshed from his nap and anxious to see Pierre's cheeses, so we crossed the muddy yard. The barn that houses his aging rooms looks as old and rustic as its companion buildings. Inside, though, the cheese-making operation is modern and computerized. Temperature and humidity are kept at the optimum levels for cheese to age properly and develop flavor. All of his cheeses start from sheep's milk, but depending on what end result he wants, Pierre exposes them to various molds, some wild ones that occur naturally in the air and some cultured ones. Some cheeses he washes in a simple brine, some in lemon juice, some in brandy or marc de Bourgogne (a potent distilled spirit made from the leftover pips and must of the Chardonnay grape after it has been crushed for wine). There were trays filled with cheeses: small brick shapes, little circles, wrinkly pyramids, bite-size squares, each shape a different cheese. Some had fluffy white molds, some cross-hatchings of blue-green mold. The entire assemblage broadcast a complex, slightly rotten aroma. Beautifully rotten, well aged. As Pascal picked up each cheese, he did so with the gentle touch of a bibliophile handling an ancient volume.

We returned to the kitchen to prepare for the arrival of guests and the night's blowout. Pierre's wife, Paule, had begun to slice a ham. It was a little more than a year old, she said. I offered to take over the knife, which afforded me the opportunity to taste as I worked.

The ham smelled as funky as the cheese. It was slightly sweet, with a hint of bananas that have been left in the sunlight on a warm afternoon. Pierre starts his hams by covering them with fine salt for ten days. On the eleventh day, he covers them again with a mixture of sugar and coarse salt (fifty-fifty) and then leaves them for forty days, after which time he washes the rind with lemon in much the same way that he washes his cheeses. He covers the ham with ground *piment d'Espelette*, the hot pepper used in the cuisine of the pays Basque. Next, the ham is smoked over pine. This surprised me, because I was under the impression that the resin from soft woods leaves a chemical, pine-tar flavor. Not so, Pierre says. He prefers it to oak because the tannins in the oak would overpower the meat.

Every French ham maker has a different opinion about which wood to use. Some think oak is the only way to go, others chestnut. Some cover their ham with the ashes of one wood or another, some use lard to retard mold, while some leave the rind exposed in order to attract mold because, they say, that is the only way to develop flavor. All these hams are delicious and all are different, proving nothing about the various methods other than the phenomenon I have observed among flyfishermen who have equal degrees of success— each with a different fly. It's all a function of what you believe in. Faith may or may not move mountains, but it surely produces hams of great sublimity.

"What do you feed your pigs?" I inquired of Pierre.

"Potatoes, root vegetables, the whey left over from cheese making, barley, lobster shells."

"Lobster shells?" I echoed. "Surely *they* aren't farm waste?"

"My chef friends in Beaune give me leftovers for my pigs."

"In other words, Pierre, this pig that we are slicing ate food from Michelin-starred kitchens?"

"Why not?" he asked.

I finished slicing the ham. The crew from the morning's killing and butchering would soon return for the big party. Paule reappeared in a slinky halter-top dress, her strawberry-blond hair pulled back in a chignon.

Paule had started as Pierre's employee, helping with the cheese business. The two fell in love, and appeared to be still deeply in it. She greeted the evening's guests in the anteroom of the cottage while Pierre set up the meal in the main room. He cut a striking figure in his white clogs. These may be standard farmer wear in Europe, but I couldn't help thinking of Hans Brinker in go-go boots.

The guests arrived shivering in the night air, clapping their hands, blowing on their fingers, the subtext being, "A drink would be a good idea right now." Most of them had brought a bottle or two of local wine. Judging from the dead soldiers above the mantel, Pierre's parties feature good wine in big bottles. There were magnums and jeroboams. Nothing less than a *grand cru:* Hospices de Beaune, Cheval-Blanc, St.-Joseph, Pommard. In New York, you would take this as evidence of an expensive wine collection. Here it was just the house red.

The ancient stone walls of the dining room glowed with honey tones in the firelight. Two wrought-iron stands provided a convenient place to warm home-baked bread. Their main function, though, was to prop up two long-handled black steel pans. Such handles allow you to place the cooking surface right on the glowing embers and to fuss with the food—flipping and rolling the ingredients in the pan—without roasting yourself from the heat. There would be much flipping and rolling, because those guests who were not wine makers or grape growers were chefs and restaurant workers.

The feast began. Pierre fried up a panful of cracklings, well salted and peppered. Hot fat, salt, crunchiness, red wine: all you need to awaken your appetite. Next, blood sausage fried in lard, both from the morning's pigs. The dark sausages bubbled and smoked in the pan. As guys will do whenever they gather around meat and fire, the men poked and pushed and debated the moment of doneness. Once a consensus was reached, Pierre passed the platters of sausage around the dining room, the fat still hissing and popping. Bite by bite, I dipped my sausage in spicy, vinegary mustard.

No sooner were the steel pans emptied of their blood sausage than Pierre filled them once again with lard. Into the foaming fat he placed chunks of fresh pork tenderloin coated with mustard, salt, and pepper. The room filled with the blue-gray haze of cooking meat, the strong, heady aroma that the ancient Greeks sent heavenward to attract the gods to their burnt offerings. We ate the hot pork on hunks of warm and crusty homemade bread. Zeus never dined better.

I own a penknife with a sweet-smelling juniper handle, the only implement I know that gives off the whiff of a martini. Oddly, since we were in wine country, there was no corkscrew except for the one on my penknife. In consequence, Frenchmen, wine makers among them, kept approaching me to borrow my knife. In the beginning, they did their business and returned the knife, but as the night wore on and folks got progressively more lit, they tended to forget to return it, so I spent much of the evening hunting down my precious penknife.

Jacques Lameloise settled into a place two seats to my left. He is the proprietor of a Michelin three-star restaurant in Beaune. Like many chefs, no matter how tony and chichi their dining room might be, he is an earthy, hyperenergetic sort. When he is not shaking and stirring six pots at once, while giving out orders as tersely as an officer directing a firing squad, he talks, laughs, whoops, eats, and drinks in a blur of motion.

Some years before, I had eaten in his restaurant. On that occasion, he uttered the most earthy colloquialism I have ever heard. As the cheese course was being offered, Lameloise came out of the kitchen to make chitchat with the diners. He turned to me and pointed to the Epoisses, which had a rich and rotten bouquet: "Try this one. We say it is *rassé*." Roughly translated, it means "as fragrant as a maiden's ass." Even in the land of Rabelais, I found this a little over the top, but then, I am not from France, a nation that divides the world into two classes: Things You Eat, and Things You Make Love To.

When I had eaten my fill of the tenderloin and then some, Paule set before us a platter of meat cooked in beans. I am usually pretty good at picking out ingredients, and since I am a food writer, this is a helpful talent. I attacked the plate in front of me, chewed ecstatically, swallowed, and pronounced to all, "This is wonderful pork."

"It's *confit de canard* [salted duck leg cooked and preserved in its own fat]," Pascal gently corrected.

Shortly, a dapper Gallic crooner took up his position at the microphone. The improvised stage was flanked by two huge speaker columns. That could mean only one thing . . . French disco! I took the first beats of the drum machine as my cue to catch some night air. Pascal joined me, along with Pierre Anthony, son of Bernard the *affineur*.

The cold was invigorating, and a night's worth of wine drinking had emboldened us, so we clambered up the rickety ladder to Pierre Moines's hayloft, where the hams were kept. Pierre Anthony went first and offered me a hand. His light shone on the carcasses of a rabbit and a rooster hanging from the rafters.

"Aging the meat," Pierre observed.

I breathed in deeply: the sweet reek of aging hams, curing in the open air, the way the Cluniac monks who lived here at the end of the Middle Ages made their hams too. Across the courtyard, we could see the silhouettes of the dancers, moving to the beat, bouncing across the same floor where randy monks had reveled centuries before the invention of disco. No doubt they made hams too.

PORCHETTA, BURGUNDY AND BROOKLYN STYLE

When I returned to Brooklyn from Burgundy I made a note to get Pierre's recipe for chunks of loin in mustard, salt, pepper, and fried with lard. After a number of miscommunications it turns out that the whole recipe is "Combine meat with mustard, salt, and pepper. Fry in lard." Even in this era of cookbooks that dumb down the recipe because common wisdom has it that no one likes to cook a long recipe (and, by the way, I love a nice three-hour recipe: it relaxes me), Pierre's is a little on the brief side.

Still, I wanted something Burgundian with the feel of Pierre's mustardy chunks. I searched and fretted, to no avail. Then one day it hit me. Christophe Barbier would bail me out.

Christophe, a native of Burgundy who once cooked in Jacques Lameloise's kitchen, owns the Verandah Deli, one block from my home in Cobble Hill, next to a pretty little park where nannies gather with their young charges and where singles sun themselves on summer weekends.

Christophe is a French chef to the core. Ask him for a sandwich and he will butter your baguette, season the tomatoes, nicely fold the cold cuts. I told him of the meal and he suggested the following. Basically he roasts a boned and rolled roast the way Italians make their porchetta, but he sticks to more Burgundy-inspired ingredients. With the assistance of his cook, Juan Carlos Avila of Puebla, Mexico, here is the delicious result.

1 boneless pork shoulder, butterflied
1/3 cup garlic, finely chopped
1/2 cup capers, finely chopped

½ cup cornichons, finely chopped

1 tablespoon salt

½ tablespoon pepper, cracked

½ tablespoon coriander seed, cracked

½ teaspoon juniper berries, cracked

2 tablespoons olive oil

3 carrots, roughly chopped

1 cup celery, roughly chopped

2 red onions, roughly chopped

2 cups mushrooms

3 Roma tomatoes, diced

2 zucchini

10 garlic cloves

2 cups white wine

⅔ cup Dijon mustard

½ cup parsley, chopped

2 cups veal or pork stock

1. Preheat the oven to 425°F.

2. Coat the inside of the boned shoulder with the chopped garlic, capers, cornichons, salt, pepper, coriander seed, and juniper berries. Film pan with olive oil and place pork in oven. Roast one hour.

3. After one hour, add vegetables, whole garlic cloves, and white wine and continue to roast for ninety minutes.

4. Remove from oven, coat with mustard and parsley, and let stand one hour.

5. Strain the vegetables and then add the stock to the pan juices. Reduce by one half.

FOUR

REBIRTH

PIERRE MOINES'S HAM WAS THE EQUAL of anything I have eaten in America. Forty years ago, when every family farm put up a few hams to cure, you would have found such homemade treasures— a little more pepper in this one, a little longer smoking in that one— all across the South and the Midwest. It was simply the ham of the region: not extraordinary, but nonetheless superb. That yesterday's regular old ham could be today's gourmet delicacy tells us not how far ham making has come but how far our faithfulness to food traditions has fallen. Good as those hams were in America, and still are in France, they are like charming folk music next to the elegant symphony of taste that the Spanish continue to compose with their beloved acorn-fed pigs.

For years, whenever serious food lovers told me about great ham, they would mentioned the *pata negra*, or black-foot pig, of Spain. They would toss this off in conversation as if it were a given for gastronomic cultural literacy in the same way that art lovers assume you know which room in the Uffizi has Botticelli's *Birth of Venus*.

Never having tasted this ham, I reflexively pigeonholed it, putting it in the same mental bin with Prosciutto *di* Parma, *jamón serrano*, and *jambon de* Bayonne: So far as I knew, it was just another Old World term that had something to do with good ham, small farms, old styles of curing, and tradition . . . a Spanish variant on the Slow Food theme of old, small, and good.

Like a Hollywood agent treading conversational water about a book he has never read, I would avoid admitting that I was faking it by falling back on my command of Spanish. "*Pata negra,* the black feet? Of course that's on my list." No one ever pressed me further and so I remained ignorant of the true meaning of *pata negra* until Pascal and I drove clear across France to Tarbes, a town that has achieved some culinary fame because of the tarbais bean; it cooks up nicely in stews. In fact, the lamb and beans that Pierre Moines had served for lunch was made with these leguminous stalwarts of peasant cookery. Our goal, however, was a farm that raised black pigs.

Once again, Pascal took the wheel, driving into the teeth of a pelting rain moving in from the Atlantic. He conceded to my ill-disguised panic by keeping the speedometer at 95 mph. We sped across Provence, then the Languedoc, to the Gers, near the foothills of the Pyrénées. After driving fruitlessly up and down pitch-dark country lanes for an hour or so, we finally arrived at Château Montus, a state-of-the-art winery built by the visionary and hard-charging Alain Brumont. He is credited with single-handedly elevating the Madiran wines of the region from average table wine to an expertly vinified product that has muscled its way onto pricey wine lists. Château Montus hulks on a remote hilltop, like the cyber lair of a James Bond villain, a combination of expensive wood, stone, and masonry, with dazzling high-tech fittings, all built into the side of a mountain.

Brumont is intense. His shortish hair is unkempt, as if an overabundance of internal electricity had made it stand on end. Like a missionary in a land of nonbelievers, he takes every encounter as an opportunity for proselytizing. He is always selling—his wine and his winery. Although he was leaving for North America at three A.M., he had waited to give us a tour and then treat us to a dinner that featured local pork.

The winery visit underscored a paradigm shift in the wine business. Twenty-five years ago, Robert Mondavi and his son Michael gave me a tour of their facility in Napa Valley. Huge stainless-steel vats and computer-controlled processing attested to Mondavi's modernity. At the same time, Mondavi *père* was quick to point out that his wine was aged in barrels made of French white oak. "Just like the great wines of Burgundy and Bordeaux," he noted with no small measure of pride.

In the intervening years, the Mondavi model has become the template for wine makers around the globe seeking to duplicate not only his commercial success but also his achievement in creating wine that is in a class with anything in the world. Brumont is, clearly, one of his disciples.

Though Pascal and I were dog tired from our trans-Gallic drive, we appeared dutifully attentive during the tour. From a NASA-style control center at ground level, we descended through subterranean levels of crushers, fermenting vats, and finally to a floor crammed full of 225-liter oak casks.

"American red oak," Brumont said proudly. "Just like California."

With the tour completed, we piled into Brumont's car and headed for dinner in the town of Plaisance. Brumont had reserved a table for us at Le Ripa Alta, a comfortably old-fashioned small-town restaurant. Since that visit it has closed, when the owner/chef retired, but it had maintained a Michelin star for twenty years, the kind of restaurant where families might drive for a Sunday-afternoon feast, the meal that is the mainstay of many restaurants in the French countryside.

The chef, Maurice Coscuella, is an avuncular type, a far cry from the classic French kitchen tyrant. He comes from the generation that produced Paul Bocuse and the Troisgros brothers—grand old men now, but revolutionaries in their time. Like them, he had apprenticed under "Le Roi" Fernand Point, the master chef at the Restaurant de La Pyramide in Vienne. I would have been happy to stop at Ripa Alta anytime, but especially so in early autumn when there was wild game on the menu and the first fresh-killed pork of the season.

Coscuella's menu included a soup of celery root and chestnut puree with foie gras slices and pieces of ham; it has since become a favorite for my family's holiday meals sans the foie gras. Next, roasted dove with a giblet gravy and crispy Jerusalem artichokes. For the meat course, grilled pork chops with tarbais beans and marjoram—a succulent, herbaceous recipe, with the deep, meaty aroma of pigs that have grazed on pasture and fattened on autumn mast, my first taste of *porc noir*, *pata negra*, and the juiciest pork chop I had tasted in thirty years, maybe more.

Joining us were Frederico Bonomelli, the owner of Salaison des Pyrénées, a local curing-and-packing operation, and Pierre Matayron, who raises pigs and cattle on his nearby farm. Like many inhabitants of the border region, Bonomelli speaks Spanish, so I did not have to labor at my less expert French.

The *porc noir* that we sampled came from a breed of French pigs related to the *ibérico* hogs of Spain, whose haunches are made into Jabugo ham. I would learn on a subsequent trip, to pig country in Spain, that Jabugo is but one town among hundreds that produce Iberian ham. In the most fashionable Parisian restaurants, though, Jabugo is the generic term for this delicacy.

"Before the Second World War, France had thirty thousand of

these pigs," Bonomelli said. "By 1986, when we decided to open the book again [i.e., began to breed them], we were down to five *machos* [boars] and thirty sows."

"Why the big decline?"

Pierre, who in addition to being a farmer also holds a degree in economics, chimed in. "After the war, farmers opted for quick-maturing 'white pigs,' such as the Large White and the Landrace. In the process, the black pigs nearly died out."

Thirty-five pigs seemed to be too small a breeding herd for reestablishing a line, but both Bonomelli and Matayron assured me that there was sufficient genetic diversity in that number. In fact, the Spanish conquistadores would leave even fewer Iberian pigs at every landfall, confident that when they returned, the fast-reproducing pigs would assure them of an adequate supply of fresh meat.

Bonomelli was a motorcycle racer until a near-fatal accident cut short his career. As Brumont is passionate and loquacious about Madiran wines, Bonomelli is well versed and equally fervent about the many virtues of black pigs.

"We can say there are two races of pig," he said, "the white [the so-called Celtic pigs, which includes all of the familiar American and northern European breeds] and the black [which includes Iberian hogs, some surviving populations in France and Italy, as well as New World offshoots such as the Ossabaw]. The fat of the black pig is naturally rich in monounsaturates, and its diet of acorns optimizes that. When fed the right diet, combined with sufficient exercise, it develops a lot of intramuscular fat. The white supposedly does not have this propensity to intramuscular fat nor monounsaturates. If you feed white pigs acorns, you will never achieve the results that you do with the black." This was a major nutritional claim. I made a note to look into it.

"*Jambon de* Bayonne," he continued, "is like Parma ham or San

Danielle prosciutto. It comes from white pigs. I think of it like white wine, if you will. The ham from the black pig is stronger, a '*pinot noir*.' It has a long taste in the mouth because of the fat. I don't say one is better than the other [nor would he, since he is in the Bayonne ham business to a much greater degree than his fledging *porc noir* operation]. When a Bayonne ham is twelve months old, it is ready, but at twelve months, a ham from a black pig is still a child. To continue the wine analogy, it is young and still closed. It must have a minimum of eighteen months."

I understood this to mean that in the same way that tannin allows red wine to develop more with age, the greater amount of fat in the flesh of the black pig allows it to develop and achieve greater expression of its inborn "hamness."

Bonomelli went on. "With the black ham, we feel we are making a signature product for the country. As Madiran went from a table wine to a *grand cru* because of Brumont, we will do the same thing with this pig and ham. Jabugo is our model, but I don't want to make a French Jabugo. In California, they don't want to make an American Bordeaux although they learned from the French. We want our ham to have its own personality."

This discourse took us through the meal, at which point Coscuella offered us a round of 1904 *bas* Armagnac. I never say no to a glass of something that's a hundred years old. Brumont declared it past its prime, but Pascal and I were content.

By the next morning, the storms off the Atlantic had blown through. The light was almost crystalline, as it is on the finest October days. The air carried the smell of wood smoke, and in the countryside around Pierre Matayron's farm, the report of shotguns echoed off the hills.

"Dove hunters," Pierre said. "Perhaps Maurice will serve doves again tonight."

I quickly forgot about hunters, doves, and dinner, though, because, in front of us, I caught my first glimpse of black pigs, about twenty of them in a field of approximately four acres. They were high legged and black skinned, some with russet streaks that gave them an iridescent glint in the sunlight. Quite beautiful and serene. Not much odor. The pigs grew frisky, scattering at our approach, but shortly they loped back across the pasture to resume their feeding on fallen acorns and chestnuts. Some never moved, preferring to loll about. From the original brood stock of the thirty-five black pigs that Bonomelli had mentioned the night before, the French herd had grown to some thousands. Though still minuscule compared to the nearly one and a half million black pigs in Spain, it is enough for a small group of farmers to have begun to set up a system like the free-range, pasture-and-acorn system of the Spanish.

"This season, early autumn, marks the beginning of what the Spanish call the *montanera* phase," Pierre said. "Piglets are fed on mother's milk until they are five weeks old. At that time, we put them in a large pen and feed them cereals—twenty percent soy, eighty percent barley, for a month and a half. As they grow, we move them to new pens every six weeks so that you basically only have pigs of the same age group vying for food. At six months, they are put out to pasture and we give them a further choice of cereal or acorns, but they prefer acorns by a factor of eight or nine to one. They like chestnuts too, which is a traditional feed, but I find that the acorn-fed pigs produce a more fatty and delicious meat."

Pierre's anecdotal evidence, I later learned, is born out by the research of the top ham expert at the University of Extremadura, Jesus Ventanas. Repeated taste tests and fat analyses show that acorns beat out an acorn-chestnut mix.

We went into Pierre's kitchen to use the phone to confirm a ham tasting at lunchtime with Frederico. Magazines and computer stuff lay about, not messy but a bit bachelory, which was not unexpected since Pierre is recently divorced. He gets the kids on the weekends. One of their drawings was taped to the refrigerator door. It was a normal, weird-perspective kid's drawing of Life on the Farm: pigs in the grass, flying pigs, lollipop-shaped trees, rain denoted by heavy red streaks, and in the upper-right-hand corner a yellow sun with a big smiley face.

I reached Frederico. He said he would meet us at his place in an hour. Pascal and I returned to town, where, as promised, Frederico welcomed us to his sizable facility in Borderes sur Gers. He led us to a salon with a long wooden table. Alongside was a large red-enameled meat slicer and a *jamonero,* or stand, to hold the ham upright while it is sliced. It cradled a ham veiled in muslin.

On the wall, I noticed a black-and-white photo of a smiling Pope John XXIII surrounded by a group of well-wishers. Frederico pointed out a trim, confidence-brimming cleric at his side. "This was taken a few weeks before John XXIII was made pope, so actually he was still Cardinal Roncalli. My great-uncle Emilio was the director of the pontifical residence at Castel Gandolfo [the pope's summer palace]."

"How is it, Frederico, that there are so many Italians in this part of Gascony?" I asked.

"After the First World War, all the *machos* were dead [although *macho* is the word for boar, Bonomelli used it here to refer to the men of the region]. Many Italians came here, married Gascon women, and took over the farms. Maurice, the chef from Ripa Alta, comes from an Italian family too. My grandfather left Italy just after the Fascists took over in 1922."

In 1927, he founded Salaison des Pyrénées (roughly translated as "cured meats of the Pyrénées"). Although the company sells about four thousand of its Bayonne hams each week, it is a medium-to-small player in the market. Its most famous product, cured *maigret de canard* (smoked salted duck breast preserved in its own fat), was invented by André Daguin, a legendary Gascogne restaurateur of recent years.

"There was already a big demand for *confit de canard* [the preserved legs]," Bonomelli said. "That left the breasts, which had to be consumed on the spot because there was no way to conserve duck [breast] meat back then. Daguin came to my father with the idea of salting and preserving the breasts. Now enough about ducks; would you like to see how we make our hams?"

I felt the inevitable factory tour coming on, but in this case, I really did want to see it, in depth. As I would find later in ham country in Spain, in fact, as I had already seen with Pierre Moines and his cheese making, the best modern producers of many ancient artisanal products employ sophisticated machinery to duplicate the climate of an ideal year—cold autumns, colder winters, and dry summers. The natural rhythm of the seasons provides a "cooking" cycle that enhances the flavor and preservation of McGee's trinity of preciously rotten foods: ham, cheese, and wine. This is not to say that the small farmers/producers of past centuries could not turn out a product equal to today's high-tech producers. It is simply that today, with climate control, one is not at the mercy of a warm winter or a long, cold summer that can ruin your ham, your grapes, your cheese. Traditional forms of preservation, of necessity, relied on the elements. One had to take the good with the bad. Now one simply moves a dial and creates the climate of a cool January, a green April, a searing August.

At Salaison des Pyrénées, the process starts, as it does everywhere, with salting. The fresh hams, with the black hoof left on, are covered with salt at low temperatures for one day per kilo. The salt penetrates the meat during this period and begins to extract water.

In the next phase—the French refer to this as recuperation, while the Spanish use the less medical and more poetic *descanso*, which means "a relaxing rest"—the meat is kept at forty degrees for about twenty weeks. "A ham is eighty-five percent water," Frederico said, "but eventually it must be dry so that it becomes bacteriologically stabilized. During this period, it loses about twenty percent of its weight."

I regarded the racks of hams, a few hundred of them. The room was wet and cold. The hams lay under a blanket of wet salt that covered them like a mantle of late-season snow. The excess water removed by the salt drained from the shelves through small spouts that dripped like ice slowly melting.

"At five months," Frederico said, "the ham is covered with grease made from lard, and seasoned with cloves and cinnamon."

Aha! That was the scent that I had been trying to place but couldn't because it was so out of context. The aromatic spices combined with the controlled aging of the pork flesh was almost inebriating in its pungency. This lard-and-spice coating is reapplied at nine months (during the twenty-week drying period) and again at sixteen months in the middle of the high-temperature (at least eighty degrees Fahrenheit) aging period.

"Our reasoning for coating the ham," Bonomelli said, "is that although we want the ham to dry, we don't want it desiccated and hard. The grease is like a moisturizing lotion you might put on your hands."

I was puzzled. "But coating the ham prevents it from developing any molds. My friends in Kentucky tell me that those molds help develop flavor."

Frederico disagreed. "The molds do nothing for the flavor."

I did not take this as the last word on molds. The ham world is quite factionalized on the question. Personally, I prefer to believe, as

Nancy Newsom does, that the molds work some magic in the long, dark months of aging and sweating.

Pascal and I had now earned our first taste of *ibérico* ham, or at least its French cousin. In the tasting room, the table was laid out for three with a wineglass and water tumbler placed at each setting. To start, Frederico cut slices of *jambon de* Bayonne and laid them on a plate. Then he removed the muslin cowl from his Jabugo and carved it in the Spanish style, with the grain. The slices came off long and thin, with a sleek sheen. They settled on the plate like falling leaves. Then he poured us each a glass of cold Sancerre. I would have thought something red for the ham, but Pascal, who often dreams up unusual wine pairings for cheeses, smelled the ham and then the wine. "The white will pick up notes of sweetness and fruit," he advised.

First we tasted the *jambon de* Bayonne. It was quite delicious and softly sweet, in the way of a prosciutto. Alongside, the plate of Jabugo shined. The soft fat from the pigs' diet of acorns and chestnuts began to melt at room temperature, giving the ham a glossy, almost wet look. The color of the flesh was a much more saturated red than the Bayonne ham. It was the taste, however, that truly moved me. Aged nearly twice as long as the Bayonne, this ham had developed levels of flavor—distinct and mature—that I had encountered only once before, in the twenty-two-month-old ham of Nancy Newsom. Add to that the texture of a free-range animal and the unctuousness of its fat. Pascal closed his eyes and savored the flavor. He looked like a man in prayer.

If this was the taste of Jabugo made by newcomers to the art, I could only imagine what it must be like in the hands of a thirtieth-generation ham maker on the Spanish frontier. At that moment I resolved to go to the *dehesa*, the vast oak park in the west of Spain where the *ibérico* hog still reigns.

POT-ROASTED PORK WITH PRUNES, ARMAGNAC, AND WALNUTS

When I returned to New York, it was a cold November, the kind of weather that cries out for the fortifying, rib-sticking cuisine of Gascony. During the first snowfall of the season, I joined Boston chef and flyfisherman Gordon Hamersley for lunch at Savoy, a wonderful restaurant in SoHo. The old buildings and the heavy snow gave the city a magical Currier and Ives feeling that freshly fallen snow brings for a moment to Manhattan. The occasion was the publication of Hamersley's new cookbook, *Bistro Cooking at Home* (Broadway Books), where I found this recipe. It is hard for complex recipes to hop across an ocean, but Gordon's book makes the leap. This is a can't-fail crowd pleaser, but only if you use good pork; Niman Ranch or a local producer is the way to go.

FROM *BISTRO COOKING AT HOME*,
BY GORDON HAMERSLEY

 2 cups Armagnac or other brandy
24 to 30 pitted prunes, cut in half if large
 1 boneless or bone-in pork shoulder, about 4 to 6 pounds (look for cuts labeled "butt" or "Boston butt"), trimmed of excess fat
   Kosher salt and freshly ground black pepper
1/4 cup vegetable oil
 3 red onions, cut into thick rounds
1 1/2 cups dry white wine

1½ cups chicken broth
   Pinch red pepper flakes
 8 whole fresh sage leaves, plus 1 tablespoon
   chopped fresh sage
 1 tablespoon tomato paste
¼ cup honey
   About 2 tablespoons chopped fresh parsley
½ cup chopped toasted walnuts

1. Bring ½ cup of the Armagnac to a boil. (Be careful, as the Armagnac may ignite, which is actually a good thing as it burns off the alcohol and concentrates flavor. If it does ignite, just leave it alone until the flames die out, which will happen quickly.) Remove from the heat and toss in the prunes. Reserve.

2. Preheat the oven to 325°F. Season the pork liberally all over with salt and pepper. Heat the vegetable oil in a large, heavy-based, ovenproof pan over medium-high heat. Add the pork and brown on all sides, about 12 minutes total. Remove the pork.

3. Add the onions to the pan and lower the heat to medium. Cook the onions, stirring occasionally, until lightly browned, about 10 minutes. Add the white wine, the remaining 1½ cups Armagnac, chicken broth, red pepper flakes, whole sage leaves, tomato paste, and honey. Bring to a boil. Put the pork back in the pan, cover tightly with a lid or aluminum foil, and cook in the oven until the pork is very tender, about 2 hours. Add the prunes, the Armagnac they were soaking in, and the chopped sage to the pot.

4. Leave the pot uncovered and cook for an additional 20 minutes. (If you want to prepare this dish a day or two ahead, stop here. Cool the pork and its cooking liquid as quickly as possible and refrigerate the pork in its cooking liquid. On the day you plan to serve it, remove any cooled fat from the dish, reheat the pork in the oven in its cooking liquid, and then continue with the recipe.)

5. Transfer the pork to a cutting board and tent with foil. Strain the cooking liquid into a saucepan and reserve the onions and prunes. Degrease the cooking liquid if necessary. Bring the liquid to a boil and cook until reduced by half. Return the prunes and onions to the pot to warm them. Slice the pork and arrange the slices on a platter. Top with the onions and the prunes and pour some of the sauce over the top to moisten everything. Sprinkle with the parsley and toasted walnuts and serve with the remaining sauce on the side.

Serves 6.

* * *

FIVE

A BRIEF HISTORY
OF PIGKIND

SPANIARDS HAVE BEEN MAKING HAM AT least since Roman times. But recent discoveries indicate that the prehumans of Iberia may have consumed pigs long before that.

Somewhere between 700,000 and 1 million years ago, a group of humanlike creatures lived and died near Sierra Atapuerca, a hill in Northern Spain midway between present-day Bilbao and Madrid. This is a very early date for the presence of our ancient relatives in Europe, perhaps the earliest known.

The modern-day discoverers of these first Iberians called them *Homo antecessor,* as in "ancestor." Since there was no land bridge to Africa at the time of their residence, it remains a mystery as to how they got to Spain, but a plenitude of bones leaves no doubt that they were there.

Judging by the evidence left by a band of these early hominids, their descendants remained in their new home for some hundreds of thousands of years. According to one school of thought, *antecessor* may have evolved into Neanderthal in Europe, while the stay-at-homes in Africa became the forerunners of modern humans.

Sierra Atapuerca is remarkable not only for the antiquity of the remains of these prehumans. It also marks the earliest signs of humanlike funerary practices. In the large pit called Sima de Los Huesos (the "Bone Pit"), there is a cave that was inhabited at times by bears and occasionally served as a shelter for humans. In it we find the remains of *antecessor*, put there on purpose, a community of the dead numbering twenty-eight individuals.

Jean Luis Arsuaga, one of the Spanish paleontologists who brought the discoveries of Atapuerca to light, believes the burial pit reflects a catastrophe that struck the whole region. He imagines an ecological crisis: "Some—the aged, the sick, the disabled, fell by the wayside . . . The survivors deposited the bodies in The Bone Pit, safe from carrion eaters, where they remained until rediscovery by cavers 4,000 centuries later."

I feel saddened by this story. It plucks a dolorous chord because it occurs to me that the people of the Bone Pit may have been among the first to comprehend that we all die someday. Even now, with the accretion of eons of religion and psychology to help us deal with the prospect of death, it is a hard reality to accept. For those who first realized death was their lot, it must have been one enormous terror.

My sympathy for the Atapuercans is tempered, however, because the evidence of bones, tools, and marks of butchery point to the possibility that the members of this group were, quite possibly, not above eating their fellows. They may have been cannibals, although some say that such activities could just as well have been part of primitive funerary rituals, namely, "defleshing" the deceased before consigning them to their last abode.

But if they were cannibals, they were not just eating each other. They ate any mammal they could lay their hands on . . . including pigs, whose bones have been found in some of *antecessors'* caves.

"This is very exciting," said Greger Larson, an American Ph.D. candidate conducting research on ancient DNA at Oxford.

I met Larson in the north of England while attending a conference, "Pigs and Humans," organized by the Pig Project, a multidisciplinary, multinational program of Durham University dedicated to the study of the ancient interactions between pigs and humans.

I was able to corral Larson for an extensive interview because he is a sports fan and my cell phone has the ability to get updated scores. The Cubs were playing the Pirates in a season finale that would decide which team went to the playoffs. By excusing ourselves from the main group at the conference and taking a position near a window upstairs (where the reception was better), I was able to provide Larson with a pitch-by-pitch account of the crucial game.

In return, Larson shared his copious knowledge of the pig's evolutionary history.

The young scholar, tall, thin, and with the ability to speak as fast as he thinks (and the much rarer ability to do both cogently), has been using DNA to study the evolution of the modern pig. Specifically, he uses a portion of mitochondrial DNA, which passes down fairly unchanged, except for a constant rate of mutation, in the maternal line.

It was through such research that scientists have been able to trace all modern humans back to a single "Eve" who walked the savannahs of Africa 200,000 years ago. In Larson's view, the presence of pigs in western Europe at Atapuerca at such an early date is testimony to a sweeping tale of evolutionary success.

The pigs of Atapuerca, in fact all pigs, are classified as *Suidae*, which makes them relatives of hippos and peccaries (the javelina of the American West). Among their distinctive characteristics, their skin lacks sweat glands, so they can only regulate their body temperature through their noses or, more efficiently, through wallowing. A pig will wallow in anything, including its own waste, which accounts for our not entirely fair estimation of the pig as a "dirty" animal. While it is true that pigs in confinement will wallow in their waste, a human confined in the same conditions would not smell that much sweeter.

"People really know virtually nothing about the origin and evolution of pigs," Larson said. "However, the fact that Atapuerca is about seven hundred thousand years old means that the modern pig (*Sus scrofa*) was in Europe quite early. Granted, the data is kind of funky, but more and more people are taking it seriously and it seems to be holding up.

"The evidence we have at the moment suggests that somewhere between two and a half and one million years ago, *S. scrofa* first evolved somewhere in Southeast Asia before radiating north into Russia and Japan and west through India, Mongolia, central Asia, Iran, Iraq, Turkey, and then a big radiation into Europe. As they move west, they are accelerating [in the expansion of their territory], and as they spread to Europe, they hit Mach two and really take off. Mitochondrially, it is hard to refute that."

I had never considered the possibility of anyone uttering the sentence "Mitochondrially, it is hard to refute that." But, given the force of Larson's argument, I had to agree . . . mitochondrially speaking.

Humans and pigs—we've been together for a long time, humans eating and pigs being eaten, both creatures of the wild. The domestication of the pig occurred comparatively late in this relationship. Nonetheless, it may, in fact, predate the domestication of all other food animals and a good number of plants.

According to the most commonly accepted interpretation, the one I learned in grad school in anthropology, humans first settled down when they came to rely on and fully exploit the abundant crops of grains in the Near East after the retreat of the glaciers. But it now appears that there are sites where domesticated animals may have predated plants.

Richard Redding—whose acquaintance I also made at the Pigs and Humans conference—is an archaeologist who looks at ancient data from an economic perspective. He and Michael Rosenberg, a fellow archaeologist at the University of Michigan, conducted a series of excavations at Hallan Cemi, a site in present-day Turkey that dates from 9000 B.C. They found that the village people domesticated the pig well before they domesticated crops (the land was rich in acorns and pistachios—the former the best pig fodder there is and the latter a nutritious source of protein and fat for humans). The tentative conclusion is that pigs were the first domesticated food animal anywhere. Only dogs, which were not for the most part exploited for food but rather for companionship and as collaborators in hunting, were domesticated earlier.

But what is domestication? To a contemporary reader, the image evoked is of the classic barnyard with pigs, cows, chickens, goats, etc. Or domestication may mean (as it does in the hog factories) a pig bred for docility, kept in a space more constricting than the belowdecks quarters of the *Amistad*. But that is today, after eleven thousand years of domestication. Assuredly, this is not the way it started.

One thing domestication is not is wild one day and tame the next. At Hallan Cemi, many of the traditional markers of domestication are not there. For example, there is no evidence of "juvenilization" of the animal (the scientific term is "neoteny"). This last refers to more playful, cuter animals with more "babyish" features, which usually indicates selection for a more docile animal.

Even wild pigs—like people, or dogs, or cats—have some juvenile characteristics (otherwise, how could we have selected for these qualities?). Where newborn cows and sheep can stand and walk within a few hours, pigs are relatively helpless and stay in the litter for weeks, where they are quite adorable. In Papua, New Guinea, this kinship is vividly underscored: Women will habitually suckle pigs and puppies along with their own children.

According to the tale that the ancient bones tell, domestication at Hallan Cemi meant that pigs were managed in reproduction and controlled in their range. There are only two age groups at the site: young males and mature females. The sows were kept for breeding purposes and the males of their litters were raised until fat enough to provide a few good meals. This pattern is husbandry in the fairly literal sense of keeping the sows pregnant and nursing.

When one speaks of the history of domestication, the implication is always that we humans were the active partners and that pigs, goats, cattle, chickens, dogs, etc. were passive. This overestimates man's input and undervalues the animal's role in the partnership. As Michael Pollan has written in *The Botany of Desire*, the relationship between humans and such varied organisms as tulips, apples, potatoes, and cannabis demonstrates that domestication is a two-way transaction between species. Both sides gain in the deal.

The terms of the Darwinian bargain with domestic animals is that in return for food and protection they provided a ready source of food for humans, who were no longer required to pick up their spears and go trekking into the wilderness. In this predomestication hunting scenario, having killed whatever it was that was being hunted, you still had to butcher the kill and carry the choice pieces to the women and children back home in the cave.

Looking at the implications of hunting and carrying, archaeologists talk about "the Schlep Effect." If you are not familiar with the term "to schlep," it is a Yiddish expression that means "to carry something." So why don't they call it the Carry Effect? Because to schlep means to carry in a way that is onerous or, at the very least, inconvenient, as in, "They made us get out of the subway because of a water-main break and I had to schlep these heavy bags six blocks in the rain." It's even more schleppy if in the course of those six blocks, one of those bags develops a hole in the bottom and two bottles of pickles and a carton of eggs spill out and break on the sidewalk.

The Schlep Effect provides the solution to a problem that puzzled archaeologists studying Ice Age Europe. From the remains of animals at various ancient sites, paleontologists appeared to be looking at two different cultures. One seemed to be highly mobile, with no sign of permanent settlement. They subsisted on animal organs and less meaty cuts. The second group, living in more permanent settlements, dined exclusively on meaty haunches and forelegs.

With further study, scientists realized that we weren't looking at two different peoples. Instead, the nonpermanent site was in all probability the kill site. There, the hunters dined on the more perishable and less portable cuts of the animal. The permanent site was where the hunters brought back the more easily "schleppable" pieces. This phenomenon was observed as recently as the last century among Plains Indians in the United States.

Domestication meant no more schlepping: It gave humans the ability to settle down, thus keeping the women and children secure. What did the animal get in return? Clearly, in the case of the individual that was butchered, not much. But in the larger Darwinian sense, the humans guaranteed the survival of the domesticated species. Pigs (and dogs), which have a gregarious temperament, may have taken the first step by hanging around human settlements or encampments where they could find protection from huge carnivores as well as a ready food source in the castoffs of human activity.

Pigs, the more I think about them, were born to be domesticated. They are the best converter of plant to meat of any large animal. They are also marvelously fecund; the average sow may give birth to fourteen or fifteen offspring each year, and every one of them will be market weight within six months. Cattle, on the other hand, produce an average of less than one calf per year, while sheep are good for about 1.2 lambs.

Add to this the fact that pigs are friendly, don't seem to mind being around people (in fact, they appear to like it), and don't require a lot of management. If there is food around, they will eat it and stay close to home. In sum, pigs are a prolific food source that recycles waste, multiplies like rabbits, and submits rather willingly to human control. Once humans started down the road to domestication, the question is not, why pigs? It really is, why would you choose any other creature first? Doubly true, I think you will find, once you have tried the ineffable hams of Spain. Although there was no way they could have known it 700,000 years ago, when Atapuercans in their prehistoric Spanish caves first dined on pig, they were starting a great Iberian tradition.

SIX

PRISONER OF LOVE

WE WERE IN THE TOWN OF Aracena, a village in the province of Huelva, in the mountains of western Andalucía, its whitewashed walls silver in the full winter moon. Acting on the recommendation of my friends in the food world, I ordered a plate of Jabugo ham. Every trendy restaurant in Paris proudly offers it, so I felt confident that here, in the heart of ham country, I was doing the right thing in the right place.

Right food, wrong name.

"It's not properly called Jabugo," Miguel Ullibarri said. "From Jerez to Salamanca, there are hundreds of towns in addition to Jabugo that make *ibérico*. For some reason, the name Jabugo and *pata negra* caught on among the French."

Ullibarri, pronounced oo-ya-bah-ree, is the general manager of Real Ibérico, a consortium of the biggest producers of Iberian ham: i.e., ham made from hogs descended, like their cousins across the border in France, from the Mediterranean wild boar. Soft-spoken, with salt-and-pepper hair, dark wire-rim glasses, and sporting a bebop Vandyke beard, Ullibarri is a passionate advocate for what Spaniards consider their greatest delicacy, *jamon ibérico puro de bellota—ibérico* ham fabricated from free-range hogs who spend their final months on a diet of acorns and grasses.

It was a cold night in Aracena. On a Monday in January, there were not a lot of dining choices, so Miguel and I, along with my traveling buddy (and frequent fishing companion) Josh Feigenbaum, wandered into Gran Via, the only place that was open and serving food and drink to a full house.

It was a loud, overlit bar. Nearly everyone had a cigarette going and still wore their outerwear to ward off the chill (in this part of Spain, central heating has yet to be perfected). A film played on the TV with a young Ann-Margret wearing a tight-fitting sweater. Inexplicably, no one (except for Josh and me) paid much attention to her. Instead, the young guys in the crowd cheered a comrade who triumphed over a video game that capitulated with a fearful chorus of blasts. We sipped Spanish beer, which is quite wonderful and always served well chilled.

Miguel brought us up to speed on his product. "Although *ibérico* ham is a billion-dollar industry, it only makes up about five percent of the forty million cured Spanish hams produced each year, while the rest are *serrano*. Spain produces roughly one cured ham per Spaniard, including both *serrano* and *ibérico*. (This is a per-capita consumption of four kilograms, or nine pounds, which is very close to one cured ham.) Although we are the leading producer of cured ham, we export less than ten percent of our total production because we love eating ham!"

Miguel went on, "*Serrano* and *ibérico* are perceived as clearly different products by Spaniards. *Serrano* is more of an everyday product, while *ibérico* is associated with special occasions. The less-expensive *serrano* ham, made from white pigs that are raised, for the most part, in confinement, is both more famous and produced in much greater quantities."

That the world regards *serrano* ham as a great delicacy is more a testament to marketing buzz than to its gastronomic superiority.

Miguel knows a lot about marketing. His previous job was with Kellogg's, the American breakfast-cereal maker. "Our big problem wasn't convincing people to eat Kellogg's," he recalled, "it was getting them to eat breakfast. Spaniards like to sleep late."

A plate of *ibérico* was borne to our table, erasing everything that was not ham from my attention. I watched the plate, a ten-inch white circle covered with pink/scarlet *lascas* (squared-off slices of ham) that truly glistened with fat, which made them lustrous indeed even under the unflattering light of the bare fluorescent bulbs. The ham was placed before us with a smaller plate full of recently harvested and freshly brined green olives.

I speared a piece of ham with a toothpick. Its fat melted in amber droplets. It had the flavor of age with hints of banana and apricot. Then, of course, there was texture, that essential, often overlooked component of taste; the ham had smoothness, yet a gentle tooth resistance. Pushing everything forward were the high, clear notes of salt. When taste is so full, so nuanced, so layered, it can best be compared to a symphony, its aftertastes like a final grand chord, a ghost harmony, slowly dying into the hush of the audience.

This may seem a little florid, but it is no less effusive and considerably less mystical than the Spaniards themselves are on the subject of ham. They often describe it in almost religious terms. "It must be consumed as if it were a Eucharistic wafer," writes gastronomer Marcos Aguiar, "to appreciate its deep flavor calls for a ritual, an anointing, that is reserved exclusively for this food."

Ibérico ham in particular, and pork in general, is quite central to the Hispanic conception of self. Throughout most of their history, Catholic Spaniards could point to two things—religion and diet—that separated them from the Muslim community that ruled them for centuries, as well as from the Jewish community that thrived all through the era of Muslim domination. After 1492, which marked the expulsion of the Moors and the Jews, Spaniards could look no further than their dining customs to define their differentness from the non-Spanish "others." Christians ate pork and preferred it to all other meats, while for Jews and Arabs, it was proscribed. Thus, in the bloody and intolerant era of the Spanish Inquisition, the depth of faith of a convert was most easily tested by requiring the "*converso*" to eat a piece of pork. As a counterstrategy, many Jews made a point of cooking pork and placing ham in their windows to fend off the attention of the inquisitors.

To the inherent deliciousness of pork as a pure food item, the Spaniards added layers of symbolic and cultural freight. But, for all of their abstract meditations on pork, Spaniards also celebrate its pure carnality, i.e., as flesh that gives pleasure.

For example, one has the delightful Renaissance poem "*Tres Cosas*," or "Three Things." I think of it as the great-great-grandfather of *Green Eggs and Ham*. The author even has a name that Dr. Seuss might have invented, Baltazar de Alcazar.

Three Things

> *A prisoner of love I am*
> *For Ines the Fair and Spanish ham*

These things my heart do greatly please
Also eggplants and some cheese.

Ines, she has me in her spell
Without her I count it time in hell
That takes my mind and self away
From Ines, whom I loved both night and day

Yes I loved her night and day
A year, at least my friends I say
And then some ham she served me once
With eggplants and cheese—a lover's lunch

Though it was Ines that first I chose
But of the three I now suppose
There is not one I hold most dear
I love them equally, I fear.

There is no difference in my heart
Of the tasting, size, or feeling part
Ines I love, I'm here to tell
But eggplants cheese and ham as well

In Aracena the ham is born
As pretty as Ines each morn
Where eggplants and some cheese complete
A Spanish trinity, a lover's feast

In truth and fairness to the three
I hold them dear all equally

Ines I love most faithfully
But also eggplants ham and cheese

At least of one thing I am sure
My love for her (and them) is pure
In her favors I find true bliss is,
Eggplants and cheese and ham and kisses

If she would keep my affections steady
She would do wise to always ready
Of ham, a most delicious slice
Some cheese and eggplants, also nice

These lines reveal that in the Spaniard's connection to his plate of ham, there is more to it than mere food. It is fair to say that in America, most consumers, if they consider the origin of their meal of pork (or any meat), will more than likely picture a piece of flesh in a plastic wrapper. There is no reason they would think farther back in the production chain. The family farm and, with it, the household pig are more and more marginalized in the modern economy. Pigs are born, raised, slaughtered, and butchered, for the most part as part of the factory-farm system. They have been totally removed from daily life. The only contact humans have with livestock is with a knife and fork.

Spaniards are no more a nation of small farmers than Americans are, but they do think beyond the plate when it comes to pork. For the Spanish, the ham stands for the pig. The pig in turn represents the way of life and the values of Spain, much as the longhorn steer does in the American image of its past. Extremadura, neighboring western Andalucía, and Salamanca to the north are as mythic to

Spaniards as the Old West is to Americans. The heart of this region, Extremadura, owes its name to its location, one extreme of the route that sheepherders would take on their way from the valley of the Duero to the summer pastures in the north. It is a rugged land, quite cold in the winter and searingly hot in the summer. During the centuries of the Reconquest, Catholic warlords completed what they felt was their divinely ordained mission to retake the territories of Al Andalus and the caliphate of Granada from the Moors. That God's work included reclaiming the lands that were the foundation of Spain's wool and ham industries was a divine bonus.

The *ibérico* hog, which grows fat and delicious on the acorns of the forests of this frontier, has come, symbolically, to stand for the feelings that Spaniards share about the purity of the old days, of a nation with a mission, and of a natural landscape that sustained this crusading people with its forest wealth. The *ibérico* hog carries the forests and the land of the Spanish frontier to the table, where families join in the communion of the meal.

The pig is, in a sense, the embodiment of a sacred landscape. But even without the quasi-religious element, the *cerdo*—which is the term most Spaniards use to refer to hogs—would still be an expression of what the French call *terroir,* which literally translates into Spanish as *tierra,* or land. But where the word "land" holds, for the most part, a practical connotation for the American (something you either exploit or leave wild), *tierra* embodies a mystical quintessence, the "soul" of the land. *Tierra* is the sum of the soil, the sun, the history of its care under human dominion. In Burgundy, it is what makes the grapes from the bottom of the hill suitable for village wine and the grapes two-thirds up the slope right for *les grands crus.* Perhaps the closest we Americans get to this sentiment is the feeling of nostalgia that the phrase "back to the land" conjures. *Tierra* is the idea of the land, with all its cultural baggage, that we

want to get back to. In Spain, the Iberian hog is the incarnation of
the land they call the *dehesa*.

In practical terms, the *dehesa* is simply the place where pigs feed
each fall in their *montanera* phase. The *montanera* is the time,
roughly between November and March (acorn season in Spain,
black truffle season in France), when the *cerdos* put on 40 percent of
their slaughter weight, most of it fat, as thick as a down comforter.
During these last few months of its life, the pig's diet consists totally
of acorns, grasses, and wild legumes. When the pig has reached a
weight of approximately 160 kilos (about 350 pounds), it is slaughtered, often at a community ritual. With Miguel's help, we set out to
find one.

SEVEN

INVITATION TO A KILLING

IF YOU WOULD KNOW A CULTURE, you can learn much from how it metes out death. Consider the public beheadings in Saudi Arabia, versus the invitees only performance that characterizes executions in the United States. Both have the same result, but the cultural context has as much to say about a people as it does about justice. The former drives a lesson home through a mass catharsis, while the latter, well, I am not sure what it accomplishes.

In contemporary Spain, now that the Inquisition no longer burns heretics in the town square (nor, for that matter, does the state take human life), there are two main rituals of public life taking, both of them linked to the killing of animals. One is the *corrida de toros*, the bullfight, where people gather to participate, some as actors, some as observers, in a death struggle that has a liturgy as formalized as a Mass.

More impromptu, and more hands-on for common folk, is the annual hog killing, which is still a yearly event in the southwest of Spain.

In America, we say a pig is "slaughtered," a description that denotes no special connection between human and swine. It's just a verb, without any moral freight. In Spain, however, the animal is "sacrificed," which implies more than the relationship between the butcher and the butchered. There is an acknowledgment that a life is given up for some greater purpose.

Though the ritual of the killing of the farm pig has been divorced from religion, it is still called a sacrifice, a type of communal rite. As in France (and as it used to be in the United States), families and friends gather. All participate in the killing of the animal, its dismemberment, and its transformation into sausages, fresh cuts of meat, and the raw material for hams. All have blood on their hands and, in so doing, they reinforce the bonds among friends and families, between people and animals, and between people and the land.

Josh and I both very much wanted to attend one of the many such gatherings that were then taking place all around Aracena. Although the *sacrificio* is a major celebration on the regional social calendar, it is not customary to invite two strangers, and foreigners at that, to such intimacies.

We began our looking-for-an-invite day with a breakfast of coffee, Valencia orange juice, and lard from a freshly killed pig. We had our choice of lards: one with salt and a little pepper, the other with salt and the coral-colored paprika for which Spain is renowned. It bears repeating that the lard of such pigs pumps up the high-density lipoproteins, or HDLs (the "good" cholesterol), and lowers the LDLs (the "bad" cholesterol). This fact astonishes most people at first, and Miguel takes great pleasure in converting the nonbeliever.

The morning's agenda brought us to the town of Jabugo and the meat-processing facility of Sánchez Romero Carvajal. Corporate communications director Ivan Llanza gave us a factory tour. Apart from a change of language, everything was familiar from our tour of Salaison des Pyrénées. Although it is highly automated, there are key steps in the ham process that are still, of necessity, in human hands. Among these is the insertion of the *cala* (usually the sharp tibia bone of a horse or cow) to judge whether a ham is ready. A worker with a highly developed sense of taste and smell inserts the *cala* first into the *cana*, or marrow, near the foot. He withdraws it and sniffs to make sure there is no spoilage. Next he wipes the *cala* and inserts it again deep into the center of the ham, next to the bone, which is known to the Spaniards as *el violin*. If the ham is perfect, the odor after both insertions should be identical.

At this point, the ham is ready to be cut, an operation that is carried out with ceremonial care. The ham is placed on the *jamonero*, which holds it so that the toe points upward for the first cut. Champion cutter Jose Sanchez demonstrated. He cut thin slices, with the grain. This orientation is very important because only then will the slice have strands of muscle fiber interspersed with lines of flavorful fat running along its whole length. The slices, or *lascas*, are just the right size to pop in your mouth. Miguel Ullibarri had mentioned that longer slices, as one finds with *serrano* ham or prosciutto, are *lonchas*, which, according to the *Oxford Dictionary of the English Language*, is the origin of the word "lunch." A master slicer's goal is to cover a nine-inch dinner plate with exactly 100 grams (about 3.5 ounces) of *ibérico* ham sliced so thinly that the meat is translucent. The squared-off slices are arranged on the plate like the petals of a flower.

This soft fat, which makes for such good ham, is the enemy of the sausage maker. It has a tendency to clog up machinery. Thus, alongside the best of hams, in Spain, you find mediocre charcuterie with soft fat. Hard fat, from grain-fed pigs (which includes factory pigs), is preferable for charcuterie. Although I love sausages, the pursuit of perfect ham takes the pilgrim on a different route than the sausage lover's.

Across from the *bodega*, where the cutting took place, the factory sells fresh pork during the killing season. On the morning of our visit, at least twenty people had lined up to buy the meat, which is rarely available outside the pig-rearing lands of the *dehesa*. Because the fresh meat is marbled with the same succulent fat as the hams, it is highly prized and correspondingly pricey, although not so dear as the sliced *ibérico* ham that I later purchased for $77 per kilo. This makes *ibérico* more than three times as costly as a piece of range-fed, prime dry-aged beef at Staubitz Meats on Court Street in Brooklyn, my local.

The ham that Ivan offered us was even better than the one we had that first night in Aracena: more nutty and buttery. Josh remarked that we had dipped into "the private stash." Dry sherry, equally nutty but with a steely backbone, was the right drink to complement it. After the sampling, we returned to Aracena. Miguel followed up some leads on a *sacrificio* and left us in the company of Susi Delgado Gonzalez, a very pretty young mother who is also the chef and, with her husband, Manuel Fernando, owner of Bar Manzano, Miguel's favorite. It fronts on the old town square of Aracena.

Susi drew heavily on her cigarette. "I'm making pork cheeks tonight; would you like to try some?"

Cheeks (pork, beef, or lamb) are a favorite chef's cut, rarely seen on most restaurant menus and even rarer in the home kitchen. I think the reason for the scarcity is a practical one—there are only two small cheeks on a 350-pound hog. The other reason, just as likely, is that Spanish chefs and butchers keep this cut for themselves, much as the butchers of Paris are rumored to keep the *onglet*, or hanger steak, for their families.

Susi invited me into her kitchen, handed me a knife and an

apron, and the two of us set about preparing the cheeks by removing the silver skin, then sweating onions and carrots in olive oil before throwing in the cheeks, cut up into bite-size chunks. Interestingly, as she added the meat, she spooned away the olive oil.

"*Ibérico* has so much fat in the meat that it is not necessary to add extra fat or oil," she said.

As soon as the meat was browned, she added a few fresh bay leaves that her mom had picked in the countryside. Next, a cup of white wine and enough water to cover the meat, which she left to simmer.

A man about sixty years old poked his head in the kitchen: by the looks of him, a farmer. Susi introduced me to Tomás Pérez, a friend of her mother's, who said he was organizing a killing for the next morning.

My ears pricked up like a dog on point. Susi read my thoughts. "Peter is writing a book about *ibérico*, do you think he could come to the *matanza* [the hog killing]?"

"Sure," he answered with a shrug. No elaborate protocol, no secret handshake, all that was needed was a native to vouch for me, which is often the way with fishing holes, duck blinds, and mushroom patches.

PORK TENDERLOIN WITH ARACENA WHISKEY SAUCE

On the night that I first visited with Susi, she sautéed a piece of pork that looked like a mini flank steak. "Do you know about the secret?" she asked.

I was puzzled.

"*El secreto*," she said. "It's a wonderful cut, about a pound. They call it the secret because it is almost hidden inside the bacon fat."

The meat shone, as all *ibérico* does, from the soft fat beginning to melt. She flipped the pork in the hot pan, seasoning it with salt and pepper. When it was done, she plated the meat and sauced it with her mother's whiskey sauce, a Spanish favorite made with pan-roasted garlic, lemon juice, olive oil, and whiskey. It is wonderfully juicy and packs a lot of flavor, but not so much that the powerful meaty taste of the fresh-killed pork flavor does not come through. *El secreto* is a splendid cut of meat, and, if you are in Extremadura in pig-killing time, I advise you to have at least one a day.

INSPIRED BY SUSI DELGADO GONZALEZ AT BAR MANZANO

WHISKEY SAUCE

6 cloves of garlic, skin on

2 tablespoons olive oil

2 tablespoons butter

2 tablespoons beef stock

Juice of two lemons

2 tablespoons bourbon

1. In an enameled saucepan, dry-roast the garlic over medium-high heat until the skin chars.

2. Add olive oil, butter, beef stock, lemon juice, and bourbon. (You can use any brown whiskey. I prefer bourbon because of its smooth smokiness.)

3. Reduce over medium flame approximately ten minutes. Set aside.

PORK

2 pounds boneless pork roast (Note: I have adapted this for pork loin because one cannot find the *secreto* in America. You may also use tenderloin.)

1. Cut a boneless pork roast into strips 1 inch by 1 inch by 4 inches. Pan-roast in a cast-iron or heavy All-Clad-type pan about 7 to 10 minutes, turning frequently.

PLATING

1. Slice the pork on the bias in long strips. Fan out three or four slices for each serving. Spoon whiskey sauce with whole garlic cloves over the pork.

Serves 4.

* * *

EIGHT

FROM PIG TO PORK

THERE IS NOTHING QUITE LIKE THE blood-curdling yell of a pig being led to slaughter. Correct that: There is nothing quite like the blood-curdling yell of a pig being led *anywhere* against its will. I recall the same sound from some gilts (young sows, yet to be bred) being led into the show ring at the state fairgrounds in Des Moines. Still, when you know that a pig has an appointment with *el matarife* ("the killer"), you can't help but project the human capacity for foreknowledge onto the pig as it emits a guttural, yet high-pitched and ear-shattering squeal.

Josh gave what I thought was quite a good imitation of the sound of the large black pig being muscled onto a low bench. Five people pitched in to restrain the pig: all of the killing party big and strong, one of them a woman, Manuela Pérez. With everybody stretching and straining to hold the pig, the group looked like a hog-killing version of the famous photo of the flag-raising at Iwo Jima.

The *matarife* was Clemente (the name means merciful), a huge man with jet-black hair, dressed in the blue trousers that are standard issue among European workingmen. Around his middle, he wore a wide leather belt, the kind that weight lifters and piano movers favor.

With all the drama leading up to it, the actual moment of truth, when Clemente slit the jugular of the pig with a short, wide knife, was relatively calm. To my surprise, the sow did not make a sound nor did she struggle very much as her life's blood spurted into a bucket.

Manuela collected this essential ingredient for blood sausage, stirring it with her hand to keep it from coagulating in the cold morning air. When she lifted her arm from the bucket, it was scarlet, right up to the elbow. A toy poodle slurped the puddle that collected on the ground as Manuela emptied the bucket. That was the only time all day that the well-behaved little dog consumed something without it being offered by a person.

The *matanza* proceeded as two more hogs were dispatched. The wives came to and fro with buckets of hot water, cleaning the butchering area while the men dismembered the carcasses. The women wore aprons and smocks, everyday housecleaning clothes. They barked commands, nonstop, to the men.

"Put it here," they said.

"Take that there."

"Watch your feet."

"Boil more water."

In addition to keeping things tidy during the butchering of the hog, they tended a fire under a large pot in the hut that served as the lounge for our party.

Dolores Delgado, Susi's mom, tossed ingredients into the cauldron: garbanzos (chickpeas), pork, chicken, carrots, onions, bacon, the stalks from the herbs that would go into the sausage, bones from the killing. It would be a Spanish pot-au-feu traditionally served at pig killings and known as a *cocido*.

Miguel came into the hut and watched. "The *cocido* is one of the most Spanish dishes. The garbanzos come from the Arabs; the stew itself was a Jewish dish cooked on Friday and served on Saturday because Jews were not allowed to cook on the Sabbath. The Christians added pork to the recipes, and it has since become the traditional meal at a *matanza*."

After each hog was killed, Clemente took a blowtorch to its hide to burn off the bristle. Once it was charred, he brushed the skin with a stiff janitor's broom.

Josh, taking it all in from a chair that he'd leaned back against the sun-washed wall of the hut, wore a sleeveless cardigan and a hat with a turned-up brim. He looked like Marlon Brando as The Godfather in his later years, resting in his garden.

Clemente and crew split each hog, using a hand ax to crack open the sternum to get at the viscera within. Once they were removed, he hacked along the backbone until the carcass was separated in two, revealing a layer of white fat three inches thick.

Miguel pointed to the fat. "That's what the *montanera* does, all that fat. When a pig has that much fat, you know that there will be a good amount that has also infiltrated the muscles. That's what makes the meat so interesting, and you only get it if the *ibérico* pig is properly developed to take full advantage of the *montanera*."

There wasn't much we could do to help, so we stayed out of the way and watched. The only sounds were the chopping of the ax, the steady *chismes* (friendly gossip) of the ladies, and the chirping of the songbirds. The ladies' talk underscored everything, a steady, light rhythm now and then punctuated by exclamations at news of a death, a birth, a scandal. Tomas's hand ax made a short rasp as it cut through bone and then a thump as it hit the chopping block. The smaller parts went into one bucket, the organs into another. Clemente concentrated on haunches and shoulders. He pushed the blood from the tissues, a maneuver that looks like a lifeguard administering artificial respiration. He trimmed the hams with a knife that he chose from his basket of well-used cutting implements, the handles nicked and dulled with age, the blades likewise, a matte gray except for the sharp, shining edges. As he finished with each ham and shoulder, he hung it by the hoof from a frame constructed for this purpose.

Dolores summoned us for a midmorning lunch of fried sardines, warm *torta del casar* (a cheese of nearby Extremadura), and red wine. One eats the sardines, which are extremely salty, just like catfish, nibbling all the meat, right down to the skeleton. A hunk of substantial peasant bread baked by another of the ladies, Loli Alcali, cut the salty oiliness of the fish and did double duty as a napkin. Holding a wineskin above his head, Tomás squirted red wine into his mouth in a daredevilishly long stream and encouraged Josh and me to do the same—a maneuver we accomplished with surprising precision. Must be something about a well-designed tool working well even in the hands of a novice.

Although it was warm in the sun, inside the cabin it was cool, and the fire from the cauldron was very cozy. Well fed from the bread, fish, and cheese, my thirst slaked by the wine, sleep came swiftly and with it a dream. I am in the middle of an endless oak savannah, half Andalucía and the rest a mix of Yellowstone Park and the Sabora Plain of the Serengeti. Josh and I come upon a trout stream from which a cloud of mayflies with purple wings hatch in great profusion. There are pigs grazing on the deep, green grass along the riverbank. Fat trout, very dark in color, like the black trout of the Pyrénées, rise to feed on the mayflies. I look for my rod, but I'm interrupted by the offstage thump of a woodsman's ax. And then, bafflingly, I hear a voice in Spanish addressing "Señor T." I awoke with a start to a dubbed Spanish version of *The A-Team* on the old TV in the cabin. Even here, in the medieval ritual of the *matanza*, schlocko American TV had managed to infiltrate.

Outside, the ladies assembled the ingredients for sausage, heaping them in a large ceramic bowl. In addition to blood, ground meat, and fat from the freshly killed pigs, they tossed in mint, parsley, garlic, and oregano from the garden. To that they added generous amounts of hot pepper flakes and ground cumin as well as canned tomatoes. Manuela dipped elbow deep into the sausage fixings and mixed them forcefully.

Next, the filling of the casings, presided over by Josefa and Antonia. In every country where sausage is made, this activity always provides an opportunity for nonstop bawdy comment. The ladies took turns fitting the white skin over a tube in the manner of a high school health-class demonstration of the proper way to put on a condom. Then they stuffed the casing with meat, stroking it up and down until it was finally firm. More comments:

"You look like you have had a lot of experience," or, "I've seen bigger," or, "Who's your boyfriend?"

Three hours and forty-two minutes after the first killing, the butchering and sausage making were completed, about twelve hundred pounds of hog. Two of the ladies brought out the cauldron with the *cocido*. Manuela ladled out huge bowlfuls. With each, Dolores handed out a big chunk of bread for mopping up the flavorful broth, and, to wash it down, cold beer for each of our party and one extra that, Tomás explained as he lifted his bottle to offer a toast, was intended *"Por uno que donde queda,"* which roughly means "For the wayfarer, wherever he may wander"—kind of like the way, at the Passover meal, a place is set for the prophet Elijah, just in case he shows up hungry.

COCIDO,
EXTREMADURA STYLE

Donna Gelb, who describes herself as "a culinary activist," is a spectacular cook who has tested many recipes for *The New York Times*. She is also someone who, in the Aquarian Decade of her youth, found herself living and working in Spain, to which she returns every year. When I told her about my *cocido* she offered the following recipe. She also pointed me to some recipes from the records of the Spanish Inquisition that were given in evidence against *conversos* (Jews who became Christians after 1492). If a woman was found to be putting lamb or beef in her *cocido*, rather than pork, it was taken as a sure sign of apostasy, in which case the *cocido* was not the only thing that was cooked.

> 1 pound dried chickpeas (garbanzos), soaked in
> water overnight
> 4 quarts water
> 1 hambone
> 1½ pounds pig's knuckle
> 1½ pounds veal neck
> 1 pound pork baby back ribs (in one piece)
> ½ pound pig's jowl or unsmoked bacon
> 6 large whole peeled cloves garlic
> 5 sprigs each of fresh thyme and flat-leaf parsley,
> tied into a bunch with string
> 3 good large bay leaves
> 8 peppercorns
> Salt and freshly ground black pepper
> 1-pound piece whole pork loin, rolled and tied

3 carrots, peeled and cut into large chunks

3 small onions, each stuck with a clove

3 leeks, white part only, thoroughly washed, each
stuck with a clove

1 rib celery, cut in half

4 medium Yukon Gold potatoes, peeled and
quartered

1/2 pound Spanish chorizo sausage, pricked with a fork

1/2 pound morcilla sausage, pricked with a fork

1 tablespoon good Spanish olive oil

1 bunch chard, washed and roughly sliced

1 large head escarole, washed and roughly sliced

1 teaspoon Pimenton Dulce de la Vera

1/2 cup chopped flat-leaf parsley

1/2 cup chopped fresh mint

FOR THE PELOTAS (MEATBALLS)

8 ounces ground veal

8 ounces ground pork

1 egg, lightly beaten

3 rounds (baguette-size) country bread

1/2 cup milk

1 large clove garlic

1/2 cup chopped flat-leaf parsley

1 teaspoon Pimenton Dulce de la Vera

Salt and freshly ground pepper

3/4 teaspoon freshly grated nutmeg

1. Rinse and drain the soaked chickpeas. Drape the soaking vessel with a large piece of cheesecloth, allowing plenty of

excess to drape over the sides. Add the chickpeas. Bring up the ends of the cheesecloth and tie into a knot over the chickpeas, forming a neat bundle.

2. Place water in a 16-quart stockpot. Add the hambone, pig's knuckle, veal neck, ribs, and pig's jowl or bacon, and bring to a boil. Remove all scum that rises to the top.

3. Add the bundle of chickpeas. Return to the boil and continue to remove all scum. Add 4 cloves garlic, thyme, parsley, bay leaves, and peppercorns. Continue to skim as it boils, carefully adjusting for salt.

4. Sliver one of the remaining garlic cloves and stud the pork loin with it. Add the loin to the pot, continuing to skim. Reduce heat. Cover the pot and simmer for 1 hour, skimming fat as necessary.

5. Meanwhile, make the pelotas. Combine the veal and pork in a large bowl, kneading with your hands. Add the beaten egg, kneading it in thoroughly. Meanwhile, have the bread soaking in the milk.

6. Mince the garlic and parsley together in a food processor. Add the soaked bread, discarding any excess milk, and pulse until well blended but not pasty. Add to the meat mixture along with the pimenton, salt, pepper, and nutmeg. Blend well, and form into flattened oval meatballs. Set aside.

7. Add the carrots, onions, leeks, celery, and potatoes to the pot. Contiunue to simmer, skimming.

8. Add the pricked sausages. Simmer gently so they don't explode. Adjust seasoning.

9. In a large deep skillet, lightly brown the pelotas. Carefully add them one by one to the stew, placing them so that they will not get crushed. Simmer until the pelotas are cooked.

10. Have ready a wide 6-quart heatproof serving dish.

11. Using tongs, remove the cheesecloth bundle to the serving dish. Remove each of the meats and vegetables to the serving dish, arranging them separately from one another. Ladle some broth over the meats to keep them moist. Adjust seasoning with salt and pepper. Cover with foil and place serving dish in a warm oven.

12. Strain and degrease the broth.

13. Mince the remaining garlic clove. Heat the olive oil in the skillet over medium heat, and stir in the teaspoon of pimenton. Add the greens, stirring until they wilt. Add the garlic and stir, cooking until the garlic is combined and the greens are done to taste. Keep warm until ready to serve.

14. To serve, remove the serving dish from the oven. Cut open the chickpea bundle and remove the cheesecloth. Adjust seasoning. Moisten with plenty of heated broth, pouring any excess into a serving pitcher. Arrange the greens on a

separate platter. Serve with chopped parsley and sprigs of mint on the side.

Serves 8.

* * *

NINE

IN THE LAND OF
SINGING HAM

EXTREMADURA IN LATE WINTER, WHEN THE almond trees burst into full pink flower, is one of those places where Mother Earth seems most motherly. Dark-green oaks cover the hillsides and spill out onto the fields of the *dehesa*, the verdant plain awash with the blossoms of sweet pea, chamomile, and clover.

Josh, Miguel, and I had passed the night in Rocamador, a former monastery converted into a luxury hotel. It is much favored by celebrities and romantic couples looking for a weekend getaway. I think some Spaniards, with their history of stern Catholicism, get lit up by the idea of a romp in a convent.

Over a delicious meal of range-fed *retinto* beef (one of the ancestors of the Texas longhorn) and a tuber called *criadillas de tierra* ("testicles of the earth"), we were introduced to a young scientist and pig farmer named Abdom Cabeza de Vaca.

"Any relationship to the explorer?" I asked.

Abdom answered, "I am his direct descendant."

Of all the conquistadores, none undertook a longer, more arduous journey in the Americas than Cabeza de Vaca. What started out as a grand armada of five ships and six hundred men at arms suffered bad logistics, conflicts with the Indians, and disease. At the end of the eight-year trek across the southeast and the southwest, the Spaniards' proud army had been reduced to three naked stragglers, Cabeza de Vaca among them.

Five hundred years after the first voyages of the Spanish to the New World, hog raising remains an important part of the regional economy of the western *dehesas*. This in itself is not particularly surprising. What I find astonishing, however, is that the way the pigs are raised and, therefore, the way the land is looked after has hardly changed. The *dehesas* are a notable example of a system of sustainable agriculture and ecological balance.

First a little explanation of what a *dehesa* is. The literature that promotes Iberian ham leads you (or at least it led me) to believe that the *dehesa* is a primeval oak-park savannah. But as Victor Gomez, one of Europe's leading ecologists and vice rector at the ancient University of Alcala de Henares, explained to me when I visited him just a few days later, the hand of man lies all over the *dehesa*, just not heavily.

The word *"dehesa,"* which I thought meant "wide-open woodlands," in fact means just the opposite, he said. "It comes from the word *'defensa,'* meaning land that could be closed in and defended by the nobleman to whom it belonged. It was common practice to reward the nobility who defeated the Arabs with a gift of the land that the Christian knights had taken by force of arms. It may look like a vast open space, but it is literally a *finca cerrada*, or 'closed farm'; that means it can be used for only one purpose [which could be cattle, horses, sheep, pigs, olives, etc]. Although this stricture has eased over time, the *dehesas* are, or were, closed to the growing of grains, to the propagation of vineyards, or to the raising of other livestock.

"The use of oak forests goes back to Neolithic times," he said.

"Before the introduction of cereals, acorns were a prime food source, selected for sweetness (lack of tannin), fruitfulness, and size. In the same epoch that the Celt-Iberos [pre-Roman occupants of Spain] harvested acorns, they were also selecting pigs for size, fat content, and fecundity. Sometime, probably in the sixteenth century, the acorn harvest and the rearing of pigs were brought together in a single managed system, the *dehesa* system of swine rearing. The practice of transhumance [seasonal migration] of sheep herds also allowed a whole other sector of the economy to exploit the *dehesa* as sheep were driven to and from their winter and summer pastures eating the grasses that pigs had left behind. Merino sheep, which the Spanish originally imported from northern Africa, represented a monopoly that produced, in the time of the Hapsburgs, more revenue than all of the gold and silver looted from the New World. It wasn't until the eighteenth century that the wool monopoly was broken when Louis XIV obtained some merinos that became the foundation of the Rambouillet breed.

"Today, ham and cork represent the two most exploitable resources of the *dehesa*. But at current prices, they are not enough to save the *dehesas*."

"However," I said, "if you could export ham to the United States and Japan, you could raise the prices. It's like *grand cru* wine: There is only so much that can be produced. In much the same way, there are a finite number of pigs that can mature on the *dehesa*, but if you open up more luxury markets, you can double your prices while keeping the investment fixed."

"That is up to your U.S. Department of Agriculture," Gomez said, "but yes, the demand would more likely be there to employ the labor to maintain the *dehesa*, to prune the trees, to mend the fences, to mind the pigs."

In fact, American consumers have been trying to import *jamón ibérico* for some time, but the USDA requires that the pigs be slaughtered in facilities that are built entirely to its specifications. It doesn't matter that the facilities I visited in Spain were at least as hygienic as any packinghouse I have seen in the United States, nor does it matter that you can buy *ibérico* everywhere in Europe; if you want to do business in the United States, you play by our rules.

Speaking to this point on the morning that we made our way to Abdom Cabeza de Vaca's farm, Miguel Ullibarri said, "To the producers in Spain, all they see is the thirteen million dollars they would have to spend on a new processing plant rather than the long-term benefits with greater exports. Their logic is, 'Why spend more money when we are selling out?' At least that is the bottom-line business version. There is also this sense among traditional producers that theirs is an artisanal product where, at a certain point, quality, and the ability to ensure it for the future, is the key factor. That is part of the reason that the consortium was formed, to introduce minimum standards in the face of no government regulation. Some producers and distributors, eager to make a quick buck, are playing around with the quality, so we, the twenty-six producers in Real Ibérico, have instituted our own denominations, just like French wine."

Abdom Cabeza de Vaca drove between the entrance pillars to his family's farm, El Naranjero, named after a type of firearm, similar to an arbalesque, favored by the conquistadores. The *dehesa* spread across the wide valley floor. Thicker stands of oak, where grazing animals were fenced out, anchored the soil on the hillsides.

"You cannot make a *cerdo* without the *dehesa*," Abdom said categorically. "The *montanera* that begins in October is actually the culmination of a process for which most pigs have been prepared for a whole year.

"Apart from when they are sucklings, they spend their whole

lives outdoors. This allows the *cerdos* to develop muscles, which means, in turn, that there is some place for intramuscular fat deposits during the *montanera*. We have a saying, 'If you finish a pig on corn or silage instead of acorns, the ham will sing it'; in other words, the mature ham tastes like the food on which the pig fattens. The acorns must be ones that the pig walks to and actively searches out. Simply feeding them acorns that you have harvested does not yield the same flavor. And if you finish white pigs the same way, the manner in which the pig puts on fat and the quality of the fat is totally different from the *ibérico*. I love the *ibérico*; as they say, 'Hasta las andares.'"

Miguel translated this; it means that he loves the pig so much that he even likes its gait. I think Miguel gave us the PG-13 translation. My guess is that Abdom admires the *ibérico* because the way it walks, swaying from side to side, is like a woman.

I watched a drove of pigs resting against the sunny side of a stone wall. Beautiful creatures indeed—black with flashes of red—but I thought I would have to spend a lot more time around them, and less time around humans, before they began to look as good as a pretty woman.

"During the *montanera*, the pigs eat in the morning, rest in midday, and eat in the late afternoon," Abdom continued.

We walked toward the pigs. They wanted nothing to do with us. They lumbered to their feet and moved along the fence line, occasionally stopping to munch a clump of blooming chamomile.

Abdom picked up a handful of acorns.

"Are they okay to eat?" I asked.

"Sure, why not?"

Josh and I each tasted the meat of a freshly fallen acorn, slightly tannic but also sweet. It had the consistency of a slightly underdone potato.

We strolled toward the pigs. Though they appeared to be so fat and ungainly, they were quite good at keeping their distance. With the sun dappling them as it slanted through the trees and the tom-tom beat of their footfalls, they brought to mind a downsized Cape buffalo in the long grass of Africa.

Moved by a spirit of malicious mischief, Josh burst out in an imitation of the howl of a pig being led to slaughter. It was alarmingly accurate, so much so that the pigs quickened their pace.

"There's a sound that you put on your voice mail and no telemarketer will cold-call you twice," he said.

Abdom took a stick and knocked a branch of the oak tree quite vigorously. Acorns rained down.

"There are the pigs, and there are the acorns," he said. "Everything depends on the acorns [in much the same way that pig production in America depends on the corn crop]. If the summer is too dry, the acorn crop is destroyed. If it rains after they fall, the acorns on the ground are destroyed. For a good harvest, you want no late spring frost so that the trees bloom well with small yellow flowers and then an autumn with moderate temperatures and equally moderate rain."

Well-cared-for trees that are properly pruned have a broad canopy. At a density of 30 to 40 trees per hectare (2.47 acres), the yield might be 10 to 15 kilos (22 to 33 pounds) of acorns per tree. A pig must eat 10 kilos in order to put on one kilo of weight, or 70 to 80 kilos during the course of the *montanera*. They put on 1 kilo per day until they reach a weight of 150 to 180 kilos. That means each pig requires just under a hectare of *dehesa*.

Although acorns fall for free, raising pigs is not cost-free. Abdom explained the math. "First there is the land, six thousand dollars per hectare, which is what a vineyard that produces good wine will cost. The saplings must be protected, the walls maintained, and the trees require pruning. This job often fell to traveling gypsies, but in recent years these folk have settled down and the trees have suffered for it. The pigs must be fed grains to prepare for the *montanera*. Edible grasses and legumes must be raised. Someone must move the pigs from field to field so that they don't exhaust the land or root up everything."

I interjected, "As precious as these pigs are, at six thousand dollars a hectare, you can't leave the ground fallow for eight months in between *montaneras*." He answered, "When the *montanera* is done, we let the sheep graze, and then the brown stubble is for cattle. So yes, there is more to the *dehesa* than the *cerdo*, but there is no question that the *cerdo* is the king of the *dehesa*."

Acorns are essential to the rearing of *ibéricos* because of their extremely high level of heart-healthy monounsaturated oleic acid (62 percent in the acorn, up to 55 percent in the *ibérico*) as well as the coronary-neutral linoleic acid (up to 10.5 percent). Although this unsaturated fat content is less than the 83 percent that is typical of some olive oil, it is well above the levels of a corn/soy pig or a feedlot steer.

As Ullibarri put it to me in an e-mail follow-up to my trip to Spain, "not even *ibérico* ham is a 'perfect' food. Instead, it must be looked at as part of an overall balanced diet." As he said, "This means that each food needs to be judged based on its potential contribution in achieving a balanced diet in conjunction with other foods. Diets are good or bad (balanced or unbalanced), not specific foods. Coming down to fat, once we understand that it is also a key nutrient . . . what's really important is the quality as well as the quantity of the fat we eat. That's where *ibérico* ham and Iberian products in general can play a relevant role in our diet, as an alternative to other meat products with a poorer fat profile."

Though the pig's acorn diet is necessary, and is, in fact, the defining feature of *ibérico* ham, it is not, by itself, sufficient, as every scientist and farmer with whom I met emphasized. The fact that the pigs get exercise on the *dehesa* means they develop the muscle mass that can integrate the oleic acid from acorns. The grasses of the *dehesa* provide balance in the diet with a high level of antioxidants. The *dehesa*, then, is a perfectly balanced environment for the production of the best pork, and the oak is the key to the *dehesa*.

Oaks. The Druids worshiped them, maybe with good reason. They provide wood for shelter; fuel for fire; food for pigs and other wild things. I looked out over the hills of the *dehesa*. Covered with oaks, they rippled all the way to the Portuguese border until they melted into the blue haze on the horizon.

SUCKLING PIG BRAISED IN SHERRY, WHITE WINE, AROMATIC SPICES, AND HERBS

My interest in Spanish pigs first took shape as a plan for a journey after I sent an e-mail to Lento Fuego, the Spanish branch of
the international Slow Food movement toward artisanal and
healthful food. The mail was passed around and finally landed in
the office of a wildly engaging polymath, Antonio Gazquez Ortiz.
He is a professor of pathology on the veterinary faculty at the
University of Extremadura; he is also an accomplished modernist
painter, a historian of Spanish gastronomy and culture, a photog-
rapher, and a great home chef. It is through Antonio that I met
Jorge Ruiz and Jesus Ventanas, two academics who did so much
to help me understand the process of raising *ibérico* hogs and making ham.

One afternoon, Antonio took me to a pig farm high up in the
dehesa, on the border with Portugal. After tramping around the
fields for a few hours, we stopped to visit a monastery where we
were told San Pedro de Alcantara, a fourteenth-century monk, had
achieved his blessed state by sleeping in a cell that measures eighteen inches in length. For this act of faith over the course of a
number of decades, and for the requisite number of miracles, he
was elevated to sainthood.

Following our visit to the anchorite's monastery, we adjourned
for Sunday dinner to Palancar, a restaurant situated on a hill over-
looking the valley. The following dish, made from suckling pig, was
both delicious and memorable—perhaps aided in this last regard by
a huge cloud that hung over the countryside. Its swirling, towering
shape—all white, pink, and purple from the setting sun—looked

like a cotton-candy version of Frank Lloyd Wright's design for the Guggenheim.

    1/4 cup extra-virgin olive oil
    3 large Spanish onions, thinly sliced
    8 cloves garlic
    8 pounds (1/2 small) suckling pig cut into serving-sized pieces
    2 cups dry sherry
    2 cups dry white wine
    1 cup veal stock
    1/2 cup cilantro leaves, measured then chopped
    1 cinnamon stick
    1 piece of star anise
    Pinch of saffron
    Salt and ground white pepper to taste

1. Preheat oven to 225°F. In a large cast-iron pot or thick stainless steel roasting pan (such as a good turkey roaster), set over medium-high heat, add olive oil.

2. Toss in the onions and garlic. Sauté until the onions are clear.

3. Add the meat to the onions and brown over medium-low heat, approximately 10 minutes. The meat should be well caramelized.

4. Add sherry, wine, and stock and season with cilantro, cinnamon, star anise, saffron, salt, and pepper.

5. Cover and place in oven until fork tender, approximately 7 hours. Serve with pan-roasted potatoes.

* * *

TEN

MOTHER NATURE, FATHER OAK

YOU WILL RECALL THAT ON MY visit to the University of Alcala Henares, Victor Gomez had corrected my romantic, but mistaken, impression of the *dehesa*: Far from being the natural landscape
that I imagined it to be, it is, in fact, very much controlled by man.
However, I was not wrong in thinking that pigs are part of a particular forest ecology and, furthermore, that environmentally healthy
husbandry can only be understood in the context of an ecological
system, the wilder the better (it's also less costly). For pigs, this ecological community is the forest. But what do we mean when we say
"forest," and did it mean the same thing to a swineherd in Bourbon
Spain, Restoration England, and colonial Virginia?

Do we mean the brooding forest of the brothers Grimm, a
primeval, dark, unbroken canopy? The shadowed lair of trolls,
sprites, and warty witches who eat naughty children? Who among us
has not felt a twinge of terror at whatever lurks in the forest shadows?

Traditional science has, for the most part, taught us that our sto-
rybook conception of the impenetrable forest was historical fact. As
the theory goes, forests, like theatrical productions, have a "story," a

progression of acts. First, a bare stage. Then, exit the glaciers, or a forest fire clears the land, or a hurricane blows down the dense tree cover. In any event, something wipes away the landscape. Then, grasses and flowers and bushes pop up. Next, pines and light-loving broadleaf trees such as oak sprout up, and, finally, in their shade, the beech and elm and other shade-tolerant species take over, establishing a wall-to-wall carpet of tree-next-to-tree-next-to-tree.

According to this narrative, the result is a dense canopy of green, and, underneath, lots of mulch from fallen leaves. In the places where light peeks through, one finds a berry tangle here and there, or perhaps a seedling. This tableau is the "old-growth forest," or to continue the theatrical metaphor (and to give it the name that modern ecological theory has appropriated from dramaturgy), this is the Climax Forest, "Climax," as in the end of a play, or an amorous encounter, or both.

Maybe we find this tale so credible because it has a beginning, middle, and end story structure, and all humans are hardwired to interpret experience through stories. But could it be that the forest primeval is a "just-so" story: appealing, but as lacking in factual basis as the myth of Shangri-la? Granted, the forest makes a perfect headquarters for Grendel and her dragonly relatives whenever they feel the inclination to devour some unfortunate Danes, but do the fairy tales depict the past or simply the psychology of the present projected into the past?

If you have taken a walk in the forest lately, say, in the Catskills just north of New York City, you will probably have passed through dense stands of oak, hemlock, and beech, broken up by occasional open patches of light-drenched scrub. These luminous spaces often mark a spot where a tree has fallen (due to old age, lightning, ice, insects, disease, or wind). Among the creatures you will not meet on your walk are the cougars that once prowled here. Neither will you see the caribou that grazed here nor the so-called forest bison. It is puzzling that this last animal, a grazer, could have survived here, since bison find their food in open, grassy areas and our "climax forest" doesn't allow enough sunlight to reach the forest floor to sustain grasses. You might see a bear, but that is the only big mammal to be found.

For sure you will not run into some earlier Catskill residents: no saber-tooth tigers or woolly mammoths, no tarpans (the wild ancestors of some modern horses) or lumbering gomphotheres (think mammoth, only bigger), or the biggest land mammal of all, the giant ground sloth that paleoecologist Connie Barlow describes as "a bear, crossed with a prairie dog or marmot and endowed with the bulk of an elephant."

All of these animals once roamed the Catskills, the Jersey meadowlands, the crags and meadows of the Bronx, and the chasm, now filled with seawater, where one of my college professors suggested that Paleo-Indians once drove herds of bison and caribou over the Bayonne cliffs and down into the Arthur Kill that separates Staten Island from New Jersey. The presence of every one of these species argues for a landscape far different from the dark and brooding forest primeval and much more similar to the parklike expanses of the African savannah.

The forest bison, as I suggested, may be misleadingly named. Bison eat grass, lots of it. If you have bison, you have grass. Mammoths, or mastodons, or gomphotheres (doesn't matter which, they are all big) ate leaves as well as large fruits from trees, but they rarely did so in a dense forest. As I have seen in the low veldt of Zimbabwe, when a herd of elephants moves through a stand of acacia or baobabs, a swath of broken and uprooted trees marks their passage. Big animals in the forest mean big spaces in between trees. Once again, more like a park than a forest.

We should put aside those images of depressing Teutonic woodlands, if they ever existed at all. For the most part, in the temperate zones, the so-called climax forest is as much a man-made artifact as the patchwork of farm fields that cover the state of Iowa. In terms of biodiversity, Iowa could well outshine any textbook old-growth forest.

When Professor Gomez told me that the *dehesa* was the creation of the last millennium rather than the last twenty thousand years, I consoled myself, thinking, "Oh well, it is still a collection of the prettiest pig farms I ever saw."

Then I came across an article in the *New York Review of Books* by the Australian ecologist Tim Flannery. It included a review of a Ph.D. thesis now published as a book, *Grazing Ecology and Forest History,* written by Frans Vera, a Dutch ecologist. I bought the book, found it brilliant, and decided that in order to understand the place of pigs, and humans as well, in the natural order, I had to go meet this guy.

An exchange of e-mails with Vera produced an appointment. Within the month, I found myself following a set of travel instructions filled with unfamiliar combinations of consonants. "Take the train to Duivendrecht," he directed. "There you have to take the train to Utrecht [the intercity]. In Utrecht, you have to change to Driebergen-Zeist (probably direction Arnhem, Nijmegen), which is next to our office. I can take you from there to your hotel in Wijk bij Duurstede."

So much for Dutch being the closest linguistic relative of English. All those *j*s and diphthongs, and none of them pronounced in keeping with my sense of linguistics. Happily, many Dutchmen speak English, and their railroads run on time, so, as promised, Vera was at the Driebergen-Zeist station when I stepped down from the train.

Trim, with sandy-gray hair and beard, and wearing a tweed jacket, Vera looks at the world through rimless spectacles, which draw your attention to a middle-distance gaze that is a little world-weary, a little bemused, and, finally, reassuring. It strikes me as the gaze of someone who has had a revelation. This explains Vera's unshakable, but easygoing confidence in what he says. He is friendly but direct, having endured the challenges that all academics—especially those with paradigm-shifting ideas—endure in the course of the intellectual keelhauling known as peer review.

We sat in his office and talked. He showed me old woodcuts from the early Renaissance: swineherds driving pigs from a forest. Then we went for a car ride through the Dutch countryside, very slowly down straight, flat roads. To our right and left, the houses of the former gentry, some fortified, some not, lent a fairy-tale aspect to a landscape of unbroken green, of woodlots and grassy fields. From the height and spacing of the trees and the grassy areas in between, Vera was able to point out to me what was being managed for timber, what was about to be felled, what still had years to grow, what would be coppiced (a form of woodland management where trees are cut down to the stump, which then sprouts shoots).

Vera stopped occasionally. He spoke quietly, as one does when hunting or viewing golf, as if he didn't want to startle the trees by speaking too loudly. It was late in the afternoon. The yellowing grass of autumn spread across the flat lowlands, and the storks overhead threw shadows, as elongated as El Greco figures, as they winged in to roost on rooftops and chimneys.

We returned to town and landed in a pub, dark and wood paneled. We drank pints of beer that foamed over the sides of tall, frosted glasses. The rousing power chords of a recording of Bruce Springsteen, who is descended from good Dutch stock, thumped over the sound system. In order to be heard, we had to lean toward one another across the table, as Vera told his story:

He had started to piece together an alternative to the standard

theory of forest growth when he took a job in the grandiloquently titled Inspectorate of Nature Conservation of the State Forestry Department. A piece of that land called, by those who can pronounce
it, Ooosvaardersplassen had begun to arouse his interest just before
he took that job. It was a type of terrain known as a "polder," or
marsh that remained after Lake IJssel had been drained with the in-
tention of turning it into arable land. In so doing, according to prevailing theory, biodiversity would be enhanced.

This didn't sound right to Vera. "I have often been amazed by
the prevailing concept among nature conservationists that agriculture in Europe is the most suitable framework for maintaining biodiversity, since I have never heard them say that the tropical rain
forests of Africa, Asia, and South America should be reclaimed for
agriculture because—like in Europe—it enriches nature."

The land of the polder turned out to be too marshy for agricultural machinery, so it was left untouched until a solution could be
found that would make it suitable for mechanized farming. "Nature
then showed a side of herself that we in the Netherlands never
knew," Vera said. "Suddenly there appeared the yellow-flowering
marsh fleawort—a plant rarely found in Holland. And along with
the rare flower, marsh species of all types, such as the common cat-
tail, began to grow. These food sources, in turn, attracted a great variety of bird species.

"We were not in charge there. Nature came up with the solution
by herself. Thousands of greylag geese—that's the wild form of the
domestic geese—discovered the area [this was in summer; previously
the geese had come for only a brief stay during their migration to
southern Spain]. They got there during a period when they are very
vulnerable, the molting period. They cannot fly for about six weeks,
so the geese look for areas that are inaccessible to predators.

"The geese started to graze the marsh's vegetation, just like muskrats. The change affected the vegetation. That was unthinkable because the prevailing theory was that there was no animal in Europe that could steer a succession of vegetation. It could only be man. It was not to be denied. I realized we can have a situation where we put nature in power again. We just have to create that circumstance, which is analogous to the pristine environment. And that was the real discovery. It was against all the ecological theories I'd grown up with as a biologist.

"Then I spoke with Harm van der Veen of the Critical Forest Foundation [a renowned ecologist as well as a mentor to Vera]. He said, 'If you look to other continents, very large animals influence the vegetation; why not in Europe? Your geese are doing what the large mammals are doing in African terrestrial habitats. The herbivores are controlling the landscape.'

"So, influenced by him, I started to think, 'If greylag geese can do it in a marshy area, why can't large animals do it on dry land? And, if those molting greylag geese are only in the marsh for six weeks, where are they other than those six weeks?' They are in grassy areas. How do they get in grassy areas? A lot of people said, 'Farmers, cattle.' We said, 'Yes, but cattle are the domestic form of a wild ox.' Because agriculture is much younger in our country than the greylag geese, marsh-living cattle must have created grassy areas for the greylag geese. We don't have such wild ox (aurochs) anymore because they became extinct in 1627 in Poland, in the wilderness of Jaktorowska, a preserve southwest of Warsaw. But we still have so-called primitive breeds of ox that carry the DNA of the auroch."

"Not too far from Bialowieza?" I said. "That's where my grandfather was born. His father was, among other things, a forester. Grandpa never mentioned Bialowieza without adding, 'It was the last virgin forest in Europe.'"

"Not exactly virgin," Vera answered. In his view, so-called virgin forests are no more than protected tree farms. While it is true that the closed-canopy climax forest of the textbooks is what grows today when we leave trees to manage themselves, to make the leap and assume that this is the way things were in ancient times is to leave a very important element out of the equation: large grazing and browsing animals, or, to use the currently accepted, and dramatic, phrase, "climax megafauna."

In post Ice Age times, when trees once again took hold in the temperate zones, there were tarpans, aurochs, mammoths, moose, and wild boar to eat young plants, girdle the bark of trees, or completely topple them over. In Vera's view, instead of speaking of virgin forests, it would be more accurate to talk of virgin ecologies: landscapes and the animals that live in them—a spectrum of thickets, grassy patches, groves of trees, and the animal species that find food and shelter there.

Aurochs—the ancient wild cattle—lived in Bialowieza until the sixteenth century. Bison, another holdover from Pleistocene times, hung on in Bialowieza until the beginning of the twentieth century (1919). It is Vera's contention that large grazing animals contributed to a plant community that was more like a mosaic of grassland and grove than a continuous forest. Grazers and browsers, by their trampling and eating, would prevent the establishment of trees and shrubs in the understory. The only place where new trees and shrubs could take secure foothold was outside the forest, in the thorny plants and grasslands that foresters call "fringe and mantle," which grazers avoid because of thorns and stickers. In other words, natural regeneration does not take place in the depths of the forest, as the standard theory maintains. Instead, light-loving trees, notably oak and hazel, would sprout up in these fringe-and-mantle thickets, their saplings protected by a shield of thorns. In fact, in America, another name for one of the common sticker bushes that serve as a nurse species for oak and hazel, Vera observed, is oakthorn. Vera also observed that the word "acre," meaning a measurement of land, is derived from an old Germanic root, *acker*, meaning acorn.

Once you start to look at landscapes with this model in mind—a dynamic, ever-changing ecology rather than a static, closed canopy, or "virgin," forest—other anomalies begin to make sense. For example, on the subject of my ancestral Bialowieza, Vera asked why " the [late medieval] Polish hunter-king Jagello built a hunting lodge . . . in the center of the area. If the area was one of the last virgin forests, as is generally assumed, the central part will certainly have been a closed forest. . . . Did he hack his way through the forest to create a large, open space in the middle and build the hunting lodge there so that he could hunt aurochs and bison? . . . In the dark virgin forest round about, there will have been hardly any wild animals such as aurochs and bison because the closed forest is not the biotope [habitat] of these animals. Why would a hunter-king go to all sorts of lengths to go miles into the dark, virgin forest if there was nothing to hunt there? One logical explanation for the fact that he did so is that there was not a closed and inaccessible virgin forest at that time at all, but vegetation comparable to wood pasture, i.e., a mosaic of grasslands and groves that was reasonably accessible. The king could have penetrated miles into this, without too much difficulty, to enjoy the pleasures of hunting . . . far from the inhabited world and in complete peace and quiet."

Likewise, in the southeastern United States, although we Americans share a similarly fabulist *Last of the Mohicans* fantasy of trees stretching from the Atlantic to midcontinent, Vera is doubtful that such forests existed until humans did away with the large animals that maintained open spaces. In other words, what we have today is not primeval at all.

Early European travelers in America, among them members of

Hernando de Soto's band in the seventeenth-century South, re-ported "a gardenlike land of fruit-bearing trees, among which a horse could be ridden without any trouble" where there was "plenty of grass for the livestock."

Well into the eighteenth century, more than two hundred years after de Soto, travelers such as John Lawson and Mark Catesby wrote of large savannahs and prairies where buffalo "ranged in droves feeding upon the open savannahs morning and night."

In much the same way that the presence in Bialowieza of a hunting lodge where one cannot today find any game indicates a dif-ferent, more open landscape in the past, our latter-day notion of an original impenetrable New World forest is contradicted by what the conquistadores and early settlers encountered.

How does one explain the existence of a mosaic of grassland shrub and wooded grove when today, if left alone, that same land would produce the closed canopy forest of the textbooks?

Many American scientists think that the Native American practice of burning off the woodlands to create new agricultural land for the raising of corn had the side effect of opening up the for-est and allowing the growth of oaks. When the practice of clearing by fire disappeared, so did the predominance of oaks.

Vera, though he acknowledges fire as a contributing factor to the development of oak-park savannah, believes that the underlying cause is the presence of large grazing animals. "Being a true grazer, it is probable that the bison created a parklike landscape in America, just as the aurochs had in Europe. In this system, oak is able to thrive in the presence of shade-tolerant species that oust oak nowadays in the so-called old-growth forests. Oak disappears not because fire has been banned, but because a true grazer like the bison disappeared from the system."

Whether you believe that humankind, through the controlled

use of fire, was the key agent in opening up the landscape, or that bison were the lead players, the bottom line is that much of the eastern United States was oak park when the Spaniards arrived. As
forest scientist Hazel Delcourt wrote in *Forests in Peril*, "By six thousand radio carbon years ago, oak forest dominated across the breadth
and width of the modern-day eastern deciduous forest region . . ."
When the Spaniards got here, they found a mosaic of oak, scrub,
and grassland, perfect conditions for the introduction of their favorite food animal . . . the pig.

Vera's notion of landscape as a community of flora and fauna
shares, and in some cases derives, some fundamental assumptions
from the work of Dan Janzen and Paul Martin. In an elegant and
paradigm-shifting paper published in 1982 ("The Fruit the Gomphotheres Ate"), they confronted the paradox of such trees as the
guanacaste of Costa Rica expending much of their life force to produce abundant crops of large fruits that rotted where they dropped
because there were no animals that consumed them.

No organism, they reasoned, would have evolved to expend so
much of its vital energy to produce trash. It was much more likely
that those large fruits were a meal served up for evolutionary partners that have long since departed — namely, the great mammals.
Their demise was part of the global ecological catastrophe that co-
incided with human advances in hunting technology. This quater-
nary extinction, as it is known, represented the disappearance of
nearly 80 percent of earth's large-animal species as a direct result of
humanity's increasing efficiency as hunters and harvesters of game.

In Europe and nontropical Asia, the job of mass extinction was
largely accomplished by about fifteen thousand years ago. In the
Americas, Connie Barlow wrote in the journal *Arnoldia*, "Thirteen
thousand years ago, the Age of Great Mammals came crashing to a
close in the Western Hemisphere. Lost were the giants of the ele-

phant clan: the mammoths, mastodons, and gomphotheres which had maintained a presence in North America for twenty million years . . . Evidence is mounting that the newly arrived humans with formidable stone-tipped spears of Clovis design were to blame. This 'extinction of the massive' that marks the end of the Pleistocene epoch ravaged the megafauna. What happened to the plants?"

Building on this scenario, Vera's argument suggests, take away the large animals that lived off the plant community and you take away the landscape that they created. Take away the large grazers and you take away the large grazing areas. But sometimes a proxy steps in and picks up the work of a long-vanished species. In this case, the vanished species was the wild auroch. Vera finds confirmation of his theory "on contemporary floodplains where wild horses and cattle roam freely. There we find oaks establishing themselves under haw-thorns."

With this in mind, I think I now understand how the Spaniards have been able to raise pigs sustainably in a semi-wild environment. Pigs, in rotation with cattle and sheep, are proxies for the now ex-tinct large animals of Europe. This is not to argue that animal hus-bandry is the preferred way to maintain biological diversity, but it does suggest that the closer husbandry is to the wild model, the more sustainable it will be.

Roaming forest and field is what pigs were born to do. Long-legged pigs are the natural form of this animal, able to move nimbly through woodlands eating acorns and grasses. That they should be raised this way is as self-evident to me as the fact that cattle should be raised on grasslands and not in feedlots on corn and soy. Grazing (as well as rooting, in the case of pigs) is the natural way for these domesticated animals to sustain themselves and us.

"Agriculture is selection," Vera writes. "All over the world, dur-ing the last 10,000–20,000 years, about 40 species of the estimated total of approximately 50,000 naturally occurring species of birds and mammals have been domesticated: that is 0.8%! . . . Only 15 species of crop (0.03%) provide 90% of the global energy intake (of domesticated animals and humans). . . . During the past thousands of years, an enormous area has been cleared using the plough, the axe and fire for the small number of selected species."

Nearly twenty years ago, more as an intellectual exercise than as a blueprint for the future, Frank and Deborah Popper of Rutgers University proposed the creation of a "buffalo commons" in the areas of the Great Plains where depopulation and depletion of the soil leads one to the conclusion that conventional subsidized agriculture makes neither ecological nor economic sense in those areas. The buffalo commons is an idea that seems less conjectural and more possible with each passing year. To turn a significant amount of land back to the buffalo will increase the biomass and support the reclamation of a biologically diverse environment, one in which people keep the animals fenced out of towns and villages rather than everywhere fencing the animals in.

The Poppers consider the buffalo as a metaphor for the whole Great Plains ecosystem. Make the environment healthy for buffalo, they say, and it will be healthier for all. Likewise, to make the Northwest healthy for its keystone species, the salmon, we will have to undam the rivers and preserve the forest. As for pigs, I would add, they help preserve a savannah-and-woodland ecology from which we humans first evolved and where, psychologically, we feel most at home.

This is not to say that everything should be returned to its "original" state; that would be both foolhardy and impossible. I certainly don't want to remove pigs from the Carolinas because they are not indigenous. But to the extent that we are able to preserve species in something approximating a wild state as, for example, the marvelous trout introduced into Patagonia a century ago, then the better chance there is for survival of all species, including our own. This will get me into trouble with some ecological purists because, in the Southern Hemisphere, trout are an exotic; but where else would you put them now that we have altered or destroyed many of their home waters in the Northern Hemisphere?

Let me return to that nameless terror of the dark forest that I mentioned at the beginning of this chapter—the anxious feeling everyone who has been in the woods after nightfall knows from their earliest camping trips. Though scientists have written about the disappearance of the evolutionary partners of the plants that produced giant fruits, I would add that the human psyche, our inner landscape, likewise expects to encounter evolutionary partners who are no longer there. In the fifteen thousand years that have passed since we have gone from small hunting bands to masters of creation, we have mostly removed the lions and tigers, elephants and wolves from our physical environment, but they persist in our psychic environment. *That* is the source of the fear that we have in the forest. It is not so much fear of the unknown as fear of the collectively remembered man-devouring known.

There are still places on earth where one can experience humankind's true place in the biological pecking order. Go fishing sometime on Slough Creek in Yellowstone Park and you will notice the way the hairs rise on the back of your neck as you consider the possibility of a grizzly-bear encounter. You are not allowed to carry a firearm in Yellowstone, so if a bear does come your way, you will know you are assuredly not at the top of the food chain. Or begin to ford the creek as the herd of buffalo on the far bank decide to make a move. If one of them gets the notion to come your way, there is nothing you can do about it as the whole herd follows.

Similarly, I remember sitting in a blind at a waterhole in southern Africa watching black rhino and elephants come in to a watering hole at sunset, slowly, purposefully, regally. "You know, kids," I said to my children, "for as long as there have been people on this planet, they have sat like this and watched big animals. You've seen them in North America and you've seen them now in Africa. Every generation before you has been able to experience this, but you may, in fact, be the last that can say you have seen such creatures in the wild."

It's a long way from elephants in the low veldt to bison in Nebraska to Ossabaw pigs in the Carolinas. But the idea that creatures can coexist with us in a natural environment—in fact, *should* coexist with us for the benefit of our collective mental health as well as the health of our planet—seems to me to be so important. As Vera says in the final chapter of his book: ". . . the wilderness shows us the framework within which our cultural landscape developed. It is only by knowing the wilderness that we can understand our cultural landscape."

Or perhaps it is better to say that we cannot understand our cultural landscape if we do not understand the wilderness. Wilderness, however, has nothing to do with a particular cultural aspect of pork that defies nutritional and gastronomic logic and which I needed to get my mind around if I truly wanted to understand the psychological community of man and pig: the pork taboo.

ELEVEN

TABOO!

INSOFAR AS GOD IS SUPREME AND omnipotent, you would think that one warning from Him about consuming pigs should have been enough. But we are instructed not to eat pigs twice in the Old Testament: once in Leviticus and once in Deuteronomy. Muslims are reminded of this twice more in the revelations given to Mohammed in suras V and VI.

Why the repetition?

It stands to reason that no deity or parent would feel the need to forbid something repeatedly unless the prohibition continued to be violated. In the age of the prophets, apparently, God-fearing people were constantly eating pork, sacrificing it, and raising it. Otherwise, why bother to proscribe it? And why did pork consumption become a transgression only after Leviticus and Deuteronomy? Does this mean that up until that time, Abraham and Isaac, Moses and Aaron presumably could consume pork and still walk in the path of righteousness? What happened in the history of the Hebrews and then the Arabs that put pork out of bounds?

Let's start with the Bible. Although Moses, as an Egyptian noble, may have shared what some scholars have suggested was a typical upper-class disdain for pigs, it does not mean that his less-prosperous followers would likewise have turned their backs on an available food source, especially in a time of privation. If the leaders of our upper classes were, for example, aficionados of Gilbert and Sullivan and foie gras, does it follow that, given the chance, they would ban macaroni and cheese and hip-hop music?

So why the taboo? I put this question to Melinda Zeder—the head archaeologist in the anthropology division at the Smithsonian—when she kindly agreed to meet with me in the midst of preparations for her wedding the following week (it's not too hard to get archaeologists to talk at any time as long as you ask them something pertinent to their field).

"Well, I don't know if I can say how the taboo got started, but what has interested me is that when you look at the various domesticated animals in the Middle East—the cattle and sheep and pigs—you begin to weigh the pluses and minuses. In terms of the nutritional pluses of pigs, while they may not have milk as a regenerative resource [as cows, sheep, and goats do], they're still the best producer of meat of any of the domesticates. And yet, with [the coming of] urbanization, they just seemed to disappear. And eventually you have the taboos. So why is something that can outcompete these other domesticates taboo?"

"Could it be disease?" I asked.

She shook her head. Fear of trichinosis is hard to justify. Its onset is just too delayed for people to have made the connection. Disease is almost assuredly an after-the-fact explanation for the pork taboo.

So, back to square one: What could logically explain the taboo? This question, which would not go away yet seemed to have no satisfying answer, compelled me to take yet another transatlantic plane ride, this time to a symposium among my fellow pig geeks that took place in the north of England. It was at that same Pigs and Humans conference that I met Greger Larson. But Larson's knowledge of the evolution of pigs was not the reason for my journey; that was just a lucky add-on. My real purpose in going to England was to learn more about the taboo.

The setting was Walworth Castle, an imposingly crenellated medieval building–turned–conference center. Battlements and escutcheons outside and, within, furniture and decor that reminded me of an American home in the late 1940s (I have often thought that when it is not being trendy, much of England looks and feels like 1945, or at least what I imagine it was like; it's as if the whole country froze on V-E day).

Among my first acquaintances was economist and archaeologist Richard Redding. In black turtleneck and gray sports coat, he looked more like the manager of a hip Tribeca restaurant than a tweedy academic. We met at the conference's kick-off cocktail party, and while waiting at the bar for our pints of bitters, we began to chat. Upon learning that his current project is at the workers' quarters of the third pyramid at Giza (the tomb of Menkaure), I posed the question that had drawn me to Walworth in the first place. "Can you offer a reasonable explanation for the pork taboo?"

"Chickens," he said.

"Chickens?" I parroted, betraying some puzzlement.

"Yes, chickens," he affirmed, but before we could explore this topic further, friends and colleagues gathered round to greet him. He excused himself, promising, "I'll fill you in tomorrow if we get a chance to break away for a few minutes."

The next morning, a talk about tooth wear in ancient pig molars offered the opportunity to "cut class." As we seated ourselves in a small meeting room, Redding unrolled a map of the workmen's quarters at the Great Pyramids.

"Over here is the entrance through the Wall of the Crows that the workers passed through each morning on their way to the pyramids," he began, pointing to areas on the map. "You can very clearly see that you have four gallery complexes. This is where the people lived who worked and built the pyramids."

I saw a layout of long rooms, probably dormitories, alongside places labeled "kitchen" and "bakery." By analyzing the trash heaps from these areas, Redding concluded that the food, provided by the state to the thousands of workers on the pyramids, was primarily sheep and goat, as well as some beef and dried fish, but no pork.

On the periphery of this workers' area, the two sides farthest from the pyramids, he pointed out a number of smaller buildings. "And here in Eastern Town, as it is sometimes called, we've got an area that is probably more residential. People lived here with their families. These overseers and master stonemasons were probably getting some subsistence resources as pay, or they were getting goods such as rocks and other materials to build their tombs, as well as land on which to site them."

There was a high percentage of pig bones in the trash middens of the overseers' village, in contrast to virtually none in the workmen's quarters. In Redding's explanation for this, one begins to understand both the important role of pigs in the ancient Near East and their scarcity in the written historical record.

Written records detail the activities of interest and importance to the central authority. Neither in Egypt, nor in Mesopotamia, as Melinda Zeder has also found, do pigs figure into the extensive records of sheep, wheat, cattle, barley, and other important foodstuffs. But there is a difference between not appearing in the written record and proof that pigs were not part of daily life (as Donald Rumsfeld said in another context, "Absence of evidence is not evidence of absence"). The analysis of trash heaps leads, in many cases, to the opposite conclusion: Namely that people, especially the middle classes, ate lots of pig when they could.

Even in villages where sheep, goat, or cattle raising was a principal industry, the value of these animals as commercial items produced a situation in which the local consumption of them was often banned. In consequence, cattle raisers kept a pig or two around the house to provide for the family's protein needs. Evidence of this arrangement has been found at an Old Kingdom site in the Nile delta as well as Abu Duwari, a third-millennium (B.C.) site in Mesopotamia that was a wool center.

Redding hypothesized that small households often raised pigs, feeding them garbage and leftovers, and, in so doing, were guaranteed a reliable and cheap meat supply that was not dependent upon the state.

Herein lies one of the problems with pigs. If a society is organized around state control of resources, then it is important that citizens be dependent on the state. In this instance, pigs become part of a "gray" economy: They are there, the government is well aware of them, but they do not figure into the planning and provisioning that the state carries out.

On this topic, Zeder has similarly said, "Where you have urbanism, you have workers who are no longer engaged in the production of food for their own consumption. They are reliant on higher-ups for resources. But what they can do themselves is raise pigs. My feeling is, while pigs are not a good resource for large-scale [agriculture], controlled by the state . . . they do make a very good resource for autonomous households. You are able to have your own garden crop of pigs. They are able to provide you with a steady meat supply, and a pretty secure one." And further, "The degree to which small-scale pig rearing provided a buffer against the vicissitudes of state-level provisioning and offered individual households some measure of economic autonomy may well have made pigs a potentially seditious force in urban economies—one which those interested in controlling the flow of marketable commodities might well have wanted to discourage."

In much the same way, marijuana, which most scientists agree is at worst a mild intoxicant, is also a hardy plant that anyone can grow. This makes it virtually untaxable, whereas many alcoholic beverages require more sophisticated industrial production and distribution, which provides many opportunities for the government to collect taxes. The result: One intoxicant is legal and widespread and one is illegal and widespread.

In Bronze Age Egypt, the pig was widely consumed. The conclusion is inescapable, if the archaeological record is accurate: The "professional" class of artisans and bureaucrats at the pyramids ate pig in great quantities. In contrast, the workers (which, if the Bible is accurate on this point, included Hebrews) ate very little pig, not because they didn't like it, but because there was not much opportunity to get any. Meanwhile, these same workers could look out from their cramped quarters and regimented lives and see other workers, and their wives and children, and all of them pork eaters. Out of such proximity it is not hard to imagine the growth of first envy, then disgust.

But one is not sure that the Bible is or means to be taken as historical fact, nor is there independent confirmation of there having been Jews in the workforce at the pyramids. What is true, however, is the transformation of the Middle East from an area low in human population and rich in game to a complex urbanized and agricultural region.

American anthropologist Marvin Harris has written that with the domestication of wheat and barley, pigs came into direct competition with humans for these valuable cultivated foods. Free-ranging pigs would destroy valuable crops. Harris writes, "People always find it difficult to resist such temptations on their own. Hence Jahweh was heard to say that swine were unclean, not only to use as food but to the touch as well. Allah was heard to repeat the same message for the same reason: It was ecologically maladaptive to try to raise pigs in substantial numbers. Small-scale production would only increase the temptation. Better, then, to interdict the consumption of pork entirely, and to concentrate on raising goats, sheep, and cattle. Pigs tasted good but it was too expensive to feed them and keep them cool, because of their inability to perspire."

Redding concurs, but he also sees other variables. "Let's say you've got pigs, you've got sheep, you've got goats and cattle," he said, presenting the economic choices open to early Iron Age farmers. "If you've got a lot of cattle and a lot of goats, you are probably raising a lot of wheat and barley. In fact, to raise grains, you need cattle to run the plow. Now if you are in a society that goes into cattle, you can also go into goats because goats and cattle have the least overlap in their diet [they don't compete]. Sheep are in the middle. Goats are easy to care for: You can let them run more or less free, and you utilize all of the vegetation along the ridges between fields that the cow can't utilize. Pigs and humans are direct competitors for wheat and barley; i.e., pigs will do an awful lot of damage to wheat and barley fields. But when you find a site with less intensive farming of grain—maybe just a few fields of wheat and barley, but lots of dates and garden crops [multicropping]—the proportion of pigs often goes up."

Although the level of state-run agriculture and husbandry can begin to explain why one finds more or fewer pigs at a particular site at a particular time, there is as yet no correspondingly clear explanation for why they disappear totally from the record. Among other reasons for the taboo, some have pointed to the natural disdain of nomadic peoples for pigs. Pigs can't be herded successfully, it is claimed, although in post-Revolutionary America, pigs by the tens of thousands were walked to market over hundreds of miles. True, they cannot be driven with the same speed as horses, goats, and cattle, so nomadic peoples have tended to steer clear of raising pigs, but there is no reason that pastoral people could not have traded for pork in the same way that they sought other products from townsfolk.

Pigs, because of their lack of sweat glands, can only cool themselves by wallowing, and are often said not to be able to survive well in the hot, dry climate of the Middle East. The eminent archaeologist Caroline Grigson has observed that this has led to a "cut-off" line of 200 centimeters (18 inches) per year of rainfall dividing pig-rearing regions from areas where it appears never to have been practiced. Nevertheless, there are, and always have been, groups of wild boar in all of these regions. "I have seen active wild pigs in the foothills of the Zagros during July," Redding says. "The pigs were active at night when the temperature had dipped to a chilly 100 degrees Fahrenheit. Daytime temperatures at the time were between 120 and 125 degrees."

If neither environment nor agricultural economics can fully explain the pig taboo, perhaps the growth of settled communities can. When pigs are kept in villages as trash recyclers, there is no getting around the fact that they are filthy. Never mind that in the wild they are clean and sociable. In villages without sewage disposal, they are smelly, rambunctious, and dirty. But they were no less unsavory and ill behaved in the villages of medieval Europe where they continued to be prized as food animals, so being generally repulsive in the squalid conditions of ancient settlements is an insufficient explanation.

So what is sufficient?

According to Redding, it boils down to one thing: poultry. "Consider the chicken," he says. "We know that by about 1000 or 1200 B.C., there is a prohibition on pigs throughout much of the Middle East, and the question is, 'Why?' I was staring at the Egyptian data, trying to look at when chickens first appeared in Egypt, and it turns out that there is one pot shard from King Tut's tomb that shows a beautiful representation of chickens scratched on it. Significantly, that's around 1400 B.C.

"It then struck me that the chicken is the only animal that is more efficient than the pig at turning plants into protein. I began to wonder what happens to the subsistence system when the chicken shows up? And it occurred to me that the pig becomes redundant because both the pig and the chicken are a personal household source of protein, but the chicken is a more efficient producer, it requires less labor, and you don't have to keep a big, mean-tempered male around to anoint the loins of the sows. Furthermore, the chicken comes in a smaller package. If you're a family raising a pig and you've got a twelve- or sixteen-month-old pig that weighs one hundred pounds and you kill it, you can't eat all of it. That probably may take several days and you run the risk of getting sick."

In a draft paper that he sent me soon after the conference in England, Redding further developed this line of thought.

Chickens are a more efficient source of protein than pigs.

They produce a secondary product, the egg, which is also a more efficient source of protein than the pig.

A household could consume one chicken at a sitting. This eliminates the need to either preserve the meat or to establish reciprocal relations for exchange of pig meat.

The chicken can be used by nomads. The pig cannot be

driven or herded effectively and hence cannot be used by nomads. Nomads at present do use the chicken and move them
by tying their legs and throwing them on packs carried by donkeys.

Although Redding does not claim outright that the introduction of the chicken led to the prohibition of the pig, he does suggest
that "the introduction of the chicken *permitted* the prohibition of
the pig to evolve."

Of course one can raise both chickens and pigs; Redding's point
is that in the highly regulated cultural environment and hard physical environment of the ancient Near East, the return on investment
of labor and resources was higher for the chicken than it was for the
pig. His conclusion: "The prohibition was the societal way of codi-
fying the best economic behavior."

Meanwhile, in Europe, pigs roamed the forests where they did
not compete with humans for food. But in Egypt and Mesopotamia,
at the time of the domestication of the chicken, an increasingly arid
climate and intensive human exploitation had just about done away
with the forests and marshes that could have harbored pigs and
given them sustenance at no cost to humans. Pigs could only be kept
in villages at a cost.

This theory, Redding will quickly underscore, is still just a theory and needs to be confirmed by more research. Still, it has the
virtue of making good, practical sense of what has always appeared
to me to be an irksome taboo. The idea of God placing pork out of
bounds "just because" never squared with the notion of a just deity.
That He did it so that His people might thrive (and eventually in-
vent chicken soup) is much more comforting.

PART THREE

A FURTHER PIG'S PROGRESS

TWELVE

A VANISHING BREED

SEEING, AND CONSUMING, THE BLACK PIGS of France and Spain left me hungry for even more delicious fresh pork, great ham, and answers to some questions of more practical consequence than the taboo issue. Like, for instance, was it nature or nurture that accounted for the deep flavor and unique aging characteristics of the ancient Mediterranean breeds? In other words, was it a diet of acorns that made such unforgettable pork or was it, as every Spaniard said, the combination of their pigs' unique genetic heritage and an equally unique ecology? And, more pressingly, why couldn't I get black pig in America?

For sure they were here once: The Arkansas Razorback, the Mississippi Mulefoot, Iowa's Piney Ridge Rooter, the Choctaw, even the ancestor of today's Duroc breed were all, to a greater or lesser degree, carriers of *ibérico* DNA. The arrival of *ibérico* pigs in the New World can be pinpointed with precision because we know that the manifest of the second voyage of Columbus lists eight pigs and, further, that those eight pigs were off-loaded in Cuba, where they thrived.

Although some anthropologists have theorized that pigs were

too slow to keep up with nomadic peoples as they swept across Iron Age Europe, there is little doubt that nimble, long-legged *ibéricos* moved at just the right speed to match the lumbering pace of fully armored sixteenth-century halberdiers. Cortés never marched without pigs, nor did his fellow conquistador Francisco Pizarro.

A persistent legend has it that Pizarro, conqueror of Peru, was a swineherd as a boy in the Extremaduran city of Trujillo, a picturesque town, reminiscent of Siena, set in the hardscrabble highlands of western Spain. Some latter-day authors say this is an apocryphal tale intended to besmirch the despoiler of the Inca civilization. On the other hand, as an adolescent occupation, looking after a drove of pigs was as common in late-medieval Spain as having a paper route or working in a hamburger franchise is today.

On the mainland of the United States, pigs made their first appearance in 1539 when Hernando de Soto, a native of the ham-making town of Jerez de los Caballeros (as was Cortés), began his journey through the Southeast with thirteen *ibéricos* that he rounded up in the forests of Cuba. He found them roaming wild in great numbers barely thirty years after Columbus. By 1542, de Soto's mainland herd had increased to seven hundred. At the conclusion of his expedition, late in 1543 (de Soto himself had died at the hands of a Chickasaw war party on May 21, 1542), there were thousands of *ibéricos* grazing and pannaging the woodlands of the Southern states.

Native Americans quickly found that pigs were a reliable alternative to wild game. In his *Travels on the Great Western Prairies*, Thomas J. Farnham reported what he took to be descendants of the de Soto herd among the Choctaws, Miamis, Shawnees, Delawares, Senecas, Kickapoos, and Cherokees. But of all the millions of Spanish pigs that once roamed the great stands of oak and hickory in early America, it appeared that none remained; they had all been replaced by the stouter, faster-growing breeds that were developed for the sties and barnyards of northern Europe, and for the meatpacking plants of the cities spawned by the Industrial Revolution and the expansion of America.

Had America's *ibéricos* suffered porcine ethnic cleansing?

I didn't think so. Somewhere, there had to be a saving remnant. In the way that eighteenth-century English ballads survived unchanged in the hills and remote hollows of Appalachia, I knew that the great-great-great-great-grandchildren of the beautiful pigs of Spain simply could not have disappeared without a trace. On a visit to my family's ancestral condo in Boynton Beach, Florida, I came across an article in the "Outdoors" column of the *Palm Beach Post* that dealt with the depredations homeowners attributed to feral hogs (descendants of domestic pigs who had reverted to a more "primitive," wild state). Those eaters of golf courses and gardens, it was theorized, were probably descended from the original Spanish pigs that arrived in Florida with de Soto.

I read everything I could find about the connection between Spanish pigs and feral hogs. It was not always easy to separate folklore from science when dealing with random sightings by agitated homeowners who swore they "saw something big, like a bear or a big pig, rearing up my zucchini patch." Still, there is some good science on this question, most notably I. Lehr Brisbin and John J. Mayer's *Wild Pigs in the United States: Their History, Morphology and Current Distribution*. In that work, the authors discuss the pigs of Ossabaw Island, a strain that the American Livestock Breeds Conservancy describes as descendants of the Iberian pigs that had been brought to the New World.

Ossabaw, I liked the name: a friendly-sounding Native American name. No warlike hard consonants as in Comanche or Mescalero.

I e-mailed Dr. Brisbin, or Bris as he is known to friends and colleagues. He wrote back that he would be glad to speak with me.

He had first gone to Ossabaw in the mid-sixties. At that time, the owners of the island, the West family, and in particular, Eleanor "Sandy" West (a filmmaker, arts patron, and lifelong activist for family planning and environmental issues), had set up a cultural retreat on the island for artists, writers, and scientists. Bris, who was at that time a young scientist, was sponsored by Sandy's foundation. He recalls, "I first set foot here as a member of the Ossabaw Island Project, which was an interdisciplinary program funded by Sandy and her brother. There were scientists, artists, authors (Ralph Ellison, Margaret Atwood, and Annie Dillard among the most notable). It was great for them. They would work on their individual projects all day, then the little bell would ring for cocktails, after which we would all sit down in jacket and tie for dinner. The only problem was that the grounds were fenced in and I wanted to be in the woods.

" 'Snakes, boars, too many dangerous things out there,' we were told, but as an ecologist, I looked at those deep, wild woods and drooled. Finally, I arranged to meet with Sandy. She saw my point, and that's how I began to explore the island and learn about these pigs."

"Are they pure Iberian?" I asked.

He explained that although DNA analysis wasn't around when he was doing his feral-hog study, the assaying that they could perform showed that this population did not come from the mainland. In other words, they were brought to the island and left on the island and appear to be Iberians. Since that time, I have sent a sample to Greger Larson's DNA project and he's reported that there was a match with the spotted Jabugo (but the same match held for a number of non-Spanish breeds. The bottom line: There is no DNA evidence that they aren't *ibéricos* and some that suggests they might be).

"They're really quite special," Bris said. "You might think about visiting Ossabaw Island."

"Who do I contact?" I asked.

"Sandy West, she was the last owner of the island and basically the only resident. She's ninety-one years old and you can e-mail her."

"Seriously?" I said, to make sure I had heard him correctly.

"She's a pretty special ninety-year-old," Bris answered with a note of affection.

I e-mailed Sandy, and got a snappy reply. We spoke on the phone and I found her to be equally sharp and funny. Age did not seem even remotely to be an issue. I was given pause, however, when she informed me that she was a vegetarian.

"That's just me," she said. "I don't care if you eat meat; I just know what horrible things they do to those animals that you find cut up into little pieces at the supermarket."

I accepted an invitation to visit her island.

THIRTEEN

OSSABAW

IT WAS A CHILLY DAY, COLD and gray in that especially depressing way that January often is. A vintage, center-console runabout awaited us at the dock in Savannah. The erratic rhythm of its idling motor sounded like the throat-clearing cough of a lifelong smoker. A northeast wind of about fifteen knots meant that the passage from Savannah to Ossabaw Island would be sloppy and chilling. We passed a number of islands on the voyage. Summer houses, docks, and condos marked them as places comfortably within the zeitgeist of our zip-coded, zoning-ordinanced world, just like almost every island on the Atlantic coast.

Not Ossabaw, whose unbroken tree line hove into view. The island is remarkable in its "unremarkableness." By that I don't mean that it is neither beautiful, nor ghostly, nor inspiring, for it is all of those. I mean unremarkable in the sense that if you were to have arrived on Ossabaw when the pigs first did, you would have thought "Hmm . . . just a plain old East Coast barrier island." There were similar islands from Montauk to Miami—more oak here, more pines there—but all would have had beaches, marshes, abundant bird life,

dunes that had built up for centuries, only to be torn down by hurri-
canes, at which time the dunes would have commenced rising again,
grain by grain.

It is that unremarkableness that kept Ossabaw wild. It is probably
what kept the Spaniards from returning once they had left their pigs
there. After all, why waste time on a windswept, snaky, mosquito-
ridden islet when there was a whole continent to explore and exploit?

My companions that day were two of Sandy's friends, Lisa
White and Louisa Abbot, the former a lawyer, the latter a judge, and
both of my generation. Once a month, they come to keep Sandy
company for a weekend during which they cook risotto, drink wine,
talk family and politics, and laugh it up a lot.

Richard Boaen met us at dockside. Like many who live by the
Savannah shore and make their living on the water, he does this and
that, including running a waterfront improvement business and
serving as the general fixer-upper on the island. It was a short drive
to Sandy's home. Her foundling dog, Queenie Mae, rushed out to
meet us and to race with our car, as she does with every motorized
vehicle on the island. After years of this mock competition, she still
has not wised up to the fact that whoever she's racing always lets her
win. If you didn't, you'd stand a good chance of running her over,
and that would be the end of your relationship with Sandy West.

Queenie Mae is a royal pain.

We moved between imposing, though crumbling, gateposts to
the grounds of the manor house. Cabbage palms, Norfolk pines, and
oak trees garlanded with Spanish moss dotted the grassy landscape.
A horse and a donkey grazed by the shore to our left, and beyond
them a vista of whitecapped seas, islands, and trees bending in the
wind.

To our right, among the fan-shaped leaves of a palmetto patch, something black and furry and about the size of a dog moved. Dogs don't grunt though. Nor do they have tusks and bristling manes. Two more creatures of the same size and color moved with it. What I was looking at, I realized, were three Ossabaw Island pigs. It was as thrilling to me as if I'd come upon the tracks of the Sasquatch. I have read countless comic books and adventure novels of lost valleys where ancient animals, long thought to be extinct, are a common sight to peoples who are similarly marooned in an ancient age. Granted, these were just three pigs, three little pigs at that, but I felt that hushed sense of coming upon a dream made real. Had a bearded conquistador with finely tooled armor and broadsword hacked his way out of the forest at that moment, I might have been startled but not incredulous.

There they were, pigdom's lost tribe, the closest thing to an *ibérico* I was going to find. I learned shortly that I was looking at Sandy West's three pet pigs: Vidal Sassoon (so-called because of his striking coiffure), Paul Mitchell (i.e., somewhat less unruly of mane), and Venus.

Pigs named after hair-care products? Curiouser and curiouser! This dream was becoming a Lewis Carroll–comes–to–Georgia tale. Having said that, what fairy tale would be complete without its palace?

Not this one: There, in the architectural style that is usually called Spanish colonial but which I think of as 1920s East Coast hacienda, stood the pink stucco home of Sandy West, built in 1924 by her father, a wealthy physician and industrialist from Grosse Pointe, Michigan. I noted a picture window through which one could see a baronial living room dominated by a hearth on which you could roast a whole deer on a spit. Louisa told me that the house had fifteen bedrooms but that only one of them was occupied, by Sandy, the last private citizen to live on Ossabaw Island, which has now passed into state hands.

A woman with white hair, and the unfailing good cheer of a

fairy godmother, steps from the entryway of the grand house to greet us. It is Sandy—she reminds me of somebody. Kate Hepburn, maybe. She has the same slangy upper-class way of talking. It makes her approachable while leaving no doubt that she was born to the finer things in life. Her blue jeans and fleecy pullover, like Hepburn's khakis and turtleneck, are as artfully matched as a Chanel suit.

Her fierce attachment to nature—animals, leaves, sunlight, the sea—maybe Rachel Carson.

The way she lives all alone on an island as big as Bermuda, in a big pink mansion—and the knowledge that she will be the last of her line to live there . . . that's pure Chekhov, although Sandy certainly does not share the anomie of the Russian doctor's lugubrious aristocrats.

Each day, she fires up her old Apple computer and dashes off e-mails—most often disapproving of the doltishness of politicians and the dereliction of the Georgia Department of Natural Resources. My guess is that Eleanor Roosevelt would be doing the same thing if she were in residence.

What it gets down to is that when you have lived ninety-one years ("Damnit, I'm still ninety and a half," she corrects) as fully as Sandy West has, there are probably any number of roles for which you would be well cast.

Onerous tax laws forced her to sell Ossabaw to the state at the fire-sale price of four million dollars, now all spent on the kids, the grandkids, the great-grandkids, patching the roof, fixing the car, paying the phone bill. Had she sold out to real estate interests, this largest wilderness island on the East Coast might have fetched hundreds of millions of dollars. But then you would have the golf courses and condos of nearby Saint Simons Island instead of mile upon mile of salt marshes, oak forest, fatwood pines, holly trees, alligators, wood storks, wild asses, and Ossabaw hogs.

A child of Grosse Point society, of deb parties, yachts, horses, and hunts, Sandy developed a lifelong, almost maternal connection to her island. Selling to the state was the only way she could extract a guarantee that Ossabaw would remain a wilderness place. "No concrete can be poured here for a hundred years," her friend Richard Boaen told me.

How, exactly, Ossabaw's hogs came to be on the island is still not entirely clear. Nearly five hundred years ago—in 1526, to be exact—a Spaniard, Lucas Vasquez de Ayllon, founded a mission off the coast of Georgia. Historians agree that the site was either on Ossabaw or the nearby islands of Saint Catherine's or Sapelo. Although the mission lasted less than a year, the pigs could well be descended from the farm animals of the short-lived priory. One cannot imagine a Spanish settlement without its complement of pigs, and one cannot imagine pigs failing to thrive in an acorn forest. Or they could have come from the mission of Santa Catalina de Guale (the local Native Americans were known as Guale Indians), which was founded four decades later.

I learned this from a notebook that Sandy loaned me compiled by Richard Dean Perry, a writer who attended the Ossabaw Island Project some years ago.

It is from the Guale that Ossabaw gets its name. In their language, it means "Place of the Yupon Holly Bush," *Ilex vomitoria*, the most potent source of caffeine in the New World. The Guale made a black tea from it. According to early chroniclers, who often embroidered the facts in the interests of a good story, the tea induced visions as well as vomiting. Sounds good, but probably not true. *Ilex vomitoria*, in spite of its name, will cause you to vomit only if taken in great amounts but no more so than too much hot water. Still, even without the visions, a caffeine source might well have been the basis for a communal drinking rite.

Santa Catalina was as far north as the Spaniards got on the East

Coast. Inevitably, they came up against the British, pushing south from their original settlement at Jamestown.

At this point in my reading of the Ossabaw saga, I encountered the rich tale of the Indian princess of the Creek Nation, born in 1700: Coosaponakeessa, known to history as Mary Bosomworth. She was the first (and last) Native American to press a successful financial claim against the British. Her mother was an Indian, her father an Englishman. She was raised by a colonial family in North Carolina, and spoke English and Muskogean (Creek) as well as Mobilan (a language of commerce used by tribes in the Southeast). When armed conflict between the British and the Creek tribe ended in 1716, the Indian princess married John Musgrove, the son of the British colonel who negotiated the peace.

The couple prospered as traders. Her cousin, Emperor (or chief) Tomo Chi Chi, in appreciation for the access to trade goods that Mary enabled, gave her clear title to five hundred acres of land on which to build a home and trading post. As a woman, under British law, she could not own real estate, but as an Indian princess, under Creek law, she could. Those five hundred acres eventually became the city of Savannah.

In 1733, James Oglethorpe arrived in Georgia with the utopian plan of establishing a colony to be settled by debtors from England. As translator for Tomo Chi Chi, and as the chief businesswoman in the territory, Mary facilitated an agreement between the new British colonists and the Creeks. In partial payment for her services, Oglethorpe presented her with a diamond ring.

After her first husband died, in 1735, she married Jacob Matthews, formerly her indentured servant. Their business prospered, so much so that Mary supplied the British with money, gunpowder, weapons, and military intelligence in the war against the Spaniards that finally drove Spain from Georgia. Apparently, the enemy never learned of Mary's true sympathies and continued to do business with her without suspecting that she was gathering information for the British.

Mary, now the successor to Tomo Chi Chi in the matrilineal line recognized by Creek culture, inherited thousands of acres along the Savannah River as well as the islands of Sapelo, Saint Catherine's, and Ossabaw. But the British continued to refuse to recognize a woman's right to own land. Her contention was that she was given the land by the Creeks, not the British.

In the midst of this quarrel, Jacob Matthews died and Mary married yet again, this time to a clergyman, Thomas Bosomworth. The couple traveled to England to press Mary's case before the British Board of Trade. To everyone's surprise, the board ruled that "In consideration of services rendered to the province of Georgia" Mary Bosomworth would be given title to Saint Catherine's, Sapelo, and Ossabaw.

She kept Saint Catherine's and sold the other islands. Ossabaw passed into the hands of a series of owners before Sandy West's father, Dr. Henry Norton Torrey, bought the island in 1924 for $150,000.

So there is symmetry in the fact that the first owner of Ossabaw was a combative and capable woman who fought for her rights, and the last owner is likewise a lifelong battler for the wilderness character of the island as well as for women's rights (Sandy will proudly tell you that she was expelled from the Michigan State Fair for distributing birth-control information).

"But don't you dare call me feisty," she threatens. She is right too. "Feisty" is a code word for a woman of advanced years who is contrary and possibly off her rocker. "Curmudgeonly" is the male equivalent. You wouldn't apply this word to this vibrant, intelligent woman with hair as silver as moonlight and deep green eyes.

Her energy is impressive. In mid-dispute she will bound upstairs to fetch a book or document in order to prove a point. I am nearly forty years her junior, and in good shape, but in such instances I will run upstairs grudgingly or not at all. Even more confoundingly, once the point has been settled, she runs back upstairs to put the book in its proper spot so that she doesn't forget where it lives.

Okay, then not feisty, but how about a woman of firm convictions that she advertises right off the bat? The decal in her office clearly states, "Keep Abortion Legal." Similarly, the bumper sticker on her old SUV reads "Keep Your Laws Off My Body!"

On the second morning of my visit, Sandy suggested that during her nap her girlfriends would show me around the island, so Lisa, Louisa, and I made a two-hour circuit. As I always do, I asked about the best fishing hole on the island. The few local men who come over from the mainland to look in on Sandy all referred to a place called Cabbage Garden. Through long experience, I have found that when more than one local sportsman casually refers to a fishing hole as if all the world knows what he is talking about, it is often worthwhile to check it out. We never did find it, though, because as Lisa drove past the main house, Queenie Mae spotted us and raced in front.

"Damn, now we'll never lose her," Lisa said.

We continued along the road. Every so often, Queenie Mae darted into the forest, chasing the scent of whatever animals were there. Then, breaking the morning calm, we heard the high and horrified squeal of a pig.

"Oh my God!" Louisa said. "It's Queenie. She's got a pig."

I jumped down from the truck and ran toward the commotion. (I was later told that this is a foolish thing to do and could have gotten me gored.) Sure enough, Queenie had brought down a pig three times her size. The pig thrashed wildly, but Queenie had a lock on her hind leg.

"Queenie, stop!" I growled at full volume, but to little effect. I looked around and picked up a stick about the size of a broom handle. What could I do with it? Smash Sandy's dog? This was a dilemma, but as I wound up to hit the dog, the pig broke free. I brought the stick down hard, right in front of Queenie. That stopped her in her tracks, and by this time, the young pig had scooted into the forest.

Dilemma solved.

* * *

So I had found my *ibéricos* . . . or at least some of their descendants. As for getting them off the island, that would be very difficult. Like many creatures in the wild, a good number of these pigs had pseudorabies, a highly contagious disease, which, if brought to the mainland, could sweep like wildfire through the closely packed quarters of industrial hog farms. However, the cause was not lost. Bris wrote me with a suggestion.

> Some REALLY exciting diabetes work has just been started at the University of Missouri School of Medicine in Columbia, MO. They are using a colony of captive Ossabaws that we brought off the island a year ago.
>
> The results are most exciting—you should contact Dr. Michael Sturek, who is the associate director of basic research at their Center for Diabetes and Cardiovascular Research.
>
> Hope this helps. We need all of the outreach and positive PR that we can get for these unique animals, since the state of Georgia, which manages the island, would like very much to exterminate them!

It sounded like the thing to do. But what did I really know about these pigs other than that they looked like the pigs in medieval woodcuts? Also, they were small, but that phenomenon, known to scientists as "insular dwarfism," I knew something about. I had seen it with deer in the Florida Keys. Basically, in the Darwinian effort to survive, animals that live on small islands tend to be smaller. Remove that selective pressure and, in a few generations, you will have normal-size animals. There were, however, other qualities of the Ossabaw hog that I needed explained to me.

I called Bris to fill in the blanks. An alarming fact that he shared with me made my project seem all the more necessary—namely, the state, having declared the Ossabaw pig an exotic pest that endangers the nests of sea turtles, has sought to exterminate them. Last year, they hired a pig assassin who is said to have shot sixteen hundred hogs, leaving their carcasses to rot where they fell. Of course, the state's action begs the question, how did the turtles manage to survive during five hundred years of coexistence with the Ossabaw pigs?

In striking contrast, the Wildlife Conservation Society (formerly, the Bronx Zoo) maintains neighboring Saint Catherine's Island as an ark, or refuge, for zebra, lemurs, eagles, et al. These animals are no less exotic to the Americas than the Ossabaw hog, and, speaking in purely numerical terms, are probably no more endangered than these marvelous pigs. If, on Ossabaw, the state continues to hunt the pigs, the only hope for this breed is that we will be able to raise them as food animals on the mainland.

But having evolved for the unique characteristics of Ossabaw, I wondered, how suited are they to the mainland?

"Bris," I asked, "these pigs have been here for about five hundred years. That's nothing in evolutionary terms. How can they tolerate brackish drinking water?"

Their salt tolerance is an example of evolution in the making, Bris answered. "There was a study done by Stamos Zervanos at Penn State in which he compared Ossabaws, Durocs, and Hampshires. He found that as you added more and more salt to their water, the pigs began to show signs of stress (the scientific term is "osmotic shock") and they eventually croak. The Ossabaws showed the most salt tolerance."

This is not to say that Ossabaws can survive by drinking only seawater, but, rather, that they can tolerate more brackish water than other pigs. "It's not so much a question of evolution as extreme selection pressures at work, although, in the long run, that is evolution," he said. Over time, those pigs that could survive a high salt intake, or, more precisely, those who could rid themselves of high quantities of salt more efficiently, had passed their genes on to succeeding hundreds of generations of swine since the Spaniards left the first pigs on the island.

But salt tolerance has other indirect benefits as well. As the year progresses, and freshwater dwindles or gets more brackish, the animals can still take in liquids as they now find themselves in what Bris refers to as "a survive or die mode."

"If you look out over the salt marshes on Ossabaw, you will see hammocks [raised wooded areas]. These are small islands in the saltwater marshes. Pigs that can survive on those small islands because of their tolerance for brackish water have access to a ready food supply in the form of acorns, and, equally important, they can bear their young in safety because predators are not drawn to cross the salty marshes to reach the hammocks."

"And the fat?" I ask. "Why can they put on fat faster than any land mammal, including other pigs?"

"The propensity toward fat is a function of what is known as 'the thrifty gene,'" he explained. "In a feast-or-famine environment, many mammals will put on fat very quickly when there is abundant food so that, in the less bountiful times, they have a store of energy to draw upon. In the presence of a constant food supply, they grow obese, just like modern-day humans."

In this context I now understood that in the same fashion, the *ibéricos* of Spain live according to a similar rhythm of the seasons. They are lean and well muscled at the end of the summer. When the acorns fall, they gorge themselves for the next four months. Abdom Cabeza de Vaca sees to this on his farm in Extremadura. Nature takes care of it on Ossabaw.

Doing what comes naturally would be the simple summing up of my projected attempt to raise great pigs. But American agriculture is a long way from the state of nature. Still, there are places—more of them all the time—where old-time agriculture is being supported by the evolving modern demand for taste, healthfulness, and doing the sane thing environmentally. Like a rose growing through a crack in a city sidewalk, it's not easy to do, but nonetheless, it happens.

Given that there were Ossabaws on the mainland and farmers interested in raising more flavorful pork, a project began to take shape, something that had been on my mind since my return from Spain: raising pigs in the Spanish style here in America. The missing link was provided by Don Bixby of the American Livestock Breed Conservancy, a splendid organization devoted to rescuing farm breeds on the brink of extinction. Bixby knew about a professor who was working with small farmers and pigs. "He's feeding them pumpkins, sweet potatoes, and other garden scraps. You might want to check him out."

He was referring to Chuck Talbott, who later helped me transport twenty-three pigs from Missouri to the Carolinas. Talbott's enthusiasm for my scheme was instant. "Damn right I'm interested. This is what I've been talking about: upscale pork for niche markets!"

Not only was he interested, but as director of his school's Small-scale Hog Producer Project, and under the terms of a grant he had received from the Golden Leaf Foundation, he also had the funds to help acquire and raise hogs. I next contacted Mike Sturek, at the NIH, who was intrigued by our idea of rearing these descendants of ancient Spanish pigs. For a hundred bucks a hog, Chuck and I had ourselves a deal.

Talbott invited me down to North Carolina to a conference of small farmers in the Piedmont region, near the coast. We would re-cruit some farmers there who were interested in the Ossabaw idea. The Piedmont: They used to raise hogs on peanuts here. No more, though. Peanuts go to people. Peanut hay, an excellent source of bulk and antioxidants, goes to cattle. Corn and soy are now, far and away, the preferred feeds for the two classes of hog raisers in the state: One class owns enormous facilities that it would be more accu-rate to call hog factories than farms; the other class is made up of small-scale farmers that Chuck Talbott is supporting through his grant. Those funds came out of the lawsuit against the tobacco com-panies and the resultant $246,000,000 settlement of 1998.

"We're trying to find something other than tobacco for them to raise. Pigs are good candidates," Talbott said.

With a scraggly beard, orange suspenders, thick glasses, and the permanent smile of a swami, Chuck is an amiable man who is hap-piest, I think, when dealing with animals. He studied at the Univer-sity of Colorado, where he received his Ph.D. in animal breeding and genetics. His résumé also includes work as a hired hand on cat-tle and sheep ranches in Colorado, Wyoming, Montana, Alaska, New Zealand, and Australia. With the air of a veteran recounting a favorite war story, he said of his Australian experience, "The ranch was five thousand square miles. For roundup, they would use chop-pers. The pilots, who had been in Vietnam, would drop down low and drive the cattle out of the woods. Sometimes they would moti-vate the more stubborn bulls with shotgun blasts."

"Techno cowboys, Chuck. Were the animals free-ranged on grass, like in Argentina?" I asked.

"Yes."

"How did they taste?"

Chuck squinted, pursed his lips in an expression that is half smile and half grimace—a gesture to which he is prone and which signals, I think, his semipermanent state of cheerful bafflement. "Some of it was great and some of it tasted like your belt," he said.

The crowd of farmers that Chuck had invited to the Piedmont meeting, mostly African Americans, had gathered at a small farm in Kenansville, North Carolina, for the summer farrowing workshop. Farrowing, in the lexicon of pig farming, is the term for a pig giving birth. Pig farmers rarely refer to the newborns as piglets. Right from the start, the young ones are known as pigs, as in, "When a mother gets ready to have pigs, she'll make a nest for them." This is how Paul Willis, another attendee at the workshop, put it.

Willis is the founder of Niman Ranch Pork, which markets the pasture-raised pork of three hundred family farmers. He is one of the major backers of Talbott's program, having donated many hogs. He had come to the workshop, in part, to show the flag of real business to the fledgling pig farmers. Another reason for his visit was to demonstrate to the newbie farmers how to castrate young boars. I expected, given the situation, that the young pigs would howl. But when Willis picked them up—gently and expertly—they let out no more than a little squeal. When he cut them, he extracted the gonads and discarded them as you would toss away two cherry pits. By this time, the little pig had quieted down. No big deal apparently.

A short way from the small Quonset huts where the mothers lay with their sucklings, a six-month-old pig was being cooked on a rig made of an oil drum cut in half and set on four legs welded to its underside. Shafts of blue smoke caught the dappled sunlight, shining through the leaves of an old chestnut tree.

An elderly man tended the smoker, although there was not much tending required. He sat in the shade, at ease in his folding beach chair. A Wilson Pickett song blared out from the speakers of the van parked next to him. The doors were opened and the windows lowered to let "Mustang Sally" ring out at full volume.

"Hey, good morning," he said, handing me a paper bag with a bottle in it. "Want some shine?"

I sniffed the corn liquor: sweet and oily, like grappa. I handed it back to him, saying, "Smells great, but a little early in the day for me."

He replied with an I've-heard-it-before shrug. "Well, I don't care if you do or you don't, 'cause I'm the one who has to deal with it." These struck me as the words of a man who is at peace with his drinking.

Paul Willis finished his neutering demo and we toured the adjoining woodlot where the pigs were given free range and where some of the mothers had chosen to farrow. So much for the canard that pigs prefer to lie in their own filth. They do so only when they don't have a choice.

With the morning's work done, we piled into the bus and headed over to the Duplin County Cooperative Extension Office. The moonshine sipper's pig arrived before us, its meat already pulled and sauced with peppery vinegar. Fried chicken, beans, macaroni salad, corn bread, biscuits, coleslaw all awaited. But first, a prayer of thanks offered by a man who clearly relished his moment at the head of the crowd. Not only did he thank the Lord for each and every menu item (which he roundly enunciated by name), he also thanked Him for the seasons, the presence of nearly everyone in the room (again by name), the earth, the animals (another litany) . . . in short, he might well have delivered a shorter invocation had he made a list of the things that we were not particularly thankful for.

I loaded up my plate and sat next to Emile DeFelice, a dark-haired, deep-tanned man who farms pigs in Saint Matthews, South Carolina, which, he informed me, is in the poorest county in that state. He got into pig farming through a nontraditional route. He was a student of French and philosophy. His French landed him a job at the Carter Center during the time that Jimmy Carter was brokering what was hoped to be a settlement to Haiti's governmental crisis in the early nineties. From there, he drifted into graduate school at the University of South Carolina. "While I was studying, I started growing basil in my backyard, mostly because that's what my dad grew in the garden. I took it down to the market and was soon selling thirty to forty pounds a week. Then I started offering it to restaurants and sold more. Nine months of mortgage payments off one crop, that basil. The business grew from there. I bought a small farm and rented some other small farms, et cetera. About that same time, I realized I couldn't work cooped up inside as a professor. I liked the people, I like writing, but I felt like I was trapped. So I wrote the school a letter saying, 'Thanks, but I'm gonna be a farmer.' "

"How did you get into pigs?" I asked.

"Pigs—well, that was sort of an accident. I knew that people used pigs to get rid of waste, and boy, did we ever have waste! I was selling greens all over the state. You left with the van at two in the morning and it always came back with waste. I got pigs to help get rid of stuff that was edible. I would feed them all my pumpkins left over after Halloween, and watermelons after the Fourth of July. Mostly I was raising pigs on the cheap. I knew pigs like acorns, so I would go around and rake up acorns and feed them."

A bell went off in my head. "You feed your pigs acorns?"

"Hell, yeah, my woods are full of them. When I let the pigs out, I know where they are by the sound of them crunching acorns."

"Let me tell you about these Ossabaw Island pigs I am getting from the NIH."

Emile wanted in, which is how, and why, at the beginning of this tale, I found myself hauling a load of pigs to the Carolinas.

FOURTEEN

HOME AGAIN

AFTER TWO DAYS ON THE INTERSTATE, traveling from the NIH facility in Columbia, Missouri, to South Carolina, Chuck, his colleague James DeLoach, and I delivered eleven Ossabaw hogs to Emile (the other dozen hogs would go to the North Carolina farm of Eliza Maclean—more about her later). The pigs appeared happy and in fine shape after their journey. We put a bale of hay next to the truck so that they could step down more easily, but, after nine months of life in the lab, serving science by eating a high-fat diet (not unlike the one consumed by the average American), they didn't know quite what to make of fresh air and sunshine. Chuck coaxed one out. She stumbled, regained her balance, and looked around.

"The Neil Armstrong of pigs," I thought.

The other pigs were reluctant to follow, so Chuck and James De-Loach encouraged them. "Go on, you pigs," James said and gently prodded them. They tumbled down the hay bale and rolled on the grass, blinking at the unfamiliar surroundings.

The newly arrived pigs gathered around in a circle, tails in, heads out. Their manes, running the length of the backbone, stood up straight. Seen in this way, with pointy snouts, long legs, and bristling manes, they looked like they would have been at home among the animals in the Bayeux tapestry.

We shooed them along. They broke ranks, only to re-form their odd circle.

"Protecting the litter," Chuck explained. "It's an instinctive behavior."

Even when we moved away, the pigs maintained their defensive position. Protecting themselves from what? I wondered.

Jim Wenzel, an associate of Mike Sturek at the University of Missouri, answered that question in an e-mail later that week.

> When doing EKGs on Yucatan pigs, a big jump is noticed if a dog barks in a room far away from the pig's quiet EKG room. This seems strange because dogs bark a lot at our laboratory. I would think the pigs would get used to it, but they do not. If the pigs see dogs in a hallway while in a cart to be weighed, they act jumpy and fearful.

The pigs weren't afraid of us. It was Ellie, Emile's cockapoo (half cocker spaniel, half poodle), that had the little Ossabaws so freaked out.

Dog barks, pig cowers; it's instinct.

Next to the paddock that had been fenced in for the Ossabaws (who quickly learned, after a few pissed-off squeals, to avoid the electrified single-strand wire that runs along the base of the fence) were the other hogs, standard modern breeds, that Emile was raising on corn and soy but who also had free range of the forest.

We walked into the woods and soon saw more pigs, some quite large, eating nuts, rooting for grubs and worms, and nibbling on greens. Funny that I should be in awe of a bunch of plain old pigs, but coming upon creatures in the wild has always seemed to me to be a bona fide thrill.

"Crunch, crunch, grunt, belch"—the pigs vocalized, less thrillingly.

"It'll be interesting," I told Emile, "to see if finishing them on nuts and greens, like the Spaniards do, will make their meat as delicious as that of the Iberian hogs."

"Way ahead of you, buddy," he said. "My pigs are already getting good and fat in the woods. They stay out for hours. Sometimes I hear them way down in the swamp. But when I open the gate, they always come back."

We returned to the farmhouse, the colonial-era home of Emile's parents. Kids ran in and out of rooms like the cast of a French farce. Emile served up a bone-in loin from one of his forest-grazing pigs, a Large Black. The meat was succulent and full of aroma, the fat crisp and salty. Like a freshly picked tomato (we had those too), fresh-killed pork, raised outside, as fit and fat as a sumo wrestler, needs nothing but a fork and knife to be enjoyed. In fact, if you are really committed, forget the flatware and go Neanderthal.

A few days later, after I returned to Brooklyn, Emile wrote:

> Hey, buddy, the Ossabaws are just great. I hope they taste as good as they act. They are like dogs, lots of gentle curiosity, but no noise! save for some obligatory grunts and token nips. Really great to see them; they ball up together in one spot, under a shady oak. Not overly active, nor do they eat everything in front of them; it's hard to picture the thrifty gene in full swing.

I lie down in the grass and they eventually come sniffing. We have absolutely got to get some semen to continue the flock.

Another first for me; I never thought I would find myself agreeing with a friend that our lives would be improved if we could just find a way to get some boar semen.

But if you want to keep making pigs, well . . .

FIFTEEN

WHY PORK TASTES GOOD
AND HAM TASTES GREAT

I THINK THAT ONE OF THE reasons I am so wild for pork in general and ham in particular is that it has more taste than almost any other meat. Why it does, and how this happens, are related questions. One could just as reasonably wonder why, of all the fermentable fruits in the world, a cult and an industry grew up around the grape. That would be a proper subject for another book. For me, it is enough to know that people have been making wine primarily from grapes for millennia and getting better at it. Working back from effect to cause, it's fair to say there's something that grapes have that other fruits don't. I think it is the ability to express more flavors with more nuance.

It is the same with ham versus other cured meats. In this regard, it took a chance discovery by a French chemist to begin to explain scientifically what ancient Roman chefs, medieval Castilian peasants, and Kentucky hillbillies all knew from experience: A long-cured ham unleashes wave upon wave of flavors and their airborne cousins, aromas.

Before the chemistry, though, there was the simple, though by no means universal, knowledge that salt preserves food. Among western peoples it was the pig-loving Greco-Romans (as opposed to the sheep, goat, and cattle-rearing people of the Middle East) who perfected salt curing and aging. That is a bit of a puzzlement though. The Egyptians were masters of the art of flesh preservation: Look at their mummies. Apparently, it never occurred to them to apply this technology to anything but an inedible ancestor. In any event, the salts used for mummification tasted horrible (when they weren't downright poisonous). Moreover, as we have seen, the pig has always held a tenuous spot in the culture and diet of the peoples of the ancient and modern Near East, so perhaps folks just never got around to preserving pork.

Pork is salted for the same reason that salmon is smoked, cheese is aged, and wine is fermented: Extending the "shelf life" of food that is harvested in times of plenty is a powerful survival strategy for the inevitable lean times. People didn't know how good ham would taste before they made the first ones. So their motivation wasn't taste as much as it was a desire to preserve food.

A similar need—how to deal with a lot of dead meat—arises from the keeping, feeding, and slaughtering of other large animals, but preserved mutton or beef is really quite blah. Gastronomically, what explains the preeminence of ham?

"It cheweth not its cud," warns the book of Leviticus, as if this were a self-evident indictment. I would say, quite to the contrary, because it cuddeth not, the pig does not transform the fats that it ingests. Ruminants digest things twice, and in so doing, transform fat. More scientifically, Dave Gerrard of the department of animal sciences at Purdue told me, "If you feed peanuts to pigs [as we were doing with our Ossabaws to supplement the acorns], they will deposit the fat as peanut oil, soft fat. On the other hand, you can feed cattle or sheep fat and it will be hydrogenated [get hard like butter]. These animals saturate their fat."

Pigs are not ruminants: They don't process the fat they eat in a second stomach. For this reason, pork fat has more of the subtle flavors of the acorns, soybeans, peanuts, and corn that the animal consumes. If the fat tastes good, so will the meat. By way of counterexample, Iberian swine in the Andes, where, instead of acorns, the pigs eat garbage, manure, or offal, are not known for their taste. For that matter, in the United States, with "hygienically produced" factory pigs that eat ground-up viscera and fish meal, the fat and, therefore, the meat cannot taste sublime.

The fat produced from acorns or peanuts contributes to the best-tasting ham, but they are soft fats that oxidize easily. In other words, they turn rancid. One solution would be to raise pigs only on feed that produces hard fat, for example, barley or wheat. But as the farmers of old-time Smithfield, Virginia, knew, along with the swineherds of southern Europe, pork with soft fat is juicier provided that the fat gets into the muscle tissue. Moreover, and this bears repeating, the oleic acid in acorns is not a henchman for cholesterol.

One cannot consider this fact in isolation. The pig doesn't; it needs a balanced diet as much as any other creature. Whether they are raised free range, as in Spain, or in pasture/paddocks, as the Niman Ranch farmers do, pigs, when given the chance, will eat clover, alfalfa, sweet peas—a whole range of grasses that provide bulk, protein, and antioxidants. These last, the antioxidants, are critical in aging ham with softer fats. Over the course of at least two years of aging, which is what a prime Iberian ham undergoes, the fat would oxidize rapidly and turn rancid before the first summer were it not for the antioxidants. That being said, Ruiz, and his mentor on the veterinary faculty, Jesus Ventanas, have found that the right rate of oxidation during the maturing process will allow some of the fat to break down into pleasing volatile, or aromatic, compounds.

So it is not simply a question of fat, but fat in the right amount aged at the right temperature for the right amount of time. Still, a great ham starts with a goodly amount of fat. When I showed pictures of a Spanish pig-killing to Duplin County small-scale farmers, a collective "Aah!" of wonderment filled the room as they saw the thick layer of fat on the splayed carcass of the *ibérico*: as white as goose down and thick as a comforter.

A word or two here in defense of fat. A combination of overconsumption and a sedentary lifestyle has no doubt contributed to the worldwide problem of obesity among "developed" peoples. Among the nutritionally conscious, fat is a modern wolfbane, reviled as a poison. In this regard, fat has been given a bum rap.

Evolutionary biologists are in accord that, without increased fat consumption (actually, the long-chain fatty acids known as omega-3s), our primate ancestors would never have developed large brains. According to one theory, a general savannahization occurred in Africa about 2.5 million years ago. One group of primates became a parallel lineage to our own, responding to the change in availability of food, occasioned by the disappearance of the forest canopy, by turning to a diet with large quantities of fibrous food that modern humans would find largely indigestible. These primates developed huge, heavily muscled jaws and molars and equally enlarged Klingon-like brows to anchor their chewing muscles. These australopithecines, as they are called, had relatively small brains.

The branch of the family tree that resulted in us—Homo sapiens—responded to the change in environment not by eating more but by eating better: a higher-quality diet with more concentrated energy, namely, more animal protein and fat. Their brains grew bigger, the large intestines smaller. They required a diet more like that of carnivores and less like the plant-based diet favored by other primates. They needed meat for the energy and the body-building qualities of protein and for the high concentration of stored energy and complex molecules in fat. Both are necessary for the development of the brain, which is a huge energy consumer (accounting for about 27 percent of our total energy expenditure). If we had stayed with the fruits-and-shoots menus of the apes, we would probably have the brainpower of a gorilla (which raises an interesting point: Will we revert to dim-wittedness if we all eat low-fat, vegetarian diets?). So although the invention of cured meat is an event of the last two thousand years, the fat in a well-developed ham exerts an attraction on us as old as our descent from the trees.

But it is not the heavy quilt of fat just under the skin of a plump pig that accounts for the superiority of certain hams. As Ruiz explained it to me, succulence and flavor are attributable to the high intramuscular fat content of Iberian hogs and its transformation, through aging, into compounds that we detect as floral, fruity, nutty . . . or, more to the point, deliciously hammy.

"But," I asked, "if that's the case, couldn't one also pasture white pigs [our conventional breeds] in the *dehesa* of western Spain, let them get really fat, and have great ham? Or, better yet, wouldn't you get a super ham from one of these conventional pigs set loose to roam in the forests of the United States?" This was the common way of raising pigs in colonial times, and it is what Emile DeFelice is doing with the conventional pigs he is raising along with the Ossabaws.

Ruiz's response, predictably patriotic, was that the *ibérico* hog is special. Frenchmen used to make the same argument about their wine being the product of France's unique *terroir*. Then, in 1976, the Russian-born wine expert Andre Tchelistcheff organized a blind tasting of French wines, mostly Bordeaux, and Napa Valley wines. To the world's surprise, and to the great satisfaction of California wine makers, their Stag's Leap came in first over the *premier crus* of France, besting such sacrosanct names as Mouton-Rothschild and Château Haut-Brion.

I pressed Ruiz with this story. "Well, theoretically, you could try white pigs," he conceded. "But on the other hand, white pigs get too fat to walk on the *dehesa*, and they don't stand the cold as well as the *ibérico*. Look, I am not saying you can't make good ham from white pigs. You can, but since they are sacrificed [slaughtered] at a lower weight, they may have developed muscle but not the necessary fat. Moreover, the key here is intramuscular fat, which the *ibérico* has in higher proportion than white pigs."

I began to pepper Ruiz with questions. What does the intramuscular fat do? How long can you age a ham? What role does smoking play? Nitrates? Molds?

He booted up his PC, threw in a CD, and ran over the highlights of *ibérico* ham production, which he had conveniently organized into a PowerPoint presentation.

When the weather turns cold, the pigs, fattened on acorns, are sacrificed. The hams are covered with salt, for about one day per kilo (2.2 pounds). It is important that the temperature be just around freezing so that while the salt penetrates the meat and draws out moisture, the flesh is kept safe from bacteria (which doesn't grow at low temperatures).

Over the next two to three months, the ham is removed from the salt and kept at low temperature while the salt that has already entered the flesh continues to penetrate the ham fully. The complete infusion of salt into the tissue in this stage of production is critical. Over the course of the next two years, Ruiz said, "it allows the ham to be kept at higher temperatures and lower relative humidity without the risk of microbial spoilage."

After the first few months, you have a piece of partially dewatered pork biologically stabilized by salt. No doubt the tannin from acorns serves further to retard spoilage. If any flavor transformation has taken place during this early aging, it is so little that you wouldn't notice. Yet at this young age, some modern purveyors in the United States have the chutzpah to call such a pipsqueak "a country-style ham."

For the next four to five months, during the *secado*, or drying stage, the temperature rises from the low seventies to the eighties and even nineties. The humidity gradually drops into the low fifties. The wonderful alchemy begins whereby fats break down and sugars and protein combine to initiate a cascade of chemical reactions that produce hundreds of flavor compounds. It bears noting that, during this phase of aging, one of the compounds produced is glutamic acid. When combined with salt, the result is monosodium glutamate, which is responsible for what flavor scientists refer to as umami "taste," but which I prefer to think of as a flavor booster and amplifier. Your ham is now about nine months down the road, the minimum age at which Nancy Newsom will sell one of her American hams, three months beyond the minimum for the current version of a Smithfield. Think of it as the first bottle from last year's vintage. If it was a good year, your wine is just getting started. So is your ham.

Say your pig was killed in November, salted and post-salted (i.e., letting the salt penetrate the meat) through February, and then dried into July or August before being left to age for another year or two. Under natural conditions, as they exist in the more mountainous areas of the Mediterranean, your ham can achieve its development simply by being kept—unheated and uncooled—in storerooms and open-air drying rooms. You could call this cuisine of a sort (adding heat to food), but all the heating and drying is accomplished not in an oven but by simply exposing the meat to the temperature fluctuations of the seasons.

It seems quite amazing to the contemporary observer that such a marvelous recipe requires little more than that the calendar complete two circuits. But it is precisely because the year progresses the way it does that ham was made in the first place. Ditto for cheese and wine. Nature presented the opportunity: It merely required that we humans discover fermentation, salting, and salubrious molds to extend the life of grapes, pork, and milk. All of these products are enhanced by controlled aging, whereas the raw product, if left to stand without benefit of these processes, will spoil.

Like a great red wine, *ibérico* hams can continue to age for years. "You won't see it industrially, but sometimes they keep sows for many years and their hams, full of fat, can age four or five years," Ruiz commented.

"And . . . ," I asked, hungrily.

"Spectacular!"

Traditionally, Spanish hams were left in lofts with open windows where they were exposed to fresh mountain breezes. In America and northern Europe, where the summers are more humid, hams are often cold smoked immediately after the initial salting. Smoke contributes an extra measure of antibacterial protection, and a number of pleasing flavor compounds as well as naturally produced nitrates. The curing solution for many American and northern European hams (but not Newsom's) often contains even more nitrates. They accelerate the penetration of salts, retard bacteria and rancidity, and enhance the deep-pink blush that we associate with cured meat. The color of *ibérico* hams is not a function of added nitrates, although some nitrates occur during the curing. The color of the flesh of animals that are pastured and allowed the freedom to exercise is due to the presence of myoglobin in the muscle fibers, and to the greater number of dark-red muscle fibers in active animals.

Myoglobin is a protein that stores oxygen in muscle fibers, allowing for a sustained release of energy. Muscles that are not exercised don't have myoglobin. The fibers of animals that begin exercise early in life (and continuously after that) remain red rather than turning white through inactivity. Think of the white meat of the domestic chicken, whose large breast muscles are not used for flight. In contrast, ducks, which fly a lot, have developed dark meat in the breast, rich in the energy stores of myoglobin and dark-red muscle fibers. Pigs in the wild, that is, pigs that forage for themselves, getting lots of exercise, have dark meat with deep flavor and plenty of intramuscular fat. Confinement pigs, or even barnyard breeds, don't get much exercise, and, therefore, have white meat and little intramuscular fat . . . which means less taste. If you want maximum taste, you must leave your pigs outdoors, in pasture and forests, and you must leave them there twice as long before they are slaughtered. Of course, this increases the time the producer must wait until the pig is converted to cash at the market—but only the older, more-developed pig has intensely flavored flesh and fat.

Most cured hams, which include country hams, *serrano*, prosciutto, Bayonne, Yorkshire, and Westphalian, are not usually made from pastured pigs, nor are they aged for much more than a year, if that. The true *ibérico* ham, however, must age for at least two years or, according to a Spanish adage, it must go through *"dos ferias de Sevilla"*—two Seville cattle fairs (an annual event). It is in that second year, while the ham is stored at natural temperatures, that much of the breakdown of fats and proteins takes place. The reactions initiated by enzymes, molds, and heat produce a delicious spectrum of flavors and aromas that are cheesy, nutty, grassy, fruity, sweet, toasted, minty, meaty, buttery, earthy, and salty, to cite the most prominent taste notes.

Through the first year of aging, all hams are created equal. Or, if not equal, then one can at least say that the huge and sublime differences between a six-month ham made from a factory-bred hog and one from an Iberian aristocrat, though surely noticeable, are not as striking as they will be. Both the similarities and, in the long run, the differences are due in large part to the hugely complex series of chemical reactions that take place in the second year. These reactions are central to cuisine, yet it was not until barely one hundred years ago that we even suspected something was going on.

In 1912, Louis Camille Maillard, a biochemist with an interest in protein, addressed the French Academy. He reported the results of an experiment in which he had taken a sugar and a protein, heating them until they combined and turned brown. He was not the first to observe this effect. The British beer expert Arthur Robert Ling had, four years previously, written on the browning effect of barley in the making of beer.

What made Maillard's work so seminal was his realization that the combination of sugar and protein produces precursor compounds, which have since been identified as Amadori products, after the chemist who first identified them. These mega molecules begin a process of combining and breaking down, generating an enormous number of flavorful compounds. This secondary process is known as the Strecker degradation, likewise eponymous, and likewise something that sounds like a Robert Ludlum title. When all of these intermediary molecules and amino acids and lipids finish their dizzying choreography, the result, in the case of ham, is taste that is full of nuance and complexity.

Maillard's discovery remained a footnote in culinary history until World War II, when the U.S. Army—which has been understandably overlooked in gastronomic history—responded to GI complaints that their powdered eggs were turning brown. Army food scientists soon realized that they were dealing with a Maillard reaction. By removing some glucose from the protein-rich eggs, the browning was stopped so that the eggs would look better even if they still tasted like army eggs.

By the late 1940s, two food scientists at the General Foods Corporation, H. M. Barnes and C. W. Kauffman, continued Maillard's work of combining amino acids and sugars. They wrote, ". . . the Maillard Reaction may also be the contributing factor in the development of many of our characteristic food flavors . . . [such as] the distinctive flavor differences in breakfast foods, the crust of baked bread, roasted coffee . . ."

Further research by flavor chemists began to identify first scores, then hundreds, then thousands of flavor compounds—many of them the products of the twin, often allied processes of the breakdown of fatty acids and the bountiful cascade of combinations and recombinations of the Maillard reaction.

The science is often bewildering, even to biochemists. There have been seven international symposia on the Maillard reaction. An Internet search for it will yield thousands of hits noting its role in understanding the aging process and diabetes, as well as the science of flavor. The chemical interactions are so complex that there is considerable debate as to whether certain reactions are or are not Maillard, with each side having vehement supporters.

Aromas and tastes are a complex but universally understood code for the foods that sustain us. Fruits have a sweet odor that our bodies know will supply quick energy. For want of another word, the "garden" smell of vegetables advertises antioxidants and other vitamins which ensure that our metabolism proceeds happily. A bitter taste or a sharp odor often indicates toxins. Fats, especially while cooking, are easy to identify as advance advertisements for palatable food: advertisements written in the sensual language of taste.

We humans have evolved so that we minimize any chance that we will ignore even the faintest whisperings of that language. There is never just one seductive compound in a food. More likely, there are hundreds. The process of stimulating appetite is, to use Freud's term for elements of a dream, "overdetermined." Therein lies the allure in the enormous complexity of wine, cheese, and ham. Their tastes haunt us like dreams. Where we judge Beethoven and Bach to be geniuses for their exquisite and varied combinations of the twelve tones of the chromatic scale, the subtle interplay of tastes and aromas in these hundreds and thousands of flavor compounds that Maillard's discovery first suggested is even more intricate and no less satisfying.

PART FOUR

SMOKE AND FIRE

SIXTEEN

THE HORSEPOWER
OF PRAYER

AS I TRAVELED AROUND THE SOUTH visiting Chuck Talbott, visiting farms, visiting Nancy Newsom, I noticed that I was incapable of passing a barbecue stand without stopping for a bite. "Okay," I reasoned, "it ain't ham, but it must be nature's way of telling me that I must look into this subject if I want to understand more fully what it is about pigs that attracts me."

On our way back from Emile's house, after an early visit to our Ossabaws, I realized that I had been in the Carolinas for days and had not eaten one bit of barbecue. Chuck's girlfriend, Nadine, took my mention of the word "barbecue" as a call to action. (Etiquette question: If she is not a wife, do you call a mother of three grown children a girlfriend? She does.) We passed through Lexington, a famous barbecue town, and I was developing an intense barbecue craving. We pulled into a service station and asked a guy pumping gas if he knew where to get good 'cue.

He directed us to Jimmy's, a single-story building that seduces the approaching customer with the odor of wood smoke and meat.

Once you are within smelling range, you could drive blindfolded and still find the place.

We parked next to a 1965 Corvette, a Stingray, in mint condition, metal-flake purple.

"Oh, man," Nadine said, "check out the 'Vette!"

On its hood, the raised center panel depicted the Crucifixion: Jesus on the Cross flanked by the two thieves. The word "Calvary" appeared in large semi-gothic script under the scene.

We entered the restaurant. Families were spread out around the dining room: Dad was most often a gaunt man in a baseball cap, a pack of smokes in his breast pocket or rolled up, James Dean style, in the sleeve of his T-shirt. The kids all managed to get sauce on their clothing, and the mothers heaved weary sighs as they applied T-shirt first aid with the Wet Naps that the restaurateur supplied for post-barbecue hand cleaning.

At one table, an older couple consumed their order without speaking a word to each other. They had been married so long, apparently, that they'd said all that needed saying, but they still ate together, if only for the company.

"None of them owns the Corvette," I said.

Chuck was not so sure. "I bet one of them does."

"Uh-uh, Chuck. Maybe that guy over there with the blow-dry haircut and the purple tie. He kind of looks like a middle-market anchorman."

"Not him—too well dressed," said Chuck.

"Him, for sure," I declared.

Sure enough, the Anchorman walked out to the car, followed by a group of middle-aged to elderly folks who, once they were assembled, looked very much like new converts at a riverside baptism.

The Anchorman lifted the hood. The 'Vette, seen from this

angle, caught all of the lights that illuminated the parking lot with midday intensity.

"This car is prayer-conditioned!" he began, as if it had just returned from the Sermon on the Mount. "See this engine? I have put seven hundred and sixty-nine horsepower in it to bring people to magnify the glory of Jesus Christ!"

Did he really mean 769 horsepower? Those are major NASCAR numbers. Maybe his point was that, over the lifetime of the car, he had put in two engines whose combined horsepower totaled 769. Either way, how does putting a mega motor in a hot car spread the Gospel?

As if in answer, Anchorman cut short his sermon to demonstrate the soul-saving horsepower of his purple machine. He got in the car and started the engine. It sounded more like three or four engines at a stock-car race burbling at a powerful idle. He threw the car in reverse, backed up, and put it in neutral with another high RPM roar. Then, slipping it into gear, he peeled rubber, laying a smoking patch on the asphalt as he shot out of the parking lot. We returned to our sandwiches of sliced pork with a spicy red sauce and a side of freshly fried hush puppies—crisp, salty, hot.

I resolved to get deeper into the study of barbecue. Most Southerners (or Northerners who have spent any time in the South) prize barbecue above all other edibles. It is the essential soul food, for white folks and black. Where did it come from? I wondered.

There are many theories, most with an apocryphal ring to them, about the origin of the word "barbecue." One plausible, but nonetheless incorrect explanation is that it comes from the French, *barbe à que*, "from beard to tail," as in, "You cook the whole hog from beard to tail."

The word "barbecue" did not enter the English language until

1661, according to the *Oxford English Dictionary*, by which time the Spanish had been using it for nearly two hundred years, their term being *barbacoa*, a corruption of the Arawak (Carib) Indian term *barbacrot*, which was a lattice upon which the Indians placed food to be cooked over a pit full of burning wood or coals.

From the American South, through the Caribbean, and down through Central America, one finds the original, the many homes of this universally loved cuisine. It may have varied in its development, using one spice here and another one there, but it always involved long, slow heat to bring out the miraculous flavor and texture of pork. I have tried it all . . . well, maybe not all, but as much as I could as often as I could.

SEVENTEEN

MAYAN TREASURE

When the Spaniards arrived on the coast, they met some
natives and asked what the area was called. The reply was
"ciuthan (we don't understand you)." The Spaniards, who did
not speak the language, believed they were being told the name
of the place. For this reason, they baptized it with the words the
Indians spoke: Yucatan.

—*From a plaque in the town of Tixkokob*

* * *

SILVIO CAMPOS PREPARES *COCHINITA PIBIL* (barbecued
pig in a pit) for the daily market in the Yucatecan town of Tixkokob
(teesh-ko-kob). He is one of those gifted people who needs only to
touch food for it to be elevated to something wonderful. He has the
knack. You might take a less talented person, put him or her through
a full course of study at the Culinary Institute of America, and your
graduate would still be gustatorially tone deaf. Show Silvio an ingredient and he will know how it wants to be cut, how long it should

cook, and what its flavors and textures will do in combination with other ingredients.

When I first met him, he made me *salpicón de venado*, a venison dish that is hard to find simply because you can no longer hunt the native Yucatán deer. In the 1970s, however, the Indians would still set up their stands on the steps of overgrown pyramids and wait for a deer to come into their sights. The dressed carcass was rubbed with a spice paste, called a *recado*, which is a mixture of chilies and spices that typifies Yucatecan cuisine. Then the deer was placed in a pit on top of a pile of rocks that sat, in turn, on top of a hot fire. The dead animal was covered with banana leaves and then buried. The next day he dug it up, shredded the meat, sauced it with bitter-orange juice, and tossed in some diced chili, sliced radish, and coriander. To eat it, you took a tortilla and grabbed a serving of the *salpicón*, which was smoky, gamey, fruity, fresh, crunchy, and hot all at once.

I was very taken with Silvio's style. So was Rick Bayless, the Chicago chef/restaurateur who is often thought to be the greatest interpreter of the many culinary traditions of Mexico. Bayless tasted Silvio's food and was so impressed that he brought him to Chicago to cook for his staff. In subsequent years, Bayless took his employees to the Yucatán to learn from the master. Despite the strong urgings of Bayless that he seek his fortune up North, Silvio preferred to return to his pretty little town.

"You get up at six, work all morning," he explained, "then you come home and drink a quart of beer at lunch. Then you take a nap with your wife and get up again in the cool of the day and walk around town making small talk with your neighbors during *la hora de chisme*, the gossip hour."

He likes the pace of life in Tixkokob. His contentment shows in his superb cooking.

As I began to research this book, I realized that Silvio's *cochinita* was just a variant of the barbecue style that Native Americans, from Georgia to Guatemala, had mastered, so I took the opportunity afforded me by a fishing assignment in the Yucatán to visit Silvio again and get his recipe down.

The town had changed a great deal in the six or seven years since I had last been there. There were far fewer trees and much less shade. When I found Silvio at his market stall, he explained that hurricane Isidore had hit Tixkokob hard; the worst hurricane ever. The winds lifted pedicabs high in the air and left them on rooftops. I imagined a platoon of Mary Poppinses floating over Tixkokob.

When I sought him out, Silvio finished serving *cochinita* to a customer at his stall in the town market. He cleaned his hands. We hopped into his truck and drove to his home to prepare *cochinita pibil* from scratch. We joked about the "secret sauces" that I find so weird among U.S. barbecuers; in the United States, after all, everyone knows that the ingredients for just about every barbecue sauce come out of a bottle and that it's a little more ketchup here, a little more vinegar there. In contrast, if you ask a three-star Michelin chef how he makes a sauce, he is likely to give you the recipe for something very complex that took a long time to develop. But U.S. grillers guard their sauce recipes as if they were formulas for the elixir of life.

As we drove up to Silvio's home, a neighbor was hard at work breaking down the carcass of a pig. He was in shorts. I was in shorts. The temperature was about ninety degrees. So much for the common wisdom in Europe and the United States that you may kill your pigs only when the weather is near freezing.

Wearing his pressed brown slacks, maroon dress shirt, and snazzy Panama hat, Silvio tossed thirty pounds of pig parts in a pan and rubbed them with salt, spices, bitter-orange juice, and *achiote* (the coral-colored seed of the annatto plant, often used as a dye). Not a drop got on his clothes. What is it about great chefs and the way they can cook the messiest things and come away spotless?

We buried the pig in the backyard where Silvio keeps a series of pits that could easily be mistaken for a graveyard prepared for a mass burial. He wrapped the pig parts in banana leaves and placed them in a large metal box, which in turn was placed in the pit on top of the hot rocks that covered a bed of hot coals. We interred the box and left the pig to cook.

This was early in the morning. We had time to kill, so we drove around. We went into the old part of town to a *cenote* (a limestone sinkhole filled with clear, cool water). The ancient Mayans used to hurl virgins, weighted down with golden chains, into *cenotes*, in return for which the god thus honored was obliged to bring good fortune or at least delay the permanent disappearance of the sun. At this particular *cenote*, legend has it that it leads to a chamber where a rattlesnake guards two pots of gold. The snake lives directly beneath the town's main cathedral. We approached the *cenote* through a store where a hybridized mariachi cum rock-and-roll band played on the radio at the speaker-distorting volume that many Yucatecan shopkeepers favor. The proprietor rents out the *cenote* for twenty pesos an hour.

"Usually to a couple," he said. "Any kind of couple as long as they have the twenty pesos," he added with a mild leer.

We walked through a barren yard strewn with the polystyrene detritus of modern civilization, approaching the revered *cenote*. It was quite beautiful, a flight of steps descending to a clear, green pool under a limestone overhang. I dove into the water, as cold, dark, and silent as death. When I was sufficiently spooked, I turned around and swam back out again, then dried myself in the sun.

When we returned to Silvio's house, his wife, Angelica, greeted us warmly. She wore a white dress with a flower-embroidered bodice, very typical of the Maya. Silvio and I retrieved the *cochinita* from its pit. He and Angelica arranged it on a glazed clay platter covered with a floral design. Silvio grabbed a handful of fresh cilantro, pressed the leaves into a tight ball, and chiffonaded them into uniform slivers the way a trained French chef cuts herbs. Alongside, he placed a bowl of pan-roasted, salted red onions pickled in bitter-orange juice.

The layers of flavor in Silvio's accompanying sauce provided an exceedingly light and bright counterpoint to the brute carnality of the meat. The orange juice was tangy, the *habañero* chilies hot in a way that gave focus to the complex taste. The cilantro, fresh and floral, pulled subtle aromas out of the stew.

It occurred to me then, as it had occurred to me once on a trip to Chile when I'd eaten *chancho con pebre* (pork with a piquant sauce of onions, cilantro, vinegar, and garlic), that the flesh of the pig can support a wider and more robust variety of sauces than most meats, which is why you rarely find pork without a sauce or spice rub. In a world of endless flavors, there are few with which pork will not harmonize. I think, partly for this reason, we Americans have learned to accept inferior pork because we can very easily disguise its inadequacies with powerhouse sauces and condiments. Nevertheless, given great pork, there is a world of sauces out there—wine sauces, herb infusions, fruit reductions, spice rubs, sweet glazes, pepper crusts . . . ad infinitum.

Add to that the marvelous transformation of the meat through the miracle of barbecue. In the hands of real chefs, whether schooled in the great restaurants of Europe or born with the talent of Silvio Campos, it is a cuisine, rustic in its roots, that is capable of great refinement, even in the franchise-dominated mall culture of the contemporary United States. Barbecue is a personal statement.

COCHINITA PIBIL

Courtney Knapp, who is responsible for much of the good research in this book and none of the mistakes, worked for some years in the kitchen of Rick Bayless's Frontera Grill. Here is Courtney's home cooking reinterpretation of Rick's reworking of the recipe that Silvio Campos serves in Tixkokob. To all three, I am indebted.

ACHIOTE MARINADE

- 1½ tablespoons *achiote* seeds, also known as annatto seeds
- 1½ teaspoons allspice
- 1 teaspoon black pepper
- ½ teaspoon cumin
- ¼ teaspoon cinnamon
- 1½ teaspoons Mexican oregano (Traditional oregano may be substituted.)
- 3 tablespoons vinegar, white or apple cider
- 6 garlic cloves, peeled
- 1 tablespoon salt
- 1 tablespoon corn or vegetable oil
- 6 tablespoons Seville orange juice (*jugo de naranja agria*), or ¼ cup fresh grapefruit juice plus 2 tablespoons fresh orange juice

PORK

- One 2-pound piece boneless pork shoulder or pork butt
- 1 large piece banana leaf, enough to wrap the pork

1 medium onion, sliced

1 tablespoon salt

1½ cups pork stock (If unavailable, use chicken or
vegetable broth.)

Fresh tortillas, 16 to be safe

GARNISHES

Pickled red onions (see following recipe)

Cilantro

Habañero salsa (see following recipe)

1. Preparing the marinade: Grind the *achiote* very finely
and place in a separate bowl. Continue to grind the allspice,
black pepper, cumin, and cinnamon. Place the spices in a
blender with the oregano, vinegar, garlic, salt, and oil. Blend
everything into a smooth paste, adding 1 to 2 tablespoons of
water if necessary for desired consistency.

2. Marinating the pork: In a large baking pan or large
bowl, cover the meat with the paste and the citrus juice. Flip
the meat and cover the other side, pressing the mixture into
the meat. Set aside, to marinate overnight.

3. Roasting: Preheat the oven to 325°F. In a large Dutch
oven or a large braiser, arrange the banana leaf or leaves to
cover the bottom and sides of the pot, with enough to cover
the top of the meat. Slice the onion. Place the meat and its
juices into the pot on top of the leaves; add the onion and additional salt. Cover with the leaves. (If you are not using the
leaves, just add the meat and marinade juices to the pot; add

onions and additional citrus juice, and salt.) Pour stock or broth along the side of the pot until about halfway full and place on the stove. Bring to a boil over medium heat, cover securely with the lid or foil, and place in the oven. Cook for 3½ to 4 hours, periodically checking the liquid.

4. Serving: Carefully remove the top layer of leaves and discard. Take the meat out of the pot and set aside to cool. The meat will be very tender and easy to shred. The liquid can be used as sauce for tacos. Place in a separate pot (you may want to strain the liquid for a smoother consistency) and reduce if necessary. Taste and adjust with salt and pepper. Shred the meat and add it to the liquid to keep it warm and moist.

5. Garnishes: The tortillas can be steamed or, if you are careful, warmed over low flame on a gas-burning stove. Serve the meat on each taco with cilantro, pickled red onions, and a few drops of *habañero* salsa.

PICKLED RED ONIONS

Peel and slice one red onion thinly. Blanch the onion in salted water for 30 seconds, then remove and put in a colander. Rinse with cool water. Add ¼ teaspoon of black pepper, ¼ teaspoon of cumin, ½ teaspoon of Mexican oregano (or dried Italian oregano), and ½ cup of vinegar to a small container. Add the onions and cover with water. Stir and let stand until the onions turn pink, about 2 hours.

HABAÑERO SALSA

Take 5 to 6 *habañero* chilies and heat them in a sauté pan or grill pan until color begins to develop. When the chilies begin to sweat and develop color, remove from pan and add to a blender. Add 1 tablespoon lime juice and salt. Blend and adjust seasonings, being very careful, as this salsa is extremely hot.

Serves 6, about 14 to 16 tacos.

* * *

EIGHTEEN

COMPETITION 'CUE

A barbequed hog in the woods and plenty of whiskey will buy birthrights and secure elections even in America.

—*William Faux*, Memorable Days in America, 1823

* * *

THE CONCEPT OF BARBECUE HAS MANY meanings in the states of the old Confederacy. To a Texan, it can only mean beef brisket, rubbed with salt, pepper, and other spices, then smoked over mesquite for many hours before being sliced and slathered in a tomato-based sauce. A North Carolinian will immediately dismiss anything that is not pork and, if from the western part of the state, will insist that the meat be sliced and that the sauce be sweet, spicy, and tomato red; if from the eastern part of the state, the barbecue lover prefers the minced flesh of a hog cooked whole and soaked with vinegar and red pepper flakes; meanwhile, the South Carolinian will want slow-cooked pork with a sweet and assertive mustard sauce.

Within each of these communities of believers, there are those who prescribe hickory as the heat source, while others call for oak or mesquite, and still others use charcoal briquettes. More technological are the adherents of the labor-saving electric smoker, but to that, the traditionalists will disapprovingly remark, "How can you ever replace the real savoriness that wood smoke and fire lend to meat?"

As it is with religious questions, it comes down to a matter of how you were raised and, therefore, what you believe. I believe that when you combine wood, smoke, meat, salt, and fire, you are appealing to an appetite so deeply rooted in the human genome that it is instinctual. If pressed, I would say that I prefer pork barbecue to beef, and then I would admit a preference for the whole hog cooked over wood, although I can think of one pork shoulder made in Alabama (by pit master Chris Lilly) that is unsurpassed by anything else I have tasted. I would also say that it is harder for me to find barbecue that I don't like than barbecue that I like. I am kind of pre-sold.

In the Barbecue Belt—roughly contiguous with the Bible Belt— even in this age of wall-to-wall franchises, one can count on finding some funky-looking roadhouse with a cutesy billboard featuring a pig, usually naked, sometimes in a cowboy hat and boots, or high-stepping like a pudgy Rockette. Such places customarily offer home-made coleslaw, hush puppies, a housebroken Brunswick stew (i.e., not made with squirrel, as called for in the original recipe), banana pudding, and sweet iced tea.

It is important, here, to distinguish "barbecue" the noun from "barbecue" the verb. The latter is what we do when we fire up the grill and throw on some burgers or a steak. It simply means the act of cooking over an outdoor fire, or the gas equivalent. The effect on the meat is tasty, but not transforming. That is not to say that nothing happens, because there is no denying that any cooking at all will produce many compounds that affect flavor in a positive way. But the same can be said of boiling, frying, or roasting.

Here is the miraculous thing about barbecue: Given that the pork from which it is made is almost always the nearly tasteless, nearly fatless product of a confinement operation, how is it that pit masters are able to create a cooked product that is, to my palate, almost always perfect, a culinary silk purse from a factory-farmed sow's ear?

I believe the secret is that barbecue chefs have mastered heat, with the very rudimentary technology of wood fire. True, pit masters may also use other means to increase flavor or tenderness; some may use brines, others may inject the meat with fruit juice, still others may have a particular understanding of the special heating and flavoring properties of oak, hickory, pecan, apple, peach, or mesquite wood, but all have in one way or another figured out how to apply heat, at low intensity, over a long time, and, while doing so, to take into account the different thicknesses, fat content, and muscular development of the parts of a pig, even an industrially raised pig.

Barbecuing a pig is like performing a song: Once you start it, the expectation is that you will carry things to a conclusion. You cannot half-barbecue a pig. You must see the process through, and though it requires little in the way of technology—just meat and heat—it does require attention and a time commitment.

When people argue, and they do argue a lot about which barbecue is the best, they are most often referring to the product of a local roadside restaurant. There is, in addition to these home-town favorites, a whole other world of barbecue: the competition circuit. All over the nation, there are mass cook-offs entered into by barbecue teams of five or six people. They drive their "rigs," the insider's term for barbecue apparatus, to the competition site. There they set up shop for a two- or three-day festival attended by similarly devoted competitors and diners. At the end of a rigorous judging, prizes are given in various categories: usually whole hog, ribs, and pork shoulder (beef has its own rites and devotees). The competition chef, with his twenty-thousand-dollar, custom-welded, transportable rig, can give the kind of minute-by-minute attention to one pig that, were he in the retail business, would quickly bankrupt him.

Memphis in May is among the largest of the nation's barbecue competitions. It is held on the banks of the Mississippi during the first week of May, when the old river town looks like Brigadoon riding on a cloud of magnolia blossoms. That, at least, is the hope, although this year, it was more like Woodstock 1969. Heavy spring rains joined with the snowmelt of the far Rockies to create a Mississippi that was particularly muddy, and carrying the fallen limbs and washed-out topsoil of half a continent on a high-speed voyage to the Gulf of Mexico. A thick blanket of humidity served as a constant harbinger of torrential downpours that were punctuated by cloud-cracking thunder and tornado sightings. The rains left the fairgrounds in a swampy condition over which hung a pork-scented cloud of wood smoke and the steam of sizzling fat.

The teams had set up camp in fancifully decorated stations that resembled floats in a small-town Fourth of July parade. They were colorfully named with the kinds of *jeux des mots* that you see on the backs of pleasure boats. Among them: Beturazz Barfbeque, the Beverly Pigbillies, the Crispy Critters, the Late-Night Porkers, Hogapalooza, Notorious P.I.G., Oscar & The Grouches, Porkosauraus, Snoop Hoggy Hogg, and my favorite, Pork Me Tender, which featured a cartoon pig done up in Elvis regalia (Late Vegas Period).

Upon entering the fairgrounds, I spotted the setup of Big Bob Gibson's of Decatur, Alabama. They are specialists in pork shoulder. The previous fall I had sampled their meat at a barbecue conference in Jackson, Mississippi. Chef Chris Lilly, a man with inborn Southern manners, courtly and low key, thinks a lot about barbecue. He favors a *chipotle* sauce (which adds layers of smokiness and heat) and a garlic-accented rub. Whenever he takes a pork shoulder from his cooker (a highly enameled affair that looks like a well-cared-for fire engine), he draws a crowd. This performance takes place on a raised platform, which puts the pork about eye level with onlookers. With the showmanly shtick of a lion tamer, he cautions the crowd to step back as he presses down on the pork shoulder with both fists. The meat sags under the weight, its sides bulging out like a tire that's low on air. With a final push, the shoulder completely collapses, releasing smoky, porky steam and juice. It is a captivating show. More important, Lilly makes a sublime piece of barbecue: a combination of the unctuous mouth feel that I associate with roast lamb and the brawniness of a full-grown porker.

I asked him about wood, a subject he has considered at length. "No question that wood imparts flavor. You will hear all kinds of opinions about wood," he said. "Some folks say they cook with nothing but hickory, but there are seven different kinds of hickory in the Southeast and I can guarantee that each hickory gives a different flavor. And then the question of aging comes in, because aged wood will burn faster and hotter, but green wood can give more taste. You need both. In the restaurant, we can't always be that selective, but when I know I am competing, we pick out some really good-looking wood and age it for four months in dry storage.

"I like hickory because it is even denser than red oak. Hickory gives an intense smoky flavor. This is good, but you have to be careful because of that intensity. I use that wood for flavor rather than as the main heat source. For that, I like oak charcoal."

For six consecutive years Big Bob Gibson's has taken the grand prize for pork shoulder at the Memphis in May competition. This is quite an achievement given that the competitors are all masters of the game. At the competition I attended, some of the smart money was on Myron Mixon from Jack's Old South BBQ Sauce cooking team in Vienna, Georgia. Mixon's setup was under a cammo tent that had the look of a deer-hunting camp.

Because of the soggy ground, he had laid wooden palettes end to end to keep the work floor out of the mud. Good thing, because just as I stepped under the tarp, the skies opened up. It was as if some foul-tempered giant had lifted up the whole Mississippi River and dropped it on top of us. Add wind gusts of about fifty miles an hour to that and you have the scene of a dark tent with half a dozen of us holding the tent poles down so that what little shelter it provided did not blow away. With the splayed carcass of a pig in front of us, and the sputtering, smoking grill, fueled with rounds of aged peach wood, it looked like Hell's own workshop, with the pig as the soon-to-be tormented sinner. The effect of torture was heightened when Myron took a very big syringe attached to a hose that ran into a five-gallon plastic container and jammed the needle into the haunch of the pig.

"Peach juice," he said. "It makes the meat sweeter and keeps it from drying out. Come back tomorrow morning and I'll give you a taste."

Dryness is the enemy of the barbecuer. Or, put another way, the trick in barbecuing is to make the meat tender and full of taste before it dries out. This takes some doing with hogs that were raised to be lean. (Fact: The average pork tenderloin has 42 percent less fat than it did in the early eighties.)

I left Mixon and continued down the midway as the rain eased up. I saw a fine-looking rig with some serious-looking barbecuers peering over a smoker. "What breed of hog do you find gives the best results?" I asked.

"Don't know."

"Well, what kind of hog do you use?"

"Don't know."

"Where do you get yours?"

"Sam's Club."

Ahh . . . there's the rub! Rigs that cost tens of thousands of dollars; a staff that may or may not be paid but nevertheless needs to be transported and lodged; pigs, spices, wood, decorations. It comes to quite a big investment in time and, given the seriousness of the competition, there is no small amount of alpha-bull pride on the line. Yet no one I ask knows what kind of pig they are using or who raised it. This strikes me as nothing short of incredible. As any chef will tell you, cooking always starts with the ingredients.

But by dint of peach juice, *chipotle* rubs, complex cookers, and a fixation on just how much heat the pork is getting, the barbecue teams manage to turn out great stuff. I just keep asking myself, "How much better would it be if the pigs were good, old-fashioned, outdoor-raised fatties?"

NINETEEN

CHEER UP, MAMA

EDDIE MITCHELL'S PHOTO-MURAL SMILE beams through his salt-and-pepper beard on the side panel of the fifty-three-foot semi that transports his cookers, hogs, and pit crew whenever the call for barbecue takes him from his home in Wilson, North Carolina.

It was Jim Early who first introduced me to Eddie. The occasion was the Barbecue Summit organized by the Southern Foodways Alliance at the University of Mississippi. It was at that same gathering that I first met Chris Lilly from Big Bob's. The event had drawn chefs, authors, and civilian barbecue lovers from all over. R. W. "Johnny" Apple was there from the *New York Times*, as was the *New Yorker's* Calvin Trillin. The chef's contingent included Ben Barker, the innovative chef of the Magnolia Grill in Durham, North Carolina, and Michael Romano from New York's shrine of modern cuisine, Union Square Cafe (he also has interest in a barbecue spot, Blue Smoke, whose chef, Ken Callahan, also attended). In short, it was a serious barbecue crowd.

Saturday night was to be the grand feed of the weekend, with music by ninety-four-year-old Otha Turner (who has since passed on) and his Afrossippi All Stars, one of the last African American fife-and-drum bands. He performed his greatest hit, "Everybody's Hollerin' Goat," in honor of the animal he prefers to barbecue. Everything was grand but the weather: cold with a misting rain that, in the pauses between misting, became an insistent chilly drizzle.

Jim Early, who has no "off" button when he starts to talk about good barbecue, told me that Eddie Mitchell's is about as good as it gets for eastern North Carolina barbecue, which means cooking the whole hog and serving with a vinegar-based sauce. Acting on Jim's say-so, I drove up to the soggy site of the event where Eddie, a man with the build of a football player (in fact, he played quarterback and running back at Fayetteville State), was in the process of muscling a couple of hogs onto the hot grate. The pink body of the pig brought to mind a human about to be cooked. Maybe it is the similarity between naked pigs and naked people that caused Polynesian cannibals to refer to human meat as "long pig," as recounted by Robert Louis Stevenson in *Tales of the South Seas*.

In the dense, cold air, the clouds rising from the hogs and the fires filled the field with swirling blue-smoke wraiths, denser and denser, like the slow dissolve into the past in a time-travel movie. Three high-spirited PR women were giving away shots of Jack Daniel's as if it were the day after the repeal of Prohibition. With enough of those under my belt, I half-anticipated the parting mists to offer a glimpse of former Oxford resident William Faulkner walking his dog and smoking a pipe.

As night fell, Mitchell's crew removed the hogs and pulled the meat from the bones, hot and steaming, the tantalizing smell of fat and flesh as heavy as August night air just before a cloudburst. Eddie piled the meat in front of him and pounded out a steady beat, chopping pork with two hatchets.

Jim Early explained the action. "See, he chops the crispy skin and then there's the part we call 'the outside brown,' the crusty, drier meat where the wood coals give it a smoky, nutty taste. Finally, there's the moist inside meat. Eddie mixes them so that you get all the flavors of the meat on your bun."

I prefer bigger pieces of meat to the finer mince commonly served in the Piedmont region. (Eddie accommodates such requests.) He serves his 'cue on a bun, drenched in piquant vinegar sauce and tempered by cool, sweet coleslaw. It is an intense, almost overpowering taste but with a comforting, stomach-filling texture. The bun—slightly soggy from the sauce and slaw—helps the barbecue slide down your gullet, in Howlin' Wolf's words, "like Baby Jesus in satin pants."

I asked Eddie if I might visit him later that month when I was due to cover the false albacore fishing in the Outer Banks. For those of you unfamiliar with the fish or the region, much of the Outer Banks is still pristine and old-timey, where churches far outnumber bars (my favorite church sign: "Jesus First Oysters Second!") and where the false albacore—a member of the tuna family—weigh twenty pounds. With the exception of one-hundred-pound tarpon, they are the fastest and most powerful fish commonly taken with a flyrod.

Early November is a picture-postcard time to drive through North Carolina, when the oak leaves are turning, not the flaming scarlets and golds of New England maples, but rather the dark red to dry brown of oak. The air is cool, but there are still remnants of summer warmth in the sea breeze. Since it was only a four-hour detour—which is nothing at all for a barbecue fancier—I didn't give a second thought to driving from the coast up to Eddie Mitchell's in Wilson, about thirty miles east of Raleigh.

I was not yet aware that "hidden" in this empty countryside was the largest concentration of hog factories in America. The major pork players have done a good job of secreting their work deep in the country, provided you are upwind of them.

The highways were numerous, well maintained, and fairly empty, a sign that it pays to have Jesse Helms as your senator: gazillions for magnificent thoroughfares with nobody on them, way out in the country. On the feeder roads, one finds another sign of government largesse; at the lunch hour, every barbecue stand has a full complement of highway-maintenance trucks parked on the roadside, as their crews sit down to trencherman portions of 'cue. In that way, those millions of highway dollars are helping to support the small barbecue businesses of the Carolinas.

Although the term "best" is a completely subjective matter when comparing things in the top tier of any enterprise, one can say with confidence that Mitchell's is as good as it gets for eastern North Carolina barbecue.

His is among the largest barbecue establishments in the state, much bigger even than his clientele would warrant. Eddie Mitchell sees his place as a future school for barbecuers who want to preserve the old-time tradition.

That tradition is never far from Mitchell's conversation. For that matter, it is never far from the customer's view: Mitchell has commissioned a mural, in the American-primitive style, that dominates the dining room with its depiction of an old-fashioned "pig pickin'."

Eddie told me that a young man in town who was "very artistic" (more on that later) had painted it. The scene, as Eddie told the story, was typical of what one would have come upon in the countryside at the end of the tobacco harvest: "Once the last truck comes to the barn, it's time for the pig pickins."

Somewhat to my puzzlement, Eddie recalled that it was a real challenge to work with the artist. "The thing with him is, if I can just keep him focused, it takes about a day to work with him to get it all doing and get it all working."

"Why is that?"

"Like I said, he's autistic."

"Oh, it's your accent," I explained. "I understood you to say 'He's artistic,' which I already knew from looking at the painting."

We laughed.

Eddie's generation is probably the last to attend these farm feasts. His youth was the swan song for the era of tobacco as the driving wheel of the North Carolina economy. The mural told the tale in pictures, beginning with the planting of tobacco in the spring and concluding with the slaughtering of the pigs, the rendering of fat, the women making sausages, the men tending a barbecue pit. A huge table with seating for fifteen stood invitingly in the foreground, a gracious old Southern mansion dominated the background. In those years, I imagine, the tobacco-plantation pig pickin' was one of the few occasions when black and white families sat down to dinner at the same table.

In addition to platters of meat, the table in the tableau is laden with watermelon, fried chicken, sweet potato soufflé, ham, corn on the cob, iced tea, cakes, black-eyed peas, lemonade. Eddie said, "You put everything out for the pig pickin', so that is why, I think, you have the term 'pig out.'" Take away the plantation home and the interracial crowd and you have the *matanza* of Spain, the *cochonaille* of France, a tradition that still lives in Europe but which, to our loss, is just about gone in our country, although it survives as folklore, as I learned when I accompanied Eddie to Joe Brewer's Meat Products Incorporated, the small, privately owned slaughterhouse where Eddie often purchases hogs.

Joe, an amiable man, received us in his office. A soap opera played on the TV. Soap operas in rural Carolina are background music in the way that the Bloomberg stock ticker provides white noise in corporate offices in New York. When the conversation turned to a discussion of old-time ways, Joe offered to dig up a monograph that his wife, Ellen, had written as part of her master's thesis. In it the following oral history appeared.

The traditional hog killing is a long and hard process of preparing meat for later consumption. . . . Because the process requires many hands, friends and neighbors help one another in exchange for "freshes" or fresh meat. The occasion has provided fellowship and a sense of pride for the workers. Each man's seasoned ham or sausage is distinct from another's.

Since cold weather is essential for preserving the meat, hog killings usually begin during December. Otis Lindsey of New Hope Community in Wilson County has "cut up some hogs around Thanksgiving." The number of hogs being slaughtered varies, but usually seven or eight are killed each time. The slaughtered hogs usually belong to farmers, but some people from the city have relatives in the country raise hogs for them and then share meat.

The busy day begins shortly after sunrise. Some folks start the vats of water heating the night before the killing, while others start that morning. Another variation occurs in Elizabeth City, where the hogs are slaughtered the previous night and left to hang overnight. After the vat of water is approximately 145 degrees, the hog is killed and dragged to the vat and scalded. Otis Lindsey remembers wrapping extra large hogs in cotton sheets and pouring hot water over them. The largest he has ever cut out weighed 1,126 pounds and dressed out to weigh 1,045 pounds. Following the scalding, the hair scraping procedure begins. Mason jar lids and homemade scrapers are used. The hogs are then hung on the gallows. "There they are weighed, the entrails, heart, liver and lungs removed, in preparation for cutting out the pork." While the heart is fried or boiled, the liver and "lights" (the lungs) are later made into haslet. "The sweet breads was pulled and saved for cooking, and the entrails taken in a tub to the hole dug at the back of the yard for ridding the chitlins." This is the women's work. After the chitlins are completely rid of hog feed, they are washed until immaculate and then left to soak. The small intestines are later stuffed for sausage. Otis Lindsey recalls stuffing his sausage three days later, while Roy Taylor remembers hanging his sausage at the end of the day. (Another informant) Sylvie Houbart reports, "In days past, local folk used to save the 'chitterlings' or hogs' intestines as food. . . . The large intestine was cut into pieces which were washed separately. The small intestine stayed in one piece. Cleaning took three days: the intestines were scrubbed in salt and rinsed in water repeatedly. They were plaited together and cooked in water, and then put in a white cloth and tied up to be kept in a cool place. The women had to cook them until tender, then chop them and fry them in a pan." After the entrails are removed, the hogs are taken from the gallows and laid on a tobacco truck to be cut out. The remains are used for making lard and sausage. The ears, nose and part of the feet are used to make souse and the brains are scrambled in eggs. Otis Lindsey recalls a misconception concerning [from] which part of the hog the tenderloin is taken. "A whole heap of folks get the strip of lean down the backbone and some call this tenderloin, but it is beside the hambone about eight to ten inches long: the tenderloins are pulled from the backbone area."

Among the tools used in the cutting procedure are a hatchet, a saw and various knives. After the meat has been cut out the hams, shoulders, backbone and fat back are taken to the smokehouse and laid on tow sheets and salted down. They are to be preserved for meat to be enjoyed throughout the coming year. "The meat remains in the smoke house for six weeks. Then the salt is knocked off and the meat is washed thoroughly. A mixture of Borax to keep bugs away and black pepper is rubbed on it. Finally the meat is hung in the smoke house until it dries. It may stay there for the rest of the year during what is called the curing process."

Some farmers continue to have traditional hog killings today, while others have the hogs slaughtered at the slaughterhouse or abattoir. After being slaughtered, the meat may be processed by the farmer. While a few farmers still enjoy the fellowship and personal satisfaction associated with a hog killing, most cannot justify the time and labor spent in processing the hog the old-fashioned way. The current price for killing and cleaning a hog is nine dollars and processing is fifteen cents per pound. Comparatively, this is an inexpensive investment.

On a nostalgic note, Mrs. Brewer concluded, "The original method of hog killing, motivated by necessity, has been replaced by a more efficient and time-saving method of meat processing. The traditional hog killing is a type of folklore in that it has been passed down orally by customary example through generations with variations. It is a performance that will never die out as long as it is enjoyed by 'certain folks.'"

Mitchell's attachment, both sentimental and financial, grows out of such folkways, but his version of old-fashioned barbecue with all the side dishes is very much a New South success story. A star athlete in high school and college, he moved up North to work with the Ford Motor Company, first in Detroit and then as a regional manager in Waltham, Massachusetts. When his father fell ill in the 1970s with the very early symptoms of the lung cancer that finally killed him, Eddie moved back South to be near his mother, who ran a mom-and-pop grocery store. To supplement this income, he took a position as assistant director for the Employment Standards Division of the State Department of Labor.

The death of his father, who hung on until 1990, threw his mother into despair and, quite naturally, dealt a blow to the family store, which had suffered declining business for some time. One night, in an effort to cheer her up, Eddie said to his mother, "Mom, I see you got some collard greens cooking; what else do you feel like eating?" And she said, "I have me a taste for some good, old-fashioned barbecue."

"That was my signal to go out to the local store and buy a little thirty-four-pound pig. I came back and put the little pig on the barbecue. Later that day, someone came in to buy a hot dog or a hamburger and he could smell the smoked meat.

"'Mrs. Mitchell, you got barbecue now?' he asked.

"I stuck my head out and answered for her, 'Yeah, we have barbecue, sell the man something'—so she made the guy a couple of sandwiches and I left to go back to work. When I returned about seven-thirty to escort her home, she was all bubbly.

"And she said, 'You know I sold that barbecue, don't you? . . . yes I did. I sold every bit of it!'

"I told her, 'It's nice to see that you have a difference in personality.' As we got ready to go out the door, someone was trying to come in, and I'm thinking someone's trying to rob us. So I put a little bass in my voice and I say, 'Yeah, who is it?'

"'We want to know if you got any more barbecue.'

"'No, we don't have any more today, but we'll have some more tomorrow,' which we didn't have, but I just played along to get the guy away from the door. For the next two weeks, everyone kept asking my mom about barbecue. So she said to me, 'You know, folks are still asking me about the barbecue and none of the other stuff is selling; the groceries are still on the shelves.'

"So I got her another pig, and when that sold out, I went and got a third one, on my own, without her having to ask. And sure enough, that went too. At that point in time, it didn't take a rocket scientist to figure out that something was going on here.

"Momma said, 'Son, you'd be surprised, you go back to cooking this stuff the old-fashioned way, you add some collard greens and mustard greens. You'd be surprised.'

"That's Momma talking, and I'm a momma's boy, so I listened, but I didn't put a lot of stock in it. But time progressed; buying a pig, buying a pig, it became too much for me, the two jobs. I found myself coming home from work in Raleigh and literally changing into my cooking clothes in the car. Finally, I was in the full-time barbecue business. And that's how I found Mr. Kirby."

I noted his use of the word "mister." In the South, among churchgoing African Americans, there is still a genteel way of showing respect for one's elders and women by the use of Mr. and Miss, often, but not always, with the first name.

Like many who grew up in the South, Eddie remembers the barbecue masters. "I would always hang around when my dad and granddad and uncle were cooking. I got interested when I was eight or nine, and I cooked my first pig when I was about fourteen. And they realized I was good at it, so the next time, the older men let me cook the pig while they hit the moonshine. It kind of evolved into a job, and once it became a job, like most kids, I wasn't interested anymore.

"Still, the cooking process was always present in my home. On the holidays, we would cook our own barbecue; my family, most of whom had migrated North [largely to New Jersey], would come home at Christmastime and we would all barbecue.

"As time progressed, the old guys died out, but the art itself had been somewhat passed on. I still knew how to cook a pig, and so did my brothers. But there were certain things the old guys did that I hadn't paid attention to. When I decided to really get into this business, my mother said to me, 'You go learning this barbecue the old-fashioned way, you'll be surprised.'

"So I asked my mom, 'Who's still alive?' She told me. I went to some of the older guys, but they weren't into getting back into it; the labor was too intense if you were serious about doing it. The last guy I went to was James Kirby."

Eddie began this tale as a prelude to a visit to Mr. Kirby, who lives in a neat little bungalow nearby. The day was fair, about seventy-five degrees or so; however, inside Mr. Kirby's knotty-pine living room, it was warm. I noted that the thermometer read 82, which, coincidentally, was the age of the handsome gentleman who sat in a recliner, holding on to a cane and half-rising to greet us while he hit the remote to turn down the volume on *General Hospital*.

"I just keep the TV on for company," he explained in a thick country accent, barely intelligible to my New York ears.

"They want to know how you got me into all this crap," Eddie said.

While Mr. Kirby nodded or interjected an occasional "Yes, that's so," Eddie continued.

"Mr. Kirby and I used to play poker together. When I first approached him about learning barbecue, he said that no, he really wasn't interested, but as it turned out, that night at the poker game his luck was down and he ended up going broke. Now James was an older guy than most of us around the table and he could get very ornery."

Mr. Kirby gave a huff, skeptical and gruff.

"So he sat there with no chips and no money. The guys who were waiting to get into the game were afraid to ask him to get up because they didn't want to face his orneriness. So he just sat there as the deal went around.

"Now my luck was pretty good, so I just reached in my pocket and gave him fifty dollars. He didn't pick it up. He just looked at me. Honestly, I didn't know if he was going to take it or not. I just did it out of a gesture. The deal went around once. He didn't throw in any money that time. The deal came around again and he picked up ten dollars and anted up.

"I had won all I wanted to win, so I got up to let another guy sit down at the table. I stood around having a drink or two while Mr. Kirby's luck caught on. He won a few hands. After a while, I was ready to go and he said, 'Wait up. I want to talk to you.' So I waited.

"He said, 'Do you still want to learn about barbecue?'

"I said, 'Yeah.'

"He said, 'I'll show ya. I'll be by your place tomorrow.'

"Now I had been searching around before Mr. Kirby came forward and I had heard about Mr. Herbert Woodard, another gentleman who was noted back then for cooking barbecue. For whatever reason, he changed from the old tradition and bought a cooker [an electric smoker] and stopped cooking in the ground. When I got into the business, I wanted to do something to speed up the process and I thought about buying that cooker. I told Mr. Woodard I would be out at his place to look at it. So when Mr. Kirby came by that next day, I asked him to come on and look at this electric cooker with me."

At this point, Mr. Kirby, a wood-smoke traditionalist, affirmed, "Yes, that's right," and at the same time gave a shiver of disapproval, as you might do in recalling a meal that gave you a stomachache.

Eddie picked up the tale. "So we go out there. Mr. Woodard had the cooker out to show how it works. Mr. Kirby is standing there. He never says a word. So I cut a deal for two hundred dollars for the cooker. I began to reach in my pocket to get my wallet to pay for it. And every time I did that, Mr. Kirby, who was standing behind me, would tug on my arm. So I would start to hesitate and carry on a meaningless conversation trying to figure out if there was something about the cooker that Mr. Kirby saw that he didn't like but also didn't want to come out and say. You see, Mr. Woodard and Mr. Kirby and all the other old-timers grew up together and were real competitive barbecue cookers, real pit masters. The bottom line was, Mr. Kirby didn't want to say anything in front of Herbert because Herbert was his friend. So the last time I tried to pay Mr. Herbert, Mr. James started to tug on my arm again. I said, 'Excuse me a minute, I'll be right back.' And I told James 'Come with me outside. I can't seem to find my money or something.' And he came on out and I said 'What is it? What is it?'

"And he looked at me and he said, like he had after the poker game, 'Do you really want to get into the barbecue business?'

"I said, 'Yeah.'

"So he said it again, 'Do you really want to get into the barbecue business?'

"And I said, 'Yeah, man, I really want to get into the barbecue business.'

"He said, 'Well, if you really want to get into the barbecue business, I will put you in the water but it will be up to you to learn how to swim.'

"And I said to him, very boastfully, 'You put me in the water and don't you worry about me learning to swim.'

"He said, 'Well, you tell Herb that you'll be back and c'mon let's go.' So I went back to tell Mr. Woodard I didn't have all my funds and that I'd be back later.

"As we went back to my car, Mr. James said, 'I don't want to waste my time with you if you don't really want to do this.'

"I did not fully understand what he was talking about, but I later came to see that what he meant was that people think they want to cook barbecue this way, but when they are standing over the hot pits it makes them have a different trend of thought. If barbecuing is in your heart—cutting the wood, shoveling, turning the hog—then all that is something you need to have a burning desire for. Although I didn't know all of that at the time, what I did understand him to be saying was 'If you want to be a true pit master, you have to be ready to go the whole way.' And if I wanted to go the whole way, he would teach me.

"At that time, we had an old storage shed out back where my mom kept crates and stuff. Mr. Kirby said, 'What you doing with all this here?' So we started to clear out the shed, and when we had cleared everything out, he got down on his knees and drew out the pit. We got a mason to come in and line the pit with cement blocks and then we filled it with sand for the 'incubating period.'"

Eddie was referring to Mr. Kirby's method of slow cooking by lining the pit with sand; it holds heat remarkably well, while using relatively little fuel and requiring less fuss.

"Then we got two old oil drums. We went to the welding shop and had them cut those barrels in half. Then Mr. James set the barrels down into the sand. Once we got the thing completed, it was a real orthodox work of art!

"After we picked up the pigs, we left them to soak in saltwater and vinegar. This is one of those steps, prepping the pig, getting him ready, that people don't do anymore, but a pig is supposed to go through a twelve-hour soaking period of vinegar and seasonings, which cuts the fresh taste.

"So the very first night we were going to try it out, I was all excited. From what I knew about barbecuing, I was thinking we had to prepare to be there all night. I went home and told my wife I was going to be up all night cooking pigs. So I made a couple of sandwiches, made me some coffee, took my flashlight. Mr. James was supposed to be there at six o'clock and we were supposed to put on the pig. Well, I was there at six o'clock and no James."

Mr. Kirby laughed as if he were recalling a delicious practical joke.

"About seven or eight, he comes up. We split some oak and some hickory and left them to soak in a tub of water. We put two twenty-pound bags of charcoal in each cooker. When the coals got good and hot, he raked them to the side, and then he put the grate on top. He took the pigs and washed them, and then he salted them down the back so that the skin would paunch up. Then we put the pigs on and shut the drafts.

"Next thing I knew, Mr. James reached over and grabbed his jacket and slung it over his shoulder. He put his hat on his head and began walking out the door, and he leaves me sitting there. I said, 'Where you going? You gonna leave me here?'

"He said, 'Oh hell, you can sit there and watch the pig if you want to, but I'm going home and going to bed.'

"Having no knowledge of the old school, I thought we had to sit there all night and tend the pig. Anyway, I couldn't wait till morning. I was like a kid on Christmas Eve. I got back about four A.M. and took a peek and there was the prettiest golden-brown pig! Mr. James came in about five-thirty and we flipped the pig and started basting. That, to me, was one of the most memorable times since I started. That was my first experience of the technique called 'banking.'"

At the mention of banking, Mr. Kirby and Eddie both shared a mutual scoundrel's grin, as if they had just let me in on a big, and funny, secret, that secret being that you didn't have to stand watch over a roasting pig like a sentry in a war zone (or for that matter, like all the other pit masters).

I bit. "Eddie, what is banking?"

"In this part of the country, we used to have wood heaters or coal heaters. When I was growing up, we would put coal or wood inside the heater and shut off all the drafts. That technique is banking; in other words, it shuts the drafts off so the fire won't burn fast, and you have a slow-burning process all night long that will radiate all over your house (back then we didn't have central heating). It was a trick that the old-timers used to keep the house warm, but Mr. Kirby, he implemented that particular technique in cooking the pig. Most people say you have to sit out there all night. Mr. Kirby, as far as I'm concerned, invented this technique."

Eddie brought the story to a close (along about the time that Mr. Kirby appeared to be settling into a light doze). "Everything I learned, I learned from him. When you use the term 'pit master,' ninety-nine percent of the time you find an old black guy like Mr. Kirby sitting there all night long, nursing a fire (or in Mr. Kirby's case, not nursing a fire). However you do it, my thing is, if you really want to get back to the original, somebody needs to preserve that and pass it on."

Mr. Kirby stirred and said, "Yeah, that's right. That's right."

RICHIE'S RIBS

I wasn't even looking for ribs when I went to Kansas City. Maybe some smoked brisket, or burgers. I was there for the *New York Times* to do a story about tailgate chefs in the parking lot at Arrowhead Stadium for the first Kansas City Chiefs game of the year. I spent three days checking in with people and following up leads while staying at a hotel in a gentrified shopping area where old stores had been turned into new outlets for upscale national brands. Pleasant enough, but about as authentic as a Wild West theme park in eastern Europe. Plus, it was hot in the particularly infernal way that the Midwest heats up after eight weeks of sweltering summer. Still, something told me that a recommendation I'd gotten to visit Richie Davis at his little farm south of town would be worth it.

The drive sure was, through green farmland bursting with vegetables at their summer peak. Richie, a quiet, confident, and supremely friendly guy, greeted me at his little clubhouse kitchen where he and his wife prepare food for the tailgate parties that fill up their social schedule during football season.

The visit was just the tonic I needed to counter my testiness at franchised NFL culture. Two days later, at six-thirty A.M. in parking lot G at Arrowhead, I found Richie and his son tossing a football as they staked out a spot for their cooking setup. Three hours later, after making the rounds of the tailgaters, many of whom talked up their recipes like salesmen for Florida real estate, I returned to Richie, who was sitting on a beach chair and sipping a beer, taking it easy. He offered me a rib, and it stopped me dead. No question about it: the best sparerib I have ever tasted.

I asked Richie for the recipe and he just looked at me and smiled. "No," he said, "have a beer."

A year later, after pleading calls and letters, he relented.

MUSTARD RUB

1	tablespoon beef boullion
8	ounces Budweiser beer
1	tablespoon minced garlic
1	tablespoon white pepper
½	cup cider vinegar
½	cup brown sugar
1	quart mustard

1. Stir boullion into beer until totally broken down.

2. Stir in remaining ingredients, adding mustard last.

RIB PREPARATION

Durkee six-pepper blend
Honey
2 racks of pork ribs

1. Remove membrane from back of rib slab.

2. Apply mustard rub liberally to both sides of slab. Rub into slab six-pepper blend.

3. Smoke 4 hours at 175 to 200°F.

4. Remove ribs and apply coat of honey to backside of slab. Wrap ribs in plastic wrap, being careful not to puncture wrap. Be generous with wrap, as an airtight seal is necessary. Place back in smoker and cook an additional 2 hours, increasing temperature to 225°F.

Serves 8.

PART FIVE

THE GOOD, THE BAD, AND THE TASTY

TWENTY

SUPERMOM

BY LATE FALL, THE OSSABAWS THAT we had trucked from Missouri were well settled in their new homes and fattening up nicely when one of the small-scale farmers, Eliza Maclean, left a memorable message on my answering machine.

"Come see my newest babies. I've just castrated them," she said with affection, adding, "They're just beautiful!"

I took her up on the invitation to visit her at her farm in Mebane, North Carolina, a name that sounds vaguely Mormon, or at least biblical. It sits on Saxpahaw Road, named after the Sissepahaw Indians (a variant spelling).

Eliza, the mother of two small children, is among the most energetic people I have ever met: coordinator of Chuck Talbott's swine program for small farmers, part-time consultant and proselytizer for the Niman Ranch Pork Company, a small farmer in her own right, a champion athlete, and a world-class partier.

Her little farm is a riot of life, full of the casual and constant quack of ducks and ducklings, the cantankerous honks of geese, a donkey whose slowly blinking eyes conveyed calm amid the cacophony of the smaller beasts, the bleating of goats who moved their mouths so little that their sound appeared to be the work of ventriloquists, the flapping of wings, the barking of dogs, the hissing feints and lunges of cats, the shuffling for position among all the animals as Eliza put out feed, and the insistent questions of her three-year-olds, Enid and Quinn.

Her conventional pigs, not to be confused with the Ossabaws, were in their own area, a fenced-in woodlot in back of the house. Millicent, an agreeable sow whose weight I underestimated by 250 pounds—Eliza said she goes an easy 600—looked like a Macy's balloon version of her piglets. Clumsy and unsteady, the little ones huddled together, more like one animal with thirty-two legs than eight animals with four legs apiece. Eliza had thrown some cut-up pumpkin into their area and they did their best to consume it, but the pieces were so big and they were so small. Their mother's breasts were still the only reliable food source.

Millicent put her head out for Eliza to pat. Eliza straddled the sow and I snapped a picture: a cowgirl on an oinking bronco.

Eliza said, "Let's go feed the others," referring to our Ossabaws.

They were in a paddock about a mile down the road on some land that Eliza leases from her elderly neighbor Silas. She was raising them on acorns and peanuts.

The drive down Saxpahaw Road took us past a low rise capped by a small cemetery. Some flowers, dried and wilted but still with brilliant color, adorned the few graves. An oak spread its limbs on top of the hill, dominating the view. I thought of the cemetery in *Our Town*. It drew your eye to the vista of the wide valley, with its rich bottomland and scrubby hillside.

"Okay, Eliza, how does a girl from upstate New York with an advanced degree and a bit of a posh accent end up raising pigs in North Carolina?"

She told me that she was born in New York City and spent her summers on Little Wolf Island, one of the Thousand Islands chain on the Saint Lawrence River. There, on her family's small farm, she developed a love for animals.

"As part of a high school project, I spent the summer, when I was seventeen, with an Amish family in Pennsylvania, the Hershbergers. They raised Amish mules and draft horses and I knew right then and there that I wanted to work with animals."

College was Mount Holyoke, where she detoured from animal studies to earn a degree in art history, spending her junior year in Florence. There followed nine years in San Francisco.

"I met and fell in love with a woman who was the best vet I'd ever worked with, and bought the Marin County Veterinary Emergency Clinic. I also worked at the Marine Mammal Center at the same time, so I just lived and breathed animals.

"I got very interested in toxicology because a lot of the local seals and sea lions were getting cancer at young ages because of the pollution in San Francisco Bay, which obviously connected with my childhood experiences on the Saint Lawrence."

"Hold on," I interrupted. "What things are you talking about on the Saint Lawrence?"

"Oh, didn't I tell you about Abbie Hoffmann?"

She hadn't. I recalled that Abbie Hoffmann, under the assumed name of Barry Freed, had lived in the Thousand Islands as an environmental activist.

Eliza continued: "My whole focus in life basically has been clean water and the wildlife that lives in and around it. A lot of that came together for the first time from being a part of Save the River with Abbie Hoffmann. When I moved to California and saw that he had committed suicide, it was so sad," she said, staring for a moment and letting out a quiet sigh.

"And how did you get from California to Saxpahaw Road, Eliza?"

"Like I said, while I was at the Marine Mammal Center, I got very interested in toxicology. So I decided, 'I need to go back and study this in college.' I got into Berkeley and Duke. Berkeley's program was more human-oriented, whereas Duke's was environmental toxicology.

"I really wanted to have children, but I couldn't conceive. So, at Duke, I worked with Grace Couchman, an infertility specialist and an endocrinologist. After a really tough four years, we managed to do it. And now I have these awesome twins."

Having children of her own transformed Eliza into a pickup truck–owning Earth Mother. Her small goat farm became the bustling menagerie of chickens, ducks, donkeys, goats, pigs, dogs, and cats that I had encountered that morning.

We arrived at her pig paddocks. There was ice in the feeders. We broke it with a stick. The Ossabaws gathered and slurped greedily. While Eliza talked, she hefted sixty-pound bales of hay with ease. No question that this very feminine woman is stronger than most men.

"After I had the kids, I came home to the farm and got with the American Livestock Breeds Conservancy. Basically, one thing led to another and I found out about this guy Chuck Talbott and his Tamworth pigs. I was interested in that from the standpoint of being a steward of a rare breed: The Tamworth were the quintessential bacon hog and they do really well on outdoor pasture. They need to be able to move around, they make beautiful nests to have their pigs, and they're fiercely protective mothers, so they do well against predators of little pigs."

"Whoomp! Whoomp!" The report of shotguns rang out—a bang, then a muffled thumping echo.

"Rabbit hunters," Eliza said, pointing out two men in orange vests walking on the hill above the farm. The smell of cordite wafted over us. The hunters climbed into their pickup truck and made their way along a lumber trail with the slow, bouncy progress of a tugboat moving up the Hudson River against the tide.

TWENTY-ONE

ANOTHER GOOD THING
ABOUT OLIVE OIL

*The white moon, enchanted, turns 'round behind the roofs,
and only I, dreamily, remain in the same place. Before me, a
transparent pig ecstatically buries its feet in the mud.*

—Marc Chagall

* * *

TWO WEEKS LATER, I RETURNED TO the Carolinas to check
on the pigs. Coincidentally, it was the night of a full moon *and* an
eclipse, an event that strikes even a skeptic like me as having gris-
gris. Silver clouds in an indigo sky raced in front of the waning
moon, so that our view of the eclipse was more like a stop-motion
series of still photos than the steady fade to the corona of a total
eclipse. Out of congenital high spirits, Eliza Maclean, for much of
the evening, danced in the parking lot to bluegrass music that
blasted from the powerhouse speakers on her truck.

The occasion was a meeting of the CFSA (Carolina Farm Stewards Association), where I had been invited to show slides and give a

talk about my visit to Spain and where Chuck came to preachify his plan to produce high-end, niche-market pork.

Such conferences for sustainable agriculture ("sustainable ag" as it is known to true believers) remind me of the early days of antiwar protests during the Vietnam era: a mix of young hippies, old activists, and everyday Americans who care a lot about the issue. The hippies at this conference were represented by young farmers with dreadlocks and the kind of weathered tan that I remember seeing on travelers hanging out in Piccadilly Circus, recently returned from India, having driven most of the way in a VW microbus covered with flower decals. These vagabonds always wore a smile of inner amusement, very yogilike and very stoned. No doubt some of their latter-day successors at the conference raised a bit of cannabis along with their organic kohlrabi.

There were lots of break-out sessions on earth-friendly ways of dealing with pests and fertilizers, on marketing cooperatives, on competing with the corporate farmers.

A call was sent forth by keynote speaker Andrew Kimbrell (of the Center for Food Safety) warning of the ecological impact of genetic engineering and an attendant loss of biodiversity. He spoke movingly about the cultural impact of fewer and fewer people having any real vocational attachment to the land. He shared a fear that as this trend progresses (fewer farmers, more intensive production), the cultural chain that has bound humanity to the land will be forever broken.

I had brought a guest from New York, Donna Lennard. She owns Il Buco, an East Village restaurant that was the first place I reviewed when I was the Underground Gourmet at *New York* magazine. Having lived in Italy, she has been trying, with mixed success over the last few years, to make her own prosciutto in the basement of her restaurant on Bond Street. She once told me that hers is the very cellar that inspired Edgar Allan Poe to write "The Cask of Amontillado."

When I told her about my Ossabaws and that a visit was in the offing, she responded, "I *have* to see them!"

We were quite a pair: Miss Hip Downtown New York Restaurateur and Brooklyn Food Writer deep in Dixie, all pumped to visit some pigs.

On the morning after the eclipse, we caravaned ninety miles down to Emile's farm. It was very cold for that time of year. The clouds pressed down, a slate-gray overcast. The wind was biting and straight out of the north. Chuck and Nadine traveled in one car, Donna and I in another, and Eliza in her pickup carrying a large self-feeder—basically a six-foot cylinder—that we would fill with peanuts for Emile's pigs in order to supplement their foraging diet.

When we arrived, Emile opened the gate to the paddock. Our Ossabaws were still small but thirty pounds heavier than they were when we'd first seen them. We needed to measure their back fat, which required our herding them into a small pen. This took some doing. We formed a semicircle with arms outstretched. Emile made a sooey sound. Not the loud "Sooey!!" of a contestant in a hog-calling contest, but a lilting, almost maternal sooey.

The pigs retreated into their pen from which we then cut out half of them. We drove them into a closed chute as wide as a pig and a half. They were not pleased, though not irritated to the point of raspy protest. "This is how they are packed together in confinement operations for their whole lives," I reflected.

Chuck directed me to record the measurements he made of the back fat, this being a good indicator of how well they were fattening up on their acorn-rich diet. I had not really thought things through to how we would actually measure the fat. I supposed it would be like reading pressure gauges in an engine room. I did not foresee six squirming pigs constantly trying to get in a more comfortable position as Eliza pulled their fur back and Chuck held a sensor to the exposed skin.

"Damn, there's no gel in the bottle," Chuck barked. Gel is needed for the probe to get a reading. Luckily, Donna had brought some of her freshly harvested olive oil as a house gift. It would work as well as scientific gel. So our rare hogs were measured with cold-pressed, first-pressed, extra-virgin Umbrian olive oil. The pigs had about three-quarters of an inch of back fat. The second group confirmed these numbers.

Back in the paddock, there were piles of fresh peanuts that Emile had put there, but the pigs were more fascinated by the shiny new self-feeder. Even though it had no food in it yet, the pigs ignored the peanuts and kept playing with the lids of the feeder, flipping them open and shut with their snouts.

Emile had slaughtered one of his standard-breed pigs (actually a Farmers Hybrid, which is the Chester White × Hampshire × Duroc × Large White cross that Niman Ranch favors). In addition to peanuts, this one had been given free access to the forest, which was full of acorns as well as hickory nuts, which the pigs sometimes eat, and black walnuts, which they ignore.

When the work was done, we repaired to the farmhouse. Emile, with bib overalls and a wide smile, like a Norman Rockwell painting of a farmer serving a bounteous meal, presented a simple roast with a salad of arugula, pan drippings, cantaloupe slices, and cinnamon. My first American pig with acorn- (and peanut-) produced fat was juicy, with deep taste and equally profound aromas. Every one of us ate every bite, no doubt helped considerably by the Sagrantino, a rare and sweetish Umbrian wine from Donna's private stash.

EMILE AND RACHEL'S ROAST LOIN OF PORK WITH GREENS AND CANTALOUPE

Here is an inventive and delicious pork recipe from Emile and his mom. Before reading through it, however, I sent a note to Emile asking about his parents. His reply was so typical and gives such a flavor of the man that I thought I would share the following e-mail with you.

hey pete! mom is from south georgia—fitzgerald. grew up with that lady who wrote under the tuscan sun. i went down there to bury grandmama a couple months ago and stood on the grave of my great great great grandfather; his father moved to fitzgerald from st matthews, but i haven't been able to find his grave yet. grandaddy drove a train for 41 years, and grandmama hung on till just recently as my last grandparent.

dad's grandfather is the one who emigrated from Italy, walked seventeen miles from a town south of napoli to the coast and got a boat to ellis island . . . my grand papa was a little bit of everything, cab driver, construction worker, liquor runner in the prohibition. one of thirteen children. dad grew up in new jersey and south florida, helping his dad on jobs. no old money in my family: hard working hard living hard playing crowd, every last one of them. mom worked as a corporate chef in Atlanta, and since dad had taken us back to live in Italy and lots of other places, and she was a farm girl to begin with, she was well versed in real food.

So that's Emile, and here is the recipe he and his mom concocted for my first meal with American acorn-fed pigs.

FOR THE PORK

1 pork loin, bone in
1 cup salt
1 teaspoon pepper, cracked

1. The day before cooking, brine the pork, adding one cup of salt to one gallon water. Refrigerate overnight.

2. Season roast with pepper. Place pork on a rack in 240°F. oven. Roast "low and slow for 9–10 hours" until the pork is fork-tender, internal temperature no higher than 140°F.

FOR THE SALAD

1 cantaloupe, cut into slices
1 teaspoon ground cinnamon
1 or 2 bunches freshly picked young arugula (or
    store-bought baby arugula)
Juice of 1 lemon
Olive oil as needed, no more than 1/3 cup
Salt and pepper to taste
Pan drippings from pork roast, degreased

1. Toss cantaloupe slices with cinnamon.

2. Toss arugula with lemon juice and olive oil to lightly coat. Add salt and pepper to taste.

3. Place arugula on serving platter. Place roast in center of platter.

4. Pour pan drippings, including the little bits, over roast and greens.

5. Arrange cantaloupe slices around the platter.

Serves 6–8.

* * *

TWENTY-TWO

THE PR GUYS

THE STORY OF HOW PIGS IN America went from creatures of the forest to products of the factory is, in one animal, a history of American farming and the transformation of a virgin landscape into a suburban-industrial continuum: a tale of staggering economic growth and alarming ecological impoverishment. As I worked my way through the literature of pork in the United States, I kept coming upon references to a surprising authority, a volume entitled *From Cave to Corn Belt*. I say surprising because both of the authors had successful careers in public relations, which is not a field that one associates with the plain truth. Nevertheless, the book, by Charles Wayland Towne and Edward Norris Wentworth, is a very well-researched and equally well-written piece that remains, fifty-five years after its publication, a most complete recounting of the history of pigs in this country.

Like Stephen Maturin, the physician-cum-naturalist in Patrick O'Brian's sea novels, the brio with which Wentworth and Towne embrace their subject is a reminder of a time when enthusiasm for a subject, a quick pen, and a bit of diligent research were enough to qualify one as an expert. Edward Norris Wentworth, who weighed 310 pounds and was an accomplished tenor, began his career as a teacher of animal breeding at Iowa State. After serving with the American Expeditionary Force in France during World War I, he went on to become a PR executive at the Armour meat-packing company as well as an editor of the *Breeder's Gazette*, a livestock-industry publication. As a sideline, he achieved a following at livestock shows for his talent as an entertaining ringmaster and effective auctioneer, a talent greatly appreciated by farmers when they called upon him to pump up the excitement for a pack of sorry-looking sows.

His partner, and cousin, Charles Wayland Towne, was a schoolmate of John D. Rockefeller Jr. at Brown University, a friendship that eventually landed him the position of publicity director of the Anaconda Copper Company. But first he had put together a classic freelancer's résumé that included reporting from the battlefield in the Spanish-American War, followed by a few seasons as publicity director for Buffalo Bill Cody's Wild West Show, and a tour of duty in France organizing entertainment for the American troops during World War I. Returning to the United States, and writing under the extremely silly pseudonym of Gideon Wurdz ("Master of Pholly, Doctor of Loquacious Lunacy, Fellow of the Royal Gibe Society"), he authored *The Foolish Dictionary*, an Ambrose Bierce–type exercise that shows off a sharp, occasionally sophomoric, sometimes politically incorrect wit. For example, two definitions picked at random:

JURY: *Twelve men chosen to decide who has the better lawyer.*

or

TITIAN: *The color a poor red-headed girl's hair becomes as soon as her father strikes oil.*

household wastes," Wentworth and Towne write, "the pig became a specialized item of farm output. From haphazard employment as a hustling gleaner of forest bounty, the hog was promoted to the honored function of marketing the biggest proportion of American corn."

By the middle of the nineteenth century, they say, the American corn crop, thanks to the impetus given to it by pork, was worth as much as wheat, hay, and cotton combined. Before the Revolutionary War, less than 10 percent of American corn was fed to hogs. By the period between the two world wars, that proportion had climbed to 55 percent. "Such mass conversion of farm crop into another form of marketing while still raw material was unprecedented in agricultural history."

In 1950, the year they wrote their book, Wentworth and Towne observe: "In the last 175 years the U.S. has fought 7 wars, and all of these soldiers have trained, marched, and fought on a meat ration, predominantly pork. In World War II, no less than half of 40 different combinations of meat put up in cans contained pork in some form." In the American Revolution, a daily pork ration of three-quarters of a pound was estimated to equal the nutritive value of one pound of beef. By the Civil War, that same measure of pork was judged, by the army, to be worth one and a quarter pounds of beef.

Beef had not become less nutritious between the eras of Washington and Lincoln, but pork, which by that time was almost exclusively corn fed, had become much fatter—that is, it provided more calories per mouthful. Bear in mind that until very recent times, fat in the diet was sought out as a necessity rather than avoided as a health threat. New breeds—the Chester White, the Duroc, and the Poland China—were efficient corn feeders that would do well in farmyards. They didn't need the high legs of the *ibérico* hogs to walk through forests, nor did they need their hardiness against cold win-

On his darker side, but par for the political course for
times, Towne wrote the following advice to Rockefeller afte
Ludlow Massacre of 1914 (where company agents killed tv
men, women, and children during a miner's strike in Color.
"You've got to popularize the facts. Get some vitality, pen-pic
and 'sobs' into your Casuistry, John, via the Press, and the tables
soon be turned in your favor."

Reality versus perception, spin versus fact, the cheerful optim
of a merchant class in the ascendant expressed with an Americ
sense of endless frontier and limitless prosperity—all of these fact
combine to make *From Cave to Corn Belt* an entertaining and infc
mative read in a field where a paper is more likely to be titled som
thing less pulse quickening like "Placental Development and Fet;
Fluids."

As one reads their work, it is clear that the history of pigs in th
United States, like the history of cattle, is the history of grain recy-
cled by animals. America's economics dictated the dominance of
two crops, wheat and corn. Never mind that the land covered by
Western prairies supported more meat on the hoof in the form of bison than it does today in the form of cattle. In like manner, the oak
groves that predominated in the East nourished plenty of pigs and
required zero investment.

The advantage corn and wheat offered is that they are more
controllable crops than forest mast and prairie grass (subject, of
course, to the normal vicissitudes of weather and disease). Once you
introduce meat animals into the equation, these crops are virtually
100 percent marketable: no surplus, all sales.

Because of their ability to convert plant protein to meat so
efficiently and so quickly, pigs were the most important source of
meat for eighteenth- and nineteenth-century Americans. "Instead
of continuing as a scavenger, or mere conserver of agricultural and

ters (they were simply put in the barn). All they had to do was eat and grow fat.

In the beginning of America's love affair with corn-fed pork, pigs were raised where the corn grew. This practice started after the French and Indian War, when western Pennsylvania and Virginia, Ohio, and Kentucky were opened up to settlement, corn cultivation, and hog raising. The corn crop—in the form of fattened pigs—was then said to be "walked to market" back East. Drovers moved their animals along roads that eventually became the routes of the New York Central Railroad, the Pennsylvania, and the Baltimore & Ohio.

With the opening of more Western territories, the Ohio River replaced the overland routes as the main artery of the pork trade. Cincinnati became such a big entrepôt that it earned the sobriquet Porkopolis, a point of great civic pride. In order to handle the by-products of pork processing, the Procter & Gamble company was born in Cincinnati and grew to become the nation's largest soap maker.

The Ohio River traffic moved cargo downriver to the port of New Orleans, but with the coming of the Civil War, the Union's meatpacking moved to Chicago. Then, in the late twentieth century, Wendell Murphy, in an effort to duplicate the success of Tyson with factory-chicken production in Arkansas, built the first hog factories; in this arrangement, feed and additives— corn and soy, animal by-products, and antibiotics—are all brought to the pigs.

Is the factory process more productive and less costly in the macroeconomic sense? By two measures it is not: America has about the same number of hogs in inventory as it did in 1915. And where hog waste was once, at worst, a smelly nuisance, like any other barnyard smell, it is now, with the concentration of animals, a severe environmental problem. In colorful, but not wildly overstated, language, Richard Manning wrote in a recent *Harper's* magazine, "Our factory farm system is a living continental-scale monument to Rube Goldberg, a black mass remake of the loaves and fishes miracle."

I don't know what Wentworth and Towne would say if they could see what has happened to pigs and pork since they wrote their book. They were such business boosters that I suppose they would have done what any honorable PR person does: Take the money and make up a nice story. But I'll give them the benefit of the doubt because they wrote these prescient words:

It is an American institution, destined to endure until our crops are forced to yield to the synthetics of the chemists— May Providence long postpone the day!

TWENTY-THREE

PIG IMPERFECT

DESPITE WENTWORTH AND TOWNE'S APPEAL TO Providence, American agriculture as we know it would be unthinkable were it not for what they call "the synthetics of the chemist." From fertilizer to feed to hormones and medicines to the very structure of the DNA of crops and livestock, agriculture today is largely an industrial enterprise more like manufacturing than the commonly shared Norman Rockwell image of the family farm.

Just how far this process has come was something that I began to comprehend at an event in Des Moines—the World Pork Expo—where the mainstream industry puts on a smiley face for its annual blowout. As I walked down the midway of the Iowa State Fair grounds, pork-industry glad-handers loaded me down with literature for top-drawer boar semen, waste deodorizers, farrowing crates, carcass incinerators, manure spreaders, liquid animal fat.

Don't get me wrong. The people were as nice as could be:

"Howdy."

"How are ya?"

"Great weather, doncha think?"

They were full of the disarming friendliness that is typical of Midwesterners. Their manner of speaking was lighthearted—not exactly jokey, yet prone to laughter anyway. Lots of ambient bonhomie, the jolliness of local weather forecasters.

It was a real Heartland scene: the exhibition barns bedecked in star-spangled bunting. The dust in the air like fireflies spiraling in the shafts of sun pouring through the skylights. All around the huge barn, proud pig owners primping their animals. Inside the show rings, the never-changing cast of prize animals coaxed along by kids in Western shirts and cowboy boots: boys with cowlicks, girls with bows and ribbons, and each with a stick to encourage the competition pigs to move along so that the judges might evaluate the animals, perhaps swayed by the adorableness of the young swineherds. Along with the kids, lots of farmers, farmers' wives, farmers' moms, and farmers' dads joining in the controlled melee that somehow sorts itself out with a first-, second-, and third-place ribbon.

Across the way, in more climate-controlled surroundings, business exhibitors had set up booths for food additives, electric pumps, hog panneling, hoop houses, vitamins, antibiotics, guaranteed "genetics" (breeding stock). The subtext was that technology had the answers: how to feed your stock, protect it from disease, winnow out stress genes, incinerate the pigs that don't make it, wash away waste, automatically turn the lights on and off. From "farrow to finish"— i.e., from birth to packing plant—everything standardized and guaranteed. The future of pork is now!

Well, I have seen the future, and it stinks.

It was shown to me in great detail by a quietly evangelical conservationist named Rick Dove. Though the dove is the bird of peace, Rick—a retired USMC colonel and military lawyer—is an avenging angel, a winged nemesis of Big Pork.

I met Dove at the Gettysburg Hog Summit, an event organized

by the Waterkeeper Alliance, an activist conservationist organization founded by Robert Kennedy Jr. Clean water is their raison d'être. Few things imperil our waters more than the metastasis of industrial pig farms—hog factories.

Dove was the keynote speaker. He stood tall at the lectern, his hair neatly parted, wearing a miltary-style Riverkeeper shirt, his pants tucked into his combat boots (as an ex-marine he could get away with that). The room was darkened so that we could clearly see the video that accompanied his presentation.

The way the lectern lamp illuminated him was like theater footlights, lending a tale-told-by-firelight sense of drama to his words. And what images! Of fish and fishermen looking as if some creature had taken a bloody bite out of their bodies, of workmen inside the hog factories pounding sick pigs to death with sledgehammers, of open-pit mass graves for diseased hogs, of rivers running red with massive sewage runoff. Counterposed to this was footage of sunsets over the immense estuary where the Neuse River flows into the sea; of nets full of healthy fish; of families swimming, canoeing, fishing.

"Clean water is one of the things that makes America strong," Dove told us. "It's the people's property. It enriches our lives. It's a wonderful thing to get out on the rivers of this country and ponder the value of all this to us and to our children. Yet there are times when our rivers and streams are not safe to use in North Carolina, and in large measure that is due to the pollution we get from hog factories. The bottom line is, the rivers are for the people yet today we have signs saying 'Don't Go in This Water.' Can you imagine that? Our public-trust water and we have signs saying you can't use it."

He laid out a long bill of particulars against Big Pork: its relatively tasteless product, environmental disasters, corrupt politics, and the intolerable living conditions of the animals. Even though the audience had heard such talks before, the crowd was moved. Dove is what was different: He projects a motivating compassion for living things.

After his talk, which was followed by an equally impassioned address from Bobby Kennedy, a number of conference goers gathered in the hotel bar. Another North Carolina activist, Don Webb, provided the entertainment on his nylon-string guitar: "On the Road Again," "Love Me Tender," "You're Nobody 'Til Somebody Loves You," sung with such savviness that it made you want to smile, the way that Willie Nelson makes you smile a little sadly at the truth in his songs. Dove, with beer in hand (which he nursed for a long time), fielded compliments and questions while his buddy played.

"I really liked your talk," I told him. "Can I come and see you?"

"Anytime you want," he answered. "I'll take you up in a plane and show you things that will make your hair stand on end."

Three months later I took him up on his invite. On a drive through Duplin County, with Rick's Aussie terrier, Kimba, he gave me the back story.

"I was born on Bear Creek, on the Chesapeake," he began. "You could hunt squirrel and rabbit there back then. Now it's all developed. I remember when I was six years old, they had built some houses on the creek and one day we went down to swim and we saw human sewage being discharged. My mom said, 'You can't swim here anymore.'

"And I said, 'That's okay, Momma, we'll just tell them to stop.'

"'The child is father to the man,'" I commented. "What lured you to North Carolina?"

"In 1965, I was stationed at Parris Island, South Carolina. We flew up to attend a meeting of the Marine Corps Bar Association at Camp Lejeune. When we landed at the airstrip, the higher-ranking

officers were met by a sedan. Since I was just a lowly second lieu-
tenant, I got left standing on the hot runway for over an hour waiting for a bus ride. It was mid-August and about a hundred and five
degrees.

"When I returned home to Parris Island, I told my young bride
that I would never let them send me to North Carolina. I went on
and on, telling her it was nothing but a hellish furnace. Later, in
1975, when I got orders to transfer there, I fought it with everything
I had. Once I got there, I saw the Neuse River—it was love at first
sight. Then I swore I would *never* leave."

The rest of his story—how he went from Marine Corps to environmental watchdog—is fully told in the transcript of his 2002 testimony in Washington to the Senate committee on government
affairs:

In 1987, after retiring as a colonel in the United States Marine Corps, I pursued a childhood dream and became a commercial fisherman. With three boats and a local seafood-outlet
store, my son Todd and I worked over 600 crab pots and more
than 2,000 feet of gill nets. Things went well for the first two
years. Then the fish began to die, many with open, bleeding
sores. At first it was only a few but, as time passed, the numbers
grew larger and larger. Soon we began to develop the same kind
of sores on our legs, arms, and hands. It took months for these
sores to heal. I also experienced memory loss. At the time I did
not connect my son's and my health problems to my work on
the water—that connection was established later.

By 1990, the situation became much worse. More and more
of the fish in the Neuse River were developing bleeding le-
sions. Regrettably, my son Todd and I had no choice but to stop
fishing. Frustrated and disappointed, I grudgingly returned to

practicing law. In 1991, the Neuse suffered the largest fish kill ever recorded in the state's history. Over one billion fish died over a period of six weeks during September and October. There were so many dead fish that some had to be bulldozed into the ground. Others were left to rot on the shore and river bottom. The stench produced by this kill was overwhelming and will never be forgotten.

In 1993, I became the Neuse Riverkeeper. In that capacity, I was a full-time, paid citizen representative of the nonprofit Neuse River Foundation, whose duty it was to restore, protect, and enhance the waters of the 6,100-square-mile Neuse River watershed. Due to ill health, attributed in large measure to my exposure to the toxins in the river, my work as Neuse River-keeper ended in July 2000.

As Riverkeeper, I was in a position personally to study the river, to work with scientists and state officials, and to closely monitor the various sources of pollution. I patrolled the river by boat, aircraft, vehicle, and waders along with a corps of approximately 300 volunteers. All sources of pollution were exhaustively documented in thousands of photographs and hundreds of hours of video. By the time the next major fish kill occurred in 1995, I was in the best position to observe, report, and document the cause and effect of one of the river's most serious problems, nutrient pollution. Volunteers working with the Neuse River Foundation documented more than 10 million dead fish.

By 1995, we knew what was killing the fish (and making people sick). It was *Pfiesteria piscicida*, a one-cell animal, so tiny 100,000 of them would fit on the head of a pin. This creature, often referred to as the "cell from hell," produces an extremely powerful neurotoxin that paralyzes the fish, sloughs their skin, and eats their blood cells. It is capable of doing the same thing to humans. This neurotoxin is volatized to the air and is known to cause serious health problems, including memory loss in humans who breathe it. Its proliferation has been directly linked to nutrient pollution from hog factories.

The fish kills continue today. Depending upon weather conditions, some years are worse than others. Many smaller kills are not even counted. Fishermen continue to report neurological and respiratory symptoms, and a dark cloud still hangs over the state's environmental reputation and economy.

"All from hogs, Rick?" I asked when I finished reading the testimony.

"Not all from hogs. There are poultry operations too, millions upon millions of chickens and turkeys. Also runoff from schools, cities, golf courses. They all contribute, but in eastern North Carolina, the hog operations are the big polluters. You'll see when we get up in the plane."

New Bern, North Carolina: From four thousand feet up, the first things you notice are the lagoons, hundreds of them, as far as the eye can see, a patchwork of red-brown sewage the color of wet clay. It stretches clear across Duplin County. Below me, the greatest concentration of hog factories in America, more than two million hogs in one small county.

Brown and red rectangles, full of waste, by Dove's calculation the equivalent of ten cities the size of New York, leaking into rivers and streams, destroying the soil. Out in plain sight, the lagoons are unmistakable, but like the card that the three-card monte dealer tells you to keep your eye on, the lagoons are diversion from the true source of the problem. It's the pigs, and those who own them.

Slightly uphill from each lagoon are rows of trim one-story buildings. You can see such structures anywhere in America, places where they might make running shoes, or toasters, or waterbeds. Your attention, drawn to acre upon acre of pig waste, doesn't immediately register what is unusual about the neat-looking buildings.

And then it hits you. No parking lots. No one comes to work here, or hardly anyone. The one or two workers who might show up every few days are all that's needed to tend the machines that do all of the "farming" work required in the hog factories of North Carolina. The rest of the inhabitants spend their short, miserable lives squeezed together in metal-and-concrete pens. When they leave, it's always a one-way trip.

When I was in kindergarten, we went on a school picnic to a pig farm in the New Jersey Meadowlands. Back then, Secaucus was famous for its pigs, which lent a distinctive odor to the town. It was a nice day in spring. The apple trees were in bloom. The farmer was a nice "old" man (probably thirty-five) who wore overalls; his wife had baked four apple pies for our snack time. The milk came from their cow that we all called Frannie, in semi-honor of our teacher, Frances Reddington.

We would not have made a kindergarten trip to what the Right-to-Farm laws of North Carolina define as hog farms. You wouldn't want five-year-olds to hear the ceaseless screams of pain and fear, nor would you want them to see the brutality, misery, and filth of these places where the fact that pigs are living creatures is seen as an inconvenience to be borne in the pursuit of lean, insipid meat and the profits it brings. If only there were some way to clone the piglets in test tubes, some way to give them an antistress gene so that they would not be terrified of people, some way to genetically engineer a pig so that it didn't produce waste products, then there would be no furor about the conditions to which one hundred million pigs all over America are subjected each year. They would be out of sight, out of smell, out of mind.

CAFO is the acronym that the industry uses to describe these facilities. Just a bunch of morally neutral letters, like NASCAR or UNICEF. CAFO stands for Concentrated Animal Feeding Operation. The lawyers for the pork industry may call these facilities farms, but any sensible person recognizes them as factories, the telling difference being, according to most state statutes, that factories must build expensive waste-treatment facilities and farms can dump their waste in lagoons or spray it on the surrounding fields. Folks expect farms to be a little smelly, after all, but they certainly are not prepared for the nauseating stench that rises off the hog lagoons. "Their profitability," Rick said of the hog factories, "is in lagoons and spray fields. If you mandate proper technology, they are out of the marketplace. Any family farmer can out-compete them."

"Integrator" is a modern term for what the trustbusters of Teddy Roosevelt's era might have called a "vertical monopolist." In the hog business, it refers to a system where, from farrow to finish, actually from grain field to supermarket, a few big companies (most notably Smithfield) control 80 percent of the total hog production in America.

The CAFO system is an ingenious way of warehousing animals and locking farmers into a form of modern debt peonage. The farmer, usually someone just marginally getting by, signs on with an integrator who gives him a contract. On the basis of the contract and the say-so of the integrator, the banks give the farmer a loan (a big loan, hundreds of thousands of dollars) to build the barns, the waste lagoon, and the systems to house and feed the hogs. The farmer assumes the debt. True, he gets his pigs for free, but then he must expend time, money, and labor to bring them to slaughter weight. If any die (typically 7 percent), that is income forgone.

Someone once figured out that when all is said and done, the average CAFO operator (the farmer, not the executives of Smithfield Farms) makes about $7.00 an hour—burger-flipping money.

How did such a thing come to pass?

It took a perfect storm of economics, technology, big universities, and state legislatures. The legislatures provide the laws that shelter CAFOs, the universities provide the "science," and business provides them both with money. It also took someone with vision. More than any single person, a former schoolteacher, Wendell Murphy, created this industry and thereby earned himself the title "Boss Hog" in a Pulitzer Prize–winning series of articles that appeared in the Raleigh *News & Observer* in 1996.

Murphy started out modestly enough. After graduating from North Carolina State University in 1960, he taught high school agriculture in Duplin County at an annual salary of $4,080. It occurred to him that a feed mill might be a good business, providing local farmers with corn for their hogs, which were still being raised outside, in the conventional way.

Taking $3,000 in savings, he persuaded his dad to cosign for a loan. Working as a teacher by day, and then doing a second shift at the mill, Murphy worked to make his business grow.

When his herd of three thousand hogs was hit by cholera, it had to be destroyed, according to state law. Fate's seemingly crushing blow turned out to be a golden opportunity. A lightbulb went off in Murphy's head—instead of raising pigs, he would buy them and pay other farmers to raise them on contract. He would provide the piglets, the fencing, and the feed and pay $1 a head to his neighbors for raising his pigs. Any environmental liabilities would fall on the contract farmers. Legally, Murphy wasn't producing any waste.

Murphy was beginning to think industrially rather than agriculturally. Like the seed of any new idea, Murphy's needed ground to take hold. The sandy countryside of eastern North Carolina, never very bountiful in the first place, was fertile soil for the growth of hog factories. The dwindling number of small farmers who had managed to hang on through the lean years were receptive: Low prices for livestock and an uncertainty about the future for their traditional cash crop of tobacco had made life precarious for the family farmers of North Carolina. Murphy offered them a way out.

In order to achieve the level of concentration that made hog factories feasible, you needed to raise hogs indoors, in close quarters, which left the disposal problem of huge amounts of waste. Animal rearing indoors had become feasible when, in the early twentieth century, it was discovered that you could keep animals inside if you supplemented their diet with vitamins A and D (this made up for the lack of exposure to sunlight).

In the 1940s, scientists found that you could pack even greater numbers of animals indoors in close quarters by giving them low doses of antibiotics. The more closely you cram the animals together, the more tendency they will have to transmit diseases, and the more antibiotics they will need. A CAFO is like two dozen jetliners crammed with passengers during flu season: One sneeze and everyone's got the bug. To prevent such epidemics and to promote rapid growth, more than 80 percent of all the antibiotics consumed in the United States are used in the livestock industry: eleven million pounds per year by animals versus three million by people. Disease-resistant bacteria will one day render this strategy self-defeating, but for the time being, medicines have been critical to the success of animal factories.

Murphy already had a business model in the poultry industry, where John Tyson had perfected intensive animal rearing through contract farming. Under Tyson's system, you could jam tens of thousands of chickens together in next to no space at all. It was not much of a stretch for Murphy to try that arrangement with hogs.

By raising pigs indoors on slats, waste would not accumulate around the animals; instead, it would fall into channels where it would be flushed into outdoor lagoons. Theoretically, most of the waste would biodegrade into ammonia gas and then dissipate, and the rest would be spread on the fields as fertilizer, although, according to Dove, 100 percent of the ammonia gas discharged into the atmosphere by hog farms falls back to earth, most of it in the form of rain on the coastal plain. This nitrate-rich rain, a downpour of fertilizer, is choking the lakes and rivers with unchecked weed growth and algae blooms.

Murphy's system was successful—astonishingly so. From two million hogs in 1970, North Carolina now produces more than ten million hogs annually. Money is being made, but not very much by the small farmers. They are a disappearing breed. In 1970, there were seventy thousand independent hog farmers in the state. By the beginning of 2004, that number was down to twenty-four hundred farmers, and most of them work under contract to Smithfield, which bought out Murphy in 1998 for more than $460 million in stocks and assumed debt.

Nationally, the trend toward concentration of swine husbandry parallels the North Carolina experience. In 1950, there were 2.1 million hog farmers in the United States. By 1999, there were 98,460. While the small farmer was on the way to extinction, the difference in output was more than made up for by the CAFOs. A disturbing statistic within those statistics is that between 1920 and the turn of the century, the number of independent African-American small farmers has gone from nearly a million (925,000) to 18,500. From an average of 31 hogs per farm, by 1999 the number had soared to more than 1,100, and since this average includes all the small farmers, it is deceptively low.

Though communities have endured the loss of taxes, jobs, and farms, the truly unspeakable suffering—that of the pigs—is kept out of sight under the peaked roofs of those buildings that Rick and I flew over. Within each factory, there may be ten thousand squealing, cramped, stressed hogs. If they are sows, they are kept in separate confinement for their whole reproductive lives. Confinement doesn't simply mean that they cannot go outdoors; it means they cannot even turn around. Though they may nurse nearly a hundred piglets in their lifetime, they will never lay eyes on their offspring.

When the young pigs are weaned, they go to the feeding and finishing barns, where they are rapidly fattened for slaughter. They are jammed together with their fellows, occasionally falling, breaking limbs, developing open sores from rubbing against the metal of their pens. They are ripe targets for airborne pathogens, which spread quickly. They are tense and terrified; when a human approaches them, they cower and shriek. They are so nervous they will chew the metal bars of their cages, destroying their teeth and gums in the process.

And the humans who work in the industry? They don't do very well either. New York Times writer Charlie LeDuff, who contributed to the Pulitzer Prize–winning series "How Race Is Lived in America," hired on at Smithfield's giant Tarheel slaughterhouse (where upwards of thirty thousand pigs are slaughtered each day). Of that experience, he wrote, "Slaughtering swine is repetitive, brutish work, so grueling that three weeks on the factory floor leave no doubt in your mind about why the turnover is 100 percent. Five thousand quit and five thousand are hired every year. You hear people say, 'They don't kill pigs in the plant, they kill people.'"

Bad labor conditions for people, bad living conditions for the animals, tasteless meat—all of that is alarming, but in all likelihood, people would not be up in arms about the hog factories were it not for the pollution. Actually, come to think of it, people will even put up with pollution. With the hog factories, it's the horrific smell that gets you.

Wendell Murphy used his political talents to establish and nurture the factory-farm system in North Carolina and to protect it from the annoying protests and lawsuits of environmentalists and everyday neighbors sickened by the stench of the lagoons. You might say that having the biggest hog producer in the state helping to write the environmental laws that protect his industry is a conflict of interest, but in the state of North Carolina, there was nothing illegal about it. Murphy, former senator Lauch Faircloth, and Governor Jim Hunt all profited from industrial pork and all helped pass laws that nurtured it.

Economists question whether this highly profitable industry could remain in business were it not for the environmental laws that treat the hog factories as farms rather than factories. Once you have farm status, your waste costs go way down. Dove told me, "If hog factories were to construct high-tech sewer plants, as cities are required to do for human waste, it would raise production costs substantially. I guess upward of a hundred and seventy dollars per hog. This is the equivalent of over sixty cents per pound at kill weight, a price that would destroy the industry's market dominance. Even alternative treatment technologies, all of them less effective than conventional sewer treatment, would still raise production costs high above market levels." In fairness, I should point out that others have looked into ways to dispose of waste much more economically, but not in such geographically concentrated amounts.

In other words, factory pigs are cheaper to raise only if you discount the social costs. We will all be paying those bills long after Smithfield offshores its operations to escape impending environmental laws.

CEO Joe Luter often uses this threat to quash what business invariably refers to as "overregulation." "If regulations become too tight in this country, we'll invest in Canada and Mexico," he said in an industry publication.

The sheer amount of waste generated by North Carolina's CAFOs is astonishing. Based on a study done by Dr. Mark Sobsey of the University of North Carolina, the number of hogs in his state alone generate more fecal matter than all of the people in the states of North Carolina, New York, California, Texas, Pennsylvania, New Hampshire, and North Dakota combined! Full of pathogens, already resistant to the low-dosage antibiotics administered to factory pigs, a poisonous broth festers in the hot Carolina sun. If ever there were conditions for incubating new and devastating plagues, none would appear riper than in the patchwork of hog lagoons that stretched from horizon to horizon on the afternoon I flew over Duplin County.

TWENTY-FOUR

COUNTRY PEOPLE

*Mad Cow is just one indication that our zealous effort to
industrialize nature, to reduce it to the molecules—the cheapest
calories—is at war finally with the way nature works and you
cannot be at war indefinitely . . . Nature always wins.*

—Michael Pollan, from an interview on NPR

* * *

IF YOU HAVE EVER COME INTO contact with a CAFO, it was
probably through a strong odor. I got my baptism by smell one cold
morning with Rick Dove and Don Webb. Don, a retired schoolteacher, is an earthy, golden-tongued country boy who has been
fighting hog pollution since he first smelled something nasty in the
water of his fishing camp up in Green County.

To get to Don, Rick, Kimba, and I drove north from New Bern.
Kimba rested his head on Rick's lap. Sunday morning, gospel time
on the radio. Even if you do not have a religious frame of mind,
there is nothing to make you consider the possibilities of the here-

after more than the ethereal voice of Ralph Stanley singing an old-time hymn. Maybe that music, or the weather—cold for North Carolina, with a dusting of snow on the fields—or simply the fact that we had spent enough time together made Rick feel like talking about a painful subject.

I asked him if his son was still working with him.

"My son Todd was murdered."

"Murdered?"

"Yes. He fell for this woman, married her. They had one son, who was born after he divorced her. Afterward, she took up with a gang of bikers. They stabbed my son more than forty times, shot him in the head, and threw his dead body into a rain-filled ditch, a 'Christmas present' for his ex."

Rick's voice was flat, but not emotionless. With such tragedies, there is never such a thing as closure except in self-help books. But Rick and his wife, Joanne, have come to terms with Todd's death. They are bringing up his child, their grandson. I won't say that Rick's loss is what made him an ecocrusader, but I do think it gave him a deeper perspective and the understanding that there are bigger fights a man can lose in life, so why not take on the rich and powerful when they overstep?

Ralph Stanley finished singing about "green pastures on the heavenly shore." We were quiet for a moment. The cotton fields, with their skeletal plants, were covered with snow. Water seeped through the snow and puddled in the fields. Rick spoke, sharing what I would call the creed that drives him.

"We all come into the world naked. We all achieve different degrees of worldly possessions. The thing that we all have and share to be enjoyed equally is nature's abundance. Black or white, poor or rich, we all get to enjoy the wonders and abundance of nature. It's overwhelming: Birds and trees, water and mountains; it surely would replace TV and a good football game any day. Even at her worst, we are drawn to nature to see a hurricane or a twister. Unfortunately, there are some people who never see because they bury their heads in television. The most wonderful things we have to share are in nature, and, best of all, they are free."

We pulled up in front of Don Webb's fish camp, a rustic but comfy clubhouse. A fire blazed in the hearth, but it was still quite cold in the room. We stood in the sunlight by the windows, looking out over his bass ponds. The coffee that Don offered helped to warm us. Don and Rick, two buddies in the same platoon, the citizen army that fights the big corporate interests. Don is the president of the Alliance for a Responsible Swine Industry. His fervor would also serve him well if he wanted to be a revivalist preacher. He described their mission. "We are an organization that was designed to help the swine industry become responsible citizens. Nobody gives a damn about country people," Don said in an accent as down-home as biscuits and gravy. "They don't care if we smell shit, they don't care if they blow us to pieces [referring to a dynamite plant that was recently built nearby]. They don't care. And somebody says, 'Oh yes they do, Don.' No, they don't care because if they cared, they wouldn't do this. I feel like country people have been neglected as Americans, and many of them feel that way too; they feel like the freedoms that they should enjoy have been taken away from them.

"Their right to domestic tranquility, guaranteed by the U.S. Constitution, is denied them. Their right to be tranquil in their home is denied them. And their right to hang their clothes out at a certain time is denied them; their right to cook out in their yards at certain times is denied them; their right to sleep in their own beds with their windows up is denied them. And that's not the American way.

"Back when I first started this fight against the factory hogs, we

had this Blue Ribbon Commission, a legislative committee established to look into the hog problem. It was dominated by represen-
tatives from the hog industry. Fortunately, the chairman of this
committee was U.S. Congressman Tim Valentine, a real straight
shooter. That helped, but his views were drowned out by hog-
industry supporters. They wouldn't let me talk. They already knew
what I was going to say, but I brought in a guest named Butch Rob-
bins. He fought in Vietnam. When he came home, he had one arm,
a head, and a torso, and that's it.

"When I rolled him up in his wheelchair, and he looked out at
the people on the commission, he said, 'I've got one favor to ask of
you. My mother and father are smelling hog feces and urine, and
we're farmers. I have given all I have to give for my country; I can't
give no more, and what I ask my country to do for my momma and
daddy is to stop the stench coming from the hog pens so that my
mother and father can die in peace.'"

"And the upshot?" I asked.

"They never did nothin'.'"

We drove farther into hog country. You could see the sprayers
sending long, watery arcs, slightly brown in color from the liquefied
sewage.

"You're allowed to spray if you are fertilizing your fields," Rick
said. "Supposedly, they are raising feed for cattle. You know what
they are raising? Bermuda grass! Oftentimes, it's so full of nitrogen
that they wouldn't dare feed it to cattle. So they just leave it to de-
compose at the side of the field."

I looked out the window of Don's car. Like thick carpets rolled
up and leaned against the wall, the grass lay rotting all around the
perimeter of the field.

We drove some more. The wet puddles in the snow, which I had
noticed before, were, I was told, evidence of the high water table of

the land, which, in turn, was evidence of its inability to absorb the waste being sprayed on the fields or leaking in from the lagoons.

We pulled up past a CAFO. Three long buildings, no car parked outside. You could hear, quite clearly, the cries of pigs crammed together. Just background noise until every so often a loud yell evidenced something more painful going on inside, maybe a broken limb.

Don stopped downwind of the lagoon next to the hog barns. Though it was cold out, he opened all the windows. Within seconds, the odor hit me, the worst thing I have ever smelled. Thick and sharp, it hurt your nose, turned your stomach, and scratched your throat.

"And this ain't bad," Don said. "It's the dead of winter and a clear day. In the summertime, on a hot, humid day, it's god-awful! I took two state senators up here. They wanted to smell hog shit, well, when I got up here, the wind was blowing the other way. And they said, 'Well, we don't smell it.' And I said, 'Well, the wind ain't right.' I took them to the other side of that hog pen over there. And we got there and I let the windows down. And it wasn't long before John Carrington [one of the senators] said, 'My God, roll these windows up!'

"The hog waste was stinking up the car, but he wanted the windows up so I rolled them up. You know what that did, it locked the smell in with us. When we had gone a ways, I finally rolled the windows back down. That senator said, 'You ain't got to tell me, damn almighty stench!' He went back to the state senate and he voted different. And he was a Republican!"

We stopped at a roadside cafe. As I entered, one of the employees, a smiling waitress, held the door open.

"Hey, how are you?" she said, as if she knew me.

"Great, thanks."

We seated ourselves. The guy behind the counter greeted us with, "Hey, good to see you."

"Do you know these people?" I asked Don.

"Never saw them before."

The next group who walked through the door got the same long-lost-friend greeting.

Rick jumped in, "You are in North Carolina. Everybody is that friendly."

The menu included burgers done a couple of different ways, a BLT, tuna salad, and a shrimp burger.

"What's a shrimp burger like?" I asked. "Is it good?"

"You never had a North Carolina shrimp burger?" the men chorused as if I had just told them that I had never seen a car before, or kissed a girl.

It goes without saying that in short order I ate a shrimp burger and that it was superb. Not frozen. Fresh shrimp, which is hard to find anywhere in America.

We left Don with a plan to come back in the spring and fish.

"Big ol' bass," he promised.

As Rick and I drove back to New Bern, Kimba snoozed. I was on the sunny, nap-inducing side of the car. But before I slipped into sleep, Rick waxed philosophic once more:

"It took Mother Nature two million years to make the Neuse River and in those years she established a balance. Water, temperature—all create an environment we can live in and enjoy. As people, we think we can destroy that balance without consequences. That is nonsense. Any, repeat any, change alters the environment. It's now a witch's brew on a massive scale.

"Mother Nature has got to be coughing and gasping. Mother Nature will fight to put this back in balance, and there will be consequences. Mother Nature can produce SARS or AIDS. When you begin to feed animals meat and they don't eat meat, you get mad cow disease. We have an opportunity as people to use our common sense to keep things more in balance. We know that sustainable agriculture has existed for hundreds of years. My feeling is that we either fix the unsustainable practices of today or Mother Nature will fix it herself. When she does, she will not just go after Wendell Murphy, Joe Luter, and the others responsible for making this mess. She can't distinguish between the good and the bad. She will take it out on all of us, including our kids and grandkids."

Rick's words cause me to reflect. Often, environmentalists (I count myself among them) appeal to our sense of guilt and shame, but the world will not change because of a guilt trip. The real heart of the matter is our survival. Destroy nature and you destroy our home, and so far there are no other planets to provide us with a new one.

TWENTY-FIVE

THE GOOD FARMER

THERE IS NOT MUCH PRAIRIE LEFT in the Corn Belt, where the bison once roamed in the tens of millions and the sky darkened when passenger pigeons in the hundreds of millions passed overhead. Paul Willis, president of Niman Ranch Pork, has joined a growing movement to restore at least a part of the prairie ecosystem. The wildflowers and grasses that he has planted or which have returned on their own have names that must surely have sprung from the tongues of poets: Blue Stem and Indian Grass, Shooting Stars and Blazing Stars, Heartbeats, Golden Alexander, Pale Purple Cornflower, Death Camus, Butterfly Milkweed, and Rattlesnake Master.

"Rattlesnake Master?" I asked Willis, who, in his early sixties, still has a fair amount of sandy hair. He is fit, in the way that people are who work hard on the land. Bib overalls and a plaid flannel shirt mark him as what he is, an American farmer.

"Yes, it's called Rattlesnake Master," he said. "There's two stories about it. Either it attracts rattlesnakes or it keeps them away. I've never seen a rattlesnake on my farm, so it must keep them away."

He waited two or three beats and then, as an aside, added, "Of course, there really aren't rattlesnakes here anyway."

Paul Willis reminds me of Bob Newhart. Midwestern, affable, even-tempered, and possessed of a deadpan humor that often leaves me about ten seconds behind him. Willis is an old-fashioned pig farmer. In our agribusiness age, this makes him as remarkable as such other passing American phenomena as a pitcher who can go nine innings, an actor who can sing without lip-synching.

"You have the right kind of shoes" were his first words as I pulled into the driveway of his farm in Thornton, Iowa. "Sometimes writers show up in sneakers and they don't do too well in the muck."

I was grateful that my muck boots helped me pass the city-slicker test. "You know, Paul, driving in here, past field after field, I couldn't help but notice that the streets were numbered, 200 Street, 300 Street, 400 Street, and so on. Whoever laid out the roads must have thought there was going to be one hell of a city here someday. The street numbers don't even go that high in New York!"

"Hey, a lot goes on in Thornton. You'd be surprised," he answered as we went inside to the kitchen, which is where most of the day's indoor activities take place on a traditional family farm. I think this has something to do with the fact that coffee drinking is an all-day activity, so people tend to stay within arm's reach of the coffeepot. Paul's wife, Phyllis, greeted me as if I were a regular visitor. No special ceremony, just, "Hi, Peter," as if we had seen each other yesterday and three days before that. Her mom, Esther Westcott, is a chatty eighty-eight-year-old who sparked at fresh company, and when she discovered I was a bass fisherman, she confessed that she too was a lifelong angler. "I loved to fish for crappie [a pan fish] out at the Pits," she told me, referring to some gravel pits out by Clear Lake. I have never been guided by an octogenarian woman, but it seemed to me an afternoon on a farm pond might someday prove pleasant for both of us.

After coffee and pie—which required my forceful turning down
of slice number three—Paul took me to see his spread. We crossed
the road to a field where young pigs gamboled in the grass, noses
twitching in a wind heavy with the scent of flowers and new grass. A
few sows lay in the shade of their farrowing huts, where their litters
suckled, slept, and moved about.

"Don't approach them too quickly; they are protective mothers," Paul said.

The sows lay there placidly, each one like a nanny sitting on a
park bench, taking in the world while her young charges played and
tumbled nearby. When one of the sows got up and walked over to
the feeder, I slowly approached the back of her hut, a piece of corru-
gated aluminum bent into a semicircle, with the floor being nothing
more than deeply bedded hay. The tiny piglets, climbing over each
other and playfully nipping, were awfully cute. The fact that the
natural position of a pig's mouth looks very much like a human
smile serves to amplify the affection that such babies elicit.

We crossed the road. An old barn serves as home base for a number of sows and, nearby, two boars. Paul pointed out a big old boar
who let fly with a grunt that sounded for all the world like a grouchy
old man lamenting the fact that the world has gone to hell.

"We call him Einstein," Willis said.

"Because he's smart?"

"Smart enough. About five years ago, two young farmers, Kyle
and Marie Holthouse, were just getting started with Niman Ranch
so they came over to Thornton, pretty excited. They wanted to buy
two boars from me. They came with this little horse trailer to pick
up the boars. The trailer was divided in two. One boar went in easy,
but the other gave them a problem. They eventually succeeded in
backing it in. They dropped the gate on the back of the trailer and
drove off. The gate was pretty high, about four feet, I would guess.

So anyway, they drove off and a little later I get a phone call from Kyle. He says they have a problem."

Paul takes a few beats before he continues. " 'Okay,' I say, 'you had better tell me about it.'

" 'Well,' he said, 'one of the boars jumped out of the trailer.'

"And I said, 'Where were you?'

" 'Well,' he said, 'we were on the interstate.'

" 'How fast were you going?'

" 'About seventy miles an hour.' And at that point, I had this picture in my mind of this four-hundred-pound boar leaping out of the back of the trailer in traffic.

"He said, 'We were kind of lucky there weren't too many cars, just a couple had to swerve, but I looked in the rearview mirror and here was this boar somersaulting down the interstate.'

"So they turned around and went back. It was late May or June, so it was pretty hot and there had been a rain so water had collected in the median strip on the interstate. The boar was just sitting in there cooling off. They backed the car up and the boar walked into the trailer none the worse, it seemed. I mean, can you imagine falling out of a trailer going seventy miles an hour on the interstate? Anyway, they took him home and he was okay. They called him Tumbler, and the one that didn't jump out was named Einstein. As Tumbler got old, he developed some arthritis problems. I like Einstein's genetics so I bought him back and I am using him for my boar lines."

Niman Ranch Pork is named after its association with Bill Niman, who owns a cattle ranch in Bolinas, California. His grass-fed beef and lamb attracted the attention of Alice Waters, the great chef and prophetess of the nationwide interest in fresh, wholesome ingredients. In retrospect, it appears that Niman and Willis, two farmers with an ecological conscience, were destined to come together, although it took a lucky visit to an old Peace Corps friend (Willis served for three years in Nigeria) to start things off.

"I grew up on this farm here," Willis said, referring to the old farmhouse that now serves as the headquarters of Niman Ranch Pork. "As a kid, my job was looking after the pigs. We had maybe thirty sows in those days, and we were field-farrowing in much the same way we're doing now. I would ride my bicycle to the field and check the pigs. It was just a chore that you did when you were eleven or twelve years old, you know. When I left Thornton and went to college, that was the end of the pigs for a while. I was gone about twelve years."

College at the University of Iowa, the Peace Corps, then a job in Minnesota with VISTA (Volunteers in Service to America) filled up those dozen years. Toward the end of his VISTA job, Willis received a call from his stepfather, Oscar Floy. "He needed help on the farm, so I left my job with VISTA and came down here to help him one year. Pretty soon we bought a sow and a few pigs for myself. We sold them, and Phyllis and I got more and more pigs—we kept saving the females as breeding sows—until we were raising maybe a thousand pigs a year, working toward a goal of two thousand to twenty-five hundred pigs a year. All through that time, I was aware of things like free-range chicken on the one hand and the poultry factories and hog factories on the other. I realized that simply raising pigs outside the way we used to was becoming pretty rare. I knew there had to be a wider market for it. I had been looking for a way to sell the type of pork that we were raising probably ten years before I met Bill Niman."

"How did that come about?" I asked.

"I was out visiting my Peace Corps friends. They were raising lamb, and at that time the lamb market had fallen apart. One of them knew Bill Niman, whose beef and lamb had begun to make inroads with restaurant customers like Alice Waters in Berkeley. I was definitely interested in meeting Bill, so he, Jeanie, and I had lunch the next day at a burger joint in San Francisco. I told him what I was doing, and he gave me some of the locally raised pork he was selling. I took it back to my sister's, in Brisbane, California, where we prepared it and it was . . . all right."

That's Paul's nice way of saying it wasn't special, so I prodded him on it.

"Actually, it was mediocre. When I returned to Iowa, we packed up a box of frozen chops and roasts and sent them to Bill. He then sent the pork around to various customers, one of them being Chez Panisse. I'd never even heard of Chez Panisse at the time [Alice Waters's restaurant]. Anyway, they all loved the pork. So Bill said, 'Send me thirty hogs.'

"This was really a far cry from what we had been used to doing, which was to call up hog buyers and whoever had the best price locally you would take your hogs in and they would write you a check and that was it. This was a different deal. The pork went to the West Coast over the weekend. So the pigs had to be at the slaughterhouse on Wednesday, killed on Thursday, chilled on Friday, and shipped out. It got there at five-thirty Monday morning. That was a pretty exciting moment.

"Bill said, 'Well, what do you want, what's your price?' That was the first time as a farmer that I wasn't really dealing in a commodity. I had something that I *could put a value on!*

"So we came to an agreement. I started out sending hogs, every other week, about thirty-five head, then we'd go to thirty-seven head, forty head, and when I couldn't keep up with the numbers, I started looking for some neighbors and some other farmers I knew. First was Glen Alden, a local, and Bob Gristoff, right from Thornton. In the spring of eighty-nine, the local paper liked the idea that we were supplying the upscale markets in San Francisco. The article came out and it was picked up by the Associated Press. We started getting calls from other farmers. That fall, Iowa Public TV ran a 'Market to Market' piece talking about what I was doing. At the time, I had about thirty, thirty-five farmers involved."

Departing from what was then the norm for farmers—selling to a packinghouse and collecting the money on the spot—Willis had to figure out a new way to get the farmer paid. "Through the Packers and Stockyard Act, farmers must be paid within a couple of days. With Niman, the cash-flow situation was different. A pig comes from the farm, goes to a packing plant, then to California, then to a customer, and you, the farmer, have to wait weeks before the money comes back to you.

"So the pork company was created to enable us to pay the farmers right away, out of cash flow. We made it a requirement that each of our farmers would pay a capital contribution each time a pig was sold. It started out at one penny a pound. That was matched by Niman Ranch in California. So we as farmers put money into the company to build up a reserve, to be able to buys pigs from ourselves, and the parent company would reimburse the pork company. That penny a pound also built the farmer's equity in the company.

"The commodity business is all about doing more and doing it cheaper, but our thinking is, if you're raising the best pork, you should be paid the best price. We had to come up with pricing that would accomplish that. We decided to pay around fifteen dollars a hog over the market price. We also established a floor for those times when the local market falls below a certain point. The farmer is not going to make much money there, but they're going to be protected. In 1998, hog prices went to eight cents a pound. Eight cents a pound is like twenty dollars a pig. It was an insult, but nevertheless, it happened. I had always heard about ten-cent hogs in the fifties. And this is eight-cent hogs in the nineties! Niman Ranch paid forty-three and a half cents at that time. The good part was that we saved people's farms; we made a big difference. The bad part was that we weren't able to buy all of everybody's pigs at the time."

Willis related to me his company autobiography in bits and snatches over the course of a day, much punctuated by incoming calls on his cell phone. We drove through the rolling green Iowa countryside, with its old-fashioned red barns, easy on the eyes, even soothing. Everything was, to outward appearances, as it has always been since the late nineteenth century with the exception that here and there, standing out from the landscape into which they would never blend, were low white buildings with peaked roofs.

"See over there?" Paul said. "That's a fifteen-hundred-sow operation." He was referring to a confinement operation. "Everybody says they don't want to see more of them, but some farmers are up against it and see it as a way out."

That remark, I was beginning to learn, was typical of Willis: nonjudgmental on the personal level, but troubled from the larger perspective.

We ended our day in Clear Lake, Iowa, at a place that turned out to hold great meaning for me. There was a large building on the main street with a long curved roof that reminded me of the old trolley barn that had been converted to an A&P in Bloomfield, New Jersey, in my boyhood.

THE SURF BALLROOM, the sign proclaimed, although the ballroom, indeed all of Iowa, is about a thousand miles from the nearest surf. DANCE SUMMER AND WINTER. IOWA'S FINEST BALLROOM. Also, in what passes for hyperbole in the understated language of the Midwest, A GOOD PLACE TO GO.

"This is the last place where Buddy Holly played right before he died," Paul said.

My mind took me back forty-five years. I was over at my friend Kenny Bernstein's house in West Orange, New Jersey. We were watching Dick Clark's *American Bandstand*.

"We have just received word," Clark told the audience, "that Richie Valens, the Big Bopper (singer of "Chantilly Lace"), and Buddy Holly have died in a plane crash in Clear Lake, Iowa."

Buddy Holly dead?!!

He was my idol, with his curly, greaser-style coiffure. I even wore horn-rimmed black glasses just like him. With songs like "Peggy Sue," "Oh Boy," "That'll Be the Day," he was one of the giants of rock and roll. The Beatles would later record his "Words of Love" and Paul McCartney eventually bought the entire catalogue of Buddy Holly's songs.

"The day the music died" was how the event is remembered in American folklore. I was quite moved when Paul told me that we were at the place where Buddy Holly had played a concert and boarded a private plane in February of 1959. Four years before JFK was killed, I experienced my first loss of a public figure whose life and death greatly affected me.

We went inside the dance barn. Cavernous is the word often used to describe such places and it was particularly apt. An oil painting of Buddy Holly stood beside the door, also a facsimile of the playbill for that night. In addition to the three stars who went down on the small charter plane, Dion & The Belmonts (another fifties group) played that night. Dion himself gave up his seat on the plane at the last minute.

I have never made a religious pilgrimage, but I imagine the feelings that washed over me as I stood in the middle of the dance floor were not unlike that of a believer at the shrine of Lourdes.

We left the hall and went for dinner across the street at a lakeside restaurant called Docks, where I ate my first Niman Ranch pork chop:

juicy and profoundly meaty, served with a smoky apricot-infused sauce. The best commercial pork I had tasted in America for many years. The soft, short fibers near the bone with some crisped fat clinging to it were even more intense in taste.

"See that guy at the next table?" Paul said, indicating a white-haired man attacking what looked to be the twin to my pork chop. "He's the guy who rented the plane to Buddy Holly." And then, raising his voice to the man, "Isn't that right, Jerry?"

"Yes, I'm the man who rented Buddy Holly the plane that went down. That's all people ever want to know about when they talk to me," he lamented.

"Well, if they're from out of town, what else about you could possibly interest them?" I said, trying to be gentle about it. "I mean you're 'the guy who . . . ' "

And with that the conversation returned to Paul's "Brief History of Niman Ranch Pork."

Willis, and most of Niman's farmers, raise a hog known as a Farmer's Hybrid, not because of extensive research but because they are the hogs that Willis has always raised. Its genetics are a multigenic stew that typically contains Chester White, Hampshire, Duroc, and Large White genes. It is bred for flavor, hardiness, and mothering ability. The former is what is most important to the consumer, but in order to achieve that flavor, the animals must be able to thrive well outdoors and raise healthy litters (it costs just as much to maintain a sow that keeps nine piglets to weaning as it does to maintain a sow who loses two of her litter).

"Basically, I am just trying to raise pigs the way we did fifty years ago when being a farmer meant being a family farmer," Willis says. "You raised some corn, some soy, some chickens, a cow or two. You planted fruit trees around the house. And you let your pigs be pigs. Which means you gave them plenty of room, the opportunity to be outdoors where they could root and graze, and lots of straw so that they could have deep, fresh bedding. In the winter, the deep bedding can absorb waste material [although given the choice most pigs will deposit most of their waste outside]. When the hay decomposes, the bed produces its own natural warmth."

Speaking about the comfort of his animals brings Willis to one of the things about which he is most proud. Niman Ranch Pork is the first, and at this writing the only, national livestock company whose practices are approved by the Animal Welfare Institute. It all started at a meeting of farm activists called to protest a proposed hog factory. Diane Halverson, a filmmaker and animal-welfare activist, was in attendance along with Willis.

As Willis recalls the meeting, "Diane was the one person who got up and said 'What about the animals?' This is not the kind of question farmers would ask at a meeting. Maybe because it would appear to be wimpy and unbusinesslike or something. Still, a lot of people like myself were thinking these things. I was impressed with what she had to say, so I contacted her, and I kind of knew what animal-welfare groups didn't want so I went to her and said, 'What do you want?' So we worked together, but I have to give Diane, and the scientists that the AWI consulted, almost all the credit for putting together the husbandry standards of how we should raise the pigs."

Those standards include:

> Pigs must be owned and raised by family farmers personally involved in the business, and they must apply AWI standards to every animal they own. ("In other words," Halverson later clarified, "you can't put three animals in a sumptuous pasture and raise the rest of the herd in confinement.")

The animals must be allowed to nest and given materials to
do so.

They may never be fed bonemeal or other animal products.

They may never be raised in close-quarter confinement and
must be given sufficient room to roam, forage, and interact
with other pigs.

No growth hormones are allowed, and antibiotics only to
treat disease.

No tail docking (clipping), and animals may not be weaned
before they are six weeks old.

"If we do treat animals with antibiotics," Willis was quick to
point out, "the farmer can still sell the pig, but not under the Niman
Ranch label."

Summing it up, Willis says, in his low-key manner, "It's not rocket
science, it's really allowing the animal to be a pig; in other words,
what are the natural inclinations of a pig?"

If Paul Willis is a farmer, then, according to the Right-to-Farm
laws, so is Joe Luter, the CEO of Smithfield. The difference between
their approaches to raising food could not be more profound, so
much so that calling them both farmers is like saying that Eminem
and Renée Fleming are both singers and leaving it at that.

The family farm—a symbol that is much praised by politicians
but which is being driven to extinction by public policy—represents
one way of dealing with the land, the plants that grow on it, the
livestock that is raised there, the wildlife that somehow manages to
find a way to freeload on the edges of fields, woodlots, and unculti-
vated set-asides. I think of this outlook as The Agricultural Way, or,
as the historians of rural life say, The Agrarian Way: agrarian, with

its connotations of populism and land stewardship—not merely planting, raising, and harvesting in the shortest period of time. What goes on in the sugar plantations of Florida, the chicken factories of Arkansas, the hog factories of North Carolina (and Iowa, and Illinois, and Colorado, and more) is decidedly not agrarian nor is it truly agriculture: It is industry.

Industry is about quantification, standardization, risk management. It consumes resources and therefore depletes them. The agrarian approach, on the other hand, is about managing resources sustainably, creating while consuming, renewing while reaping. There are no factories, that I know of, that have been around for five hundred years, yet there is land the world over that has been managed agriculturally for hundreds if not thousands of years: the vineyards of France, the cattle-supporting pampas of Argentina, the oak savannahs of western Spain, the rice paddies of Indochina. The industrial model seeks to control nature; the agrarian seeks to manage it. The former consumes more and more resources to maintain output; the latter can go on producing forever.

The argument that advocates of the industrial approach often raise is that their way is more economical, practical, and the unstoppable wave of the future. Not likely. When, in the form of fossil fuel (dead plants and animals), more energy is expended to raise food (living plants and living animals) than the energy we derive from eating that food (dead plants and dead animals again), we should not be lulled into a sense of nutritional security if farm subsidies and the oil industry can, until the oil runs out, deliver artificially cheap food.

Forget about the money for the time being. If more calories are expended getting food to our plate than we consume on that plate, then calorically the world is in debt, and it's deeper in debt every day. The "bank" that holds that debt is the same one that ultimately owns all the oil fields of Saudi Arabia, Iraq, Venezuela: It is The Earth. Using fossil fuel to transport and process food, and to replace the nutrients in eroded land with fertilizers and minerals derived from petroleum, is a strategy that will only grow more costly as supplies of oil dwindle and, finally, become exhausted. Right now, it takes anywhere from two to ten calories of fossil fuel to get back one calorie of food. This is a business model that could not sustain a corporation, much less a planet. As Aldo Leopold, the founding prophet of the modern ecological ethic, wrote, "Having to squeeze the last drop of utility out of the land has the same desperate finality as having to chop up the furniture to keep warm."

Defenders of factory farming advance so-called pragmatic arguments of economies of scale to justify their practices. These "economies" do not take into account the diseconomies or social costs of pollution, the loss of resistance to pestilence through the shrinking of biodiversity, the dislocation of communities, the loss of middle- and working-class jobs, the evolution of ever more invincible diseases in the face of overused antibiotics, and the degradation or loss of millions of square miles of soil, as we have seen in the case of America's former prairies, which are yearly washing into the Gulf of Mexico. Industrial agriculture is strip-mining the biosphere, but where mining companies can always close down one operation and move on to the next, once the living community of the planet is cut off from nourishment, there is no place for earth's living things to go.

When I consider the predicament that industrialized agriculture presents, I think of the gypsy moths that plague my part of America every few years. Spring comes as usual. The trees come into leaf. Then, sometime in June, the leaves start to disappear. Whole swaths of the mountainsides look as barren as they do in winter. The gypsy moths have arrived. For the next two months, they will eat the

leaves from the broadleaf trees until it appears that all of the green-
ery will be gone and the trees will die.

Then one day, the moths have eaten all the plants that they can
and they have no more food. The next day, they are all dead. A very
simple calculus—food equals survival, no food equals extermination.
Or think of the dinosaurs—their evolution took millions of years,
but if, as scientists theorize, a volcanic eruption or the impact of a
meteor sent up a sky-darkening rain of dust—it only required the
die-off of that year's crop of plants for the dinosaurs to starve and
thus disappear. The end arrives quickly in these situations. Humankind may not come to such a quick end, but relying on just a few
domesticated crops and animals, and raising them through the use
of rapidly diminishing resources, does appear to be a recipe for widespread famine and disease, maybe not enough to destroy humanity,
but certainly enough to threaten the survival of complex society.

"An agrarian economy is always a subsistence economy before it
is a market economy," Wendell Berry writes. "Agrarian people of the
present, knowing that the land must be well cared for if anything is
to last, understand the need for a settled connection, not just between farmers and their farms, but between urban people and their
landscapes." Seen in this light, sustainable agriculture is not merely
an alternative that elitists support to feel better about themselves.
Either agriculture is sustainable or it will disappear.

"Today, according to the USDA, about 350,000 hogs were
slaughtered last week," Willis told me. "Niman, with about 286 family farms, does 2,500 in a week. So I don't claim to be able to do much
about the whole big picture, but nevertheless, it's visible. I mean,
you've been all over the country and you've seen Niman Ranch pork.
People ask for it; people want to support this. One of our real big
problems is finding enough farmers to produce enough pigs for our
market. Right now, the demand is there for double that amount."

With his small, multigenerational family farm, with his acres of reclaimed prairie, his woodlots with soil-conserving trees, his use of manure from his animals to fertilize the fields that produce the feed that sustains the animals that, completing the circle, produce the manure that starts the cycle all over again, Willis represents one thread of American agricultural history. The other thread—the one of the endless frontier and the genetically engineered and petrochemical-based "Green Revolution"—has been wildly profitable (for the shareholders of agribusiness corporations), but it is inevitably ruinous for the ecology. In *Larding the Lean Earth*, a thoughtful history of agriculture in the early nineteenth century, Steven Stoll argues persuasively for an agriculture that embraces land as a renewable rather than a consumable resource. "The deterioration of soil is the inescapable injury of agriculture to the environment," he writes, "so its severity is a sign of the failings of any people who husband the land." I can't help but note here that the word "husband," and the obligations it imposes on stewards of the land, is not that different from husbanding as it is understood in marriage, for what are we humans if not "married" to this planet?

Stoll speaks of what he calls the "land-killing" practices of early American farmers who rapidly exhausted the nutrients in much of the soil that they farmed in the original thirteen colonies and continuously moved west, where they repeated their wasteful practices. They initially reaped bumper crops, but soon the topsoil that had taken millennia to form was degraded. The rich forests and prairies of Lewis and Clark became the dust bowl of Woody Guthrie and the ruined Appalachia of Walker Evans. What we were doing was consuming the soil that had been formed with the retreat of the glaciers, soil that had been left largely undisturbed for 13,000 years, building up nutrients. Uninhabited by man and agriculturally unexploited, the American continent represented a huge "trust fund" of virgin soil. And we cannot be viewed as anything but spendthrift inheritors of this gift from the Ice Age.

The alternative to this approach is diversified farming of the
kind that typified family farms and which, in some measure, is practiced by supporters of sustainable agriculture such as Willis. He is
among the most influential of a very few who are employing modern
business practices in the service of traditional agriculture, but there
are thousands of other farmers as well who have seen the logic of
sustainability. About an hour from his home, another Iowa pig
farmer, Kelly Biensen, has put together an association of twenty-two
farmers raising Berkshire pigs outdoors on pasture, producing pork
known for its tenderness and marbling. His pork is served at the
French Laundry in the Napa Valley, often rated as the top restaurant
in America. In New York City, Gray Kunz, Peter Hoffman, Tom
Colicchio, Waldy Malouf, Dan Barber, and Charlie Palmer, among
other concerned chefs, are longtime supporters of sustainable agriculture.

Because Niman Ranch Pork has kept faith with its husbandry
principles while managing to put together nationwide distribution
under a well-known brand name, Willis is much sought after as a
speaker and adviser for farmers interested in raising hogs in some
way other than the factory system.

A few years ago, Smithfield began a still ongoing attempt to
start big hog factories in Poland. As a final step, Smithfield purchased the state-owned Animex processing facilities with a plan to
process 900,000 hogs annually. The AWI took this up as a cause
célèbre.

"AWI brought a bunch of Polish farmers over here," Paul said.
"First, they went to North Carolina. Then they went to Missouri,
and then they visited some of the Niman farms, and they said
'These animal-feeding operations, there's nothing good about them;

they're inhumane, and terrible working conditions for the people who have to work there. We don't want to raise our pigs in concentration camps.'

"Then, AWI sent some of our Niman farmers over there as consultants and they helped set up three farms using a Polish breed famous for its hams.

"The Polish peasants' farmers union had a conference. They had farm leaders, veterinarians, animal-welfare people, environmentalists—and this really impressed me—they had philosophers and they gave them equal billing! It made sense. I mean, the whole idea was about basic questions of how we and the animals live. And the thought struck me, 'Gee, I wonder if at our next conference at Iowa State we could get some philosophers.' You know, in the farm business they never want to make decisions unless they are based on sound science. But you can manipulate science to whatever your objective is. Philosophers could help."

"You mean like Wendell Berry at your next farrowing conference?"

"Sure, why not?" he said.

LAST HELPINGS

WHEN THE PHONE RINGS AT SEVEN A.M., I ignore it. My wife, Melinda, who gets up early because she teaches school, taps me on the shoulder.

"It's Donna Lennard. Something about a guy and a truck and a pig."

I know Donna is expecting the carcass of one of the Ossabaws. Her sausage-and-ham crew have come all the way from Italy to cure this pig. But the pig isn't due until later in the day.

"I just got a call from Roy," Donna says in her best Southern-truck-driver drawl. "He's somewhere in Brooklyn and I haven't got a clue. Can you talk to him?"

So I call Roy and his accent isn't too far from Donna's imitation of Andy Griffith.

"Roy, this is Pete. I'm a friend of Donna's in Brooklyn. How can we hook up to get this pig?"

"Well, I am not too familiar with these parts. I'm on Utica Avenue, near Atlantic."

Utica Avenue is one of those Brooklyn streets that goes from

nowhere to nowhere, cutting across wide swaths of the borough. It is
terra incognita to most Manhattanites.

"Okay, Roy, where do you have to go once we pick up the pig?"

"I'm taking Atlantic Avenue to 278."

In the rest of America, that would indicate something, but in
New York City, no one refers to highways by their numbers. You talk
about the Belt, the BQE, the FDR, the Deegan, etc.

"Roy, have you done it before?"

"Yes, sir, I have."

"Well then, did you end up going by the airport or down by the
river?"

"By the river. I took 278 to the Verizono Bridge [like many out
of towners, he pronounces "Verrazano" like the phone company,
only with an *o* tacked on]."

Beats me how he is going to take Atlantic to do that. It seems
like the long way around.

"Roy, do me a favor; stay where you are. You say you are on
Utica. We'll come to you."

Donna picks me up at my house and we head for Deepest Brooklyn. We make a right on Utica and look for Roy's white truck. Every
time I see a truck with a refrigeration unit, I slow to see if it's Roy. Finally, just as we pass New York Avenue, there is Roy, baseball hatted
and goateed.

The pig is in the back. The box says "1 BBQ Pig."

"I didn't order a barbecue pig," Donna says, "I wanted an Ossabaw."

"Well, that's the only pig I have, ma'am," Roy says.

I call Eliza on her cell phone. "Check the snout," she advises. I
do. It is long, definitely Ossabaw.

Riddle solved. Donna begins to tell Roy there is an easier
route back, but I cut her off. "People always get lost in Brooklyn. Let

him use the way he knows. Take it from an old cabbie." This is my standard, and truthful, line for settling driving issues in New York City.

Picking up a cold carcass in a box and driving through the toughest neighborhoods in Brooklyn inevitably puts us in mind of a cop show, but we are very unlikely hit men.

In the basement at Il Buco, Donna's partner, Alberto, awaits us with an architecture professor cum sausage and prosciutto maker, Efisio Tossa. Also on hand is a carpenter who works on framing in a climate-controlled box for aging prosciutto and *lonza* (loin).

Donna needs to do this if she is serious about making ham. Humid New York summers will not allow aging of a ham that hasn't been smoked. Prosciutto isn't smoked. Like *ibérico*, it is air dried in a climate with low humidity. The prosciuttos she put up last year, without benefit of a controlled environment, were, in her words, "lousy." Now, thanks to a dehumidifier, refrigeration, and a skilled carpenter, she can build a thousand cubic feet of highland Umbria.

It takes two men to heft the Ossabaw down the stairs and onto the table where Efisio butchers it.

Donna looks at me. "Christ, Roy must be strong; he picked up the box like it had a Barbie doll in it!"

Working slowly, looking for every scrap of meat hidden in the copious fat, Efisio fills one tub with chunks of fat, another with meat, and a third with bones. The bones and head are sent upstairs where Chef Eddie Witt begins work on *coppa*, head cheese.

An unfortunate name, head cheese. It sounds like something stinky that you eat with pickles and wash down with dark beer— food that a paunchy, middle-aged man with mustard stains on his lederhosen could uniquely withstand.

But Umbrian *coppa* is complex and light tasting, seasoned with *suk*, a spice mixture that includes cinnamon, orange peel, lemon, nutmeg, and pepper. It derives its name, I imagine, from the souk, or bazaar, where Arab traders sold their spices.

Alberto and Efisio are very excited when they see the Ossabaw's thick layer of fat and its wine-dark meat.

Efisio cuts away the *capicola*, the top of the loin that passes by the neck and shoulder. Well exercised and dark, it has the marbling we are looking for.

"Eddie," I say to the chef, "why don't you roast it off in a pan with salt and pepper and we'll compare it with those upstate hogs you got from your supplier [corn fed and semi free ranged]."

"Sure, when you break for lunch," he says.

Alberto, who is wild in his enthusiasms and his dislikes, loves the way the meat looks. Or maybe he just likes the idea of it, the romance. He grabs a handful from the plastic tub and inhales deeply, as you might do with fresh-roasted coffee beans.

"This is authentic meat. Look how dark. Even in Italy, it is hard to find it. Our commercial prosciuttos are made from Dutch or Danish pigs—very pale. Who would want such a thing?"

The question is not merely rhetorical. Alberto asks it to test the worth of your soul; if you want a ham made from insipid meat, you are a gastronomic criminal, and Alberto is a pitiless judge.

Efisio and Bernardo (the Mexican-born sous chef at Il Buco) place the meat grinder on the table. As it was in Spain, and France before that, the urge to comment on the way the casing firms up like an aroused phallus proves irresistible. It's just a question of who says something first. On this day, the race goes to Alberto, but we are all thinking it. Someday I would like to bring a chimp to a sausage-making session. I'm guessing he would find it funny and suggestive too.

When the sausages are tied off, I head straight for the kitchen. Eddie opens the oven and pulls out the loin, seared to a crusty finish in a much used black steel pan. I can see from the way the meat springs back when he pokes it that it's done. The question is, how tender is it?

He slices it in the pan and I grab a piece in my hand—hot, fatty, tender. Not meltingly tender like the *secreto* that I tried on that January night in Aracena, but still quite good and very juicy.

My friend Daniel Boulud calls. He is considered one of the greatest chefs in America. We have talked about ham making ever since we visited his family's small farm outside Lyons a few years ago. Lately, he has said he wants to make hams the way his dad did in France. Daniel bought one of Emile's Ossabaws and now has the problem of where to cure the meat. Should he clear out some shelves in his wine cellar, where thousand-dollar bottles of *grands crus* Burgundies reside? I think he would were he not afraid of his sommelier going berserk. Still, he has to do something with the meat, and he has expressed an interest in seeing Donna's setup.

"Get down here, Daniel," I tell him, "we have some megapork."

I join Alberto, Efisio, and Donna at the table. Eddie brings out a plate of crusty sliced loin. Alberto tastes and pronounces it a marvel. Next, so that we might compare, Eddie brings some of the upstate pork as well as an acorn-fed Farmer's Hybrid chop. Alberto puts a forkful of the upstate pork in his mouth, chews twice, and deposits the meat in his napkin.

"I am sorry, this meat is a catastrophe," he declares. "There is no comparison."

A bit histrionic, but not totally off the mark. The upstate meat is okay, but the Ossabaw is simply much better. Equally good, however, is a Niman Farmer's Hybrid, fed on the same diet. We discuss the nature versus nurture question for a while. About all we can conclude is that as long as the pig is a robust breed, forest feeding makes for great-tasting meat. Ten minutes later, Daniel arrives.

Eddie, who used to cook for Daniel, greets him with a plate of charred Ossabaw loin.

Will the great chef approve?

Daniel chews purposefully, concentrating on the taste. Then, without speaking, he takes another bite. We wait. Finally, he speaks. "You know, when I was a kid, we had pork all the time on my parents' farm. I think for a whole year and a half I ate pork every day and I never tired of it." Then, addressing the room in general, "I think I'd like a glass of red wine with this." Daniel rarely drinks wine during the workday unless the food is *special.*

It is midafternoon. The sun has already moved to the south, a second dawn in older sections of Manhattan, especially in the East Village where the sunlight reflects off the facades of the cast-iron buildings across the street. The secondhand sunlight floods Il Buco. If I were a cat, I would crawl up on the seat under the window and fall asleep in the warmth.

Though I hear the excited conversation between Daniel and Donna, planning hams and sausages, I don't register their presence. It is as if I am looking and listening in to an apartment across the way where an old movie plays loudly. My friends' talk is there but not foremost in my consciousness; it's just the background music of food lovers, setting me to thinking about my pork pilgrimage. It has been a full fifty years since my grandma got off the 29 bus from Newark, via Kearny, my hometown at the edge of the Jersey Meadows. The ham she brought me then, I know now, was not comparable to the country hams of Kentucky or the *ibéricos* of Aracena. Still, because I was hooked by Grandma's ham, I followed the road to Spain. That I did so and also learned truths that were new to me about how people relate to the plants and animals they consume was something I had not anticipated at the start of this trip but for which I am thankful.

Having been an outdoorsman for so many years, and a student of food for nearly as long, these pigs and farmers and forests that I have encountered have filled in something that was missing between the rod and gun, on the one hand, and the plate, on the other. I can see myself becoming as obsessed with agriculture as I was with trout when I first picked up a fly rod in my mid-twenties. There was no question about it—it felt right. In the same way, the emerald *dehesas* of Spain felt right. The fat *ibérico* hogs, swollen with acorns, felt right. The patch of prairie next to Paul Willis's farm felt right.

Though our Carolina pork was delicious, it was not yet up to the mark set by the piece of meat that Susi Delgado threw into her hot, black steel pan on that cold night of the winter moon in Aracena. But, in fairness to Chuck, Eliza, Emile, and myself, the Spanish have been raising pigs the right way since the thirteenth century. That's enough time to get it right.

I feel confident, though, on the basis of our experiment, that almost any pig farmer with a woodlot and oaks can turn out pigs that taste better than anything on the market. I know the pigs will be happier. I am sure of one more thing: If we let the pigs, and the plants that sustain them, live and grow at nature's pace, then man, beast, and our shared planet will all come out ahead.

It all comes down to something I learned from some hospitable Croatian tailgaters in the parking lot of Arrowhead Stadium right before the Kansas City Chiefs' first game of the year. Longtime tailgater Kenny Yarnevich gave me a present, a whole *povitica*, which is a strudel-like pastry. It was made by Caroline Rozgaj Kobe, a baker in Sugar Creek, Missouri. Her business card reads "If you put good things in it, it'll taste good."

I cannot think of a better plan for farmers, cooks, or the rest of us who simply like to eat.

SELECTED READINGS

General: Pigs

Daniel W. Gade, "Hogs," in *The Cambridge World History of Food*, ed. Kenneth F. Kiple and Kriemhild Coneè Ornelas, Cambridge University Press, 2000.

John McGlone and Wilson G. Pond, *Pig Production: Biological Principles and Applications*, Delmar, 2003.

Valerie Porter, *Pigs: A Handbook to the Breeds of the World*, Helm Information, 1993.

John Pukite, *A Field Guide to Pigs*, Penguin, 2002.

Jeffrey Steingarten, *It Must Have Been Something I Ate: The Return of the Man Who Ate Everything*, Alfred A. Knopf, Inc., 2002.

Ossabaw

I. Lehr Brisbin and John J. Mayer, *Wild Pigs in the United States: Their History, Comparative Morphology and Current Status*, University of Georgia Press, 1991.

H. B. Graves, "Behavior and Ecology of Wild and Feral Swine (*Sus scrofa*)," *Journal of Animal Science*, vol. 58, no. 2, 1984.

David Hurst Thomas, *St. Catherine's: An Island in Time*, Georgia Humanities Council, 1988.

Eleanor Torrey West, "Maria Bosomworth and William Rodgers," Darien News-Review, 1990.

Perry Dean Young. Notebook in private collection of Eleanor Torrey West.

Stamatis M. Zervanos, William D. McCort, and H. B. Graves, "Salt and Water Balance of Feral Versus Domestic Hampshire Hogs," *Physiological Zoology*, vol. 56, no. 1, 1983.

Barbecue

Joseph E. Dabney, *Smokehouse Ham, Spoon Bread & Scuppernong Wine: The Folklore and Art of Southern Appalachian Cooking*, Cumberland House Publishing, 1998.

Jim Early, *The Best Tar Heel Barbecue: Manteo to Murphy*, Best Tarheel Barbecue, Special Olympics North Carolina, Inc., 2002.

Bob Garner, *North Carolina Barbecue: Flavored by Time*, John F. Blair, 2002.

John Thorne with Matt Lewis Thorne, *Serious Pig: An American Cook in Search of His Roots*, North Point Press, 2000.

James Villas, *Between Bites: Memoirs of a Hungry Hedonist*, John Wiley, 2002.

Robb Walsh, *Legends of Texas Barbecue*, Chronicle Books, 2002.

Taboos

Caroline Grigson, "Shiqmim: Pastoralism and Other Aspects of Animal Management in the Chalcolithic of the Northern Negev, Israel," in *Shiqmim 1*, ed. T. E. Levy, BAR International Series, British Archaeological Trust, Oxford, 1987.

Marvin Harris, *Cows, Pigs, Wars, and Witches: The Riddles of Culture*, Vintage Books, 1989.

Brian Hesse and Paula Wapnish, "Pig Use and Abuse in the Ancient Levant: Ethnoreligious Boundary Building with Swine," MASCA Research Papers in Science and Archaeology, vol. 15, 1998.

Richard A. Lobban, "Pigs in Ancient Egypt," MASCA Research Papers in Science and Archaeology, vol. 15, 1998.

Richard Redding, "The Pig and the Chicken: A Parable," unpublished draft paper.

Melinda A Zeder, "Pigs and Emergent Complexity in the Ancient Near East," MASCA Research Papers in Science and Archaeology, vol. 15, 1998.

Ham

For grain-fed beef, The Danish Ministry for Food and Veterinary Research, www.foodcomp.dk/fcdb_foodcomplist.asp?CompId=0004.

T. Antequera and L. Martin, *Composicion quimica general del jamon ibérico*.

C. Lopez Bote, G. Fructuoso, and G. G. Mateos, "Sistemas de Producción Porcina y Calidad de la Carne. El Cerdo Ibérico," XVI Curso de Especialización FEDNAI, 2000.

Jose Carlos Capel, *Jamon*, El Pais, 1992.

R. Cava, A. I. Andres, J. Ruiz, J. F. Tejeda, J. Venatas, *Influencia de Alimentacion Sobre el Perfil De Acidos Grasos*, Jornadas Sobre el Cerdo Ibérico y Sus Productos, Estación Tecnológica de La Carne de Castilla y León, 1999.

Camilo Jose Cela et al., *Del Jamon De Cerdo Ibérico Puro De Bellota*, Plaza and Janés Editores, 1998.

A. Drewnowski, "Taste Preferences and Food Intake," *Annual Review of Nutrition*, vol. 17, 1997.

C. B. Gonzalez and H. W. Ockerman, "Dry-Cured Mediterranean Hams: Long Process, Slow Changes and High Quality: A Review," *Journal of Muscle Foods*, vol. 11, 2000.

Jeanette Higgs, "The Beneficial Role of Peanuts in the Diet, Part 2," *Nutrition and Food Science*, vol. 33, no. 2, 2003.

Sharon L. Melton, "Effects of Feeds on Flavor of Red Meat: A Review," *Journal of Animal Science*, vol. 68, no. 12, December 1990.

Herbert W. Ockerman, Lopa Basu, Francisco Leon Gespo, and Francisco J. Céspedes Sánchez, "Comparison of American and European Systems of Production and Consumption of Dry-Cured Hams," The National Pork Board, 2002. www.porkscience.org/documents/other/Q-DRYCURED%20HAMS.pdf.

Juan Muñoz Ramos, *Enciclopedia del Gourmet*, Editorial Planeta, 2000.

J. Ruiz et al, "Development of Meat and Carcass Quality Characteristics in Iberian Pigs Reared Outdoors," *Meat Science*, vol. 52, no. 3, 1999.

Jorge Ruiz, Elena Muriel, and Jesus Ventanas, "The Flavour of Iberian Ham: The Quality of Meat and Meat Products," Fidel Toldra, Research Signposts, 2002.

Luis Silio, "Lord of the Mediterranean Woodlands," *Gourmetour*, May–August 1999.

Rex Stout, *Too Many Cooks: A Nero Wolfe Mystery*, Bantam, 1938.

Anke van Wijck, "Ibérico Ham: A Secret Unveiled," *Gourmetour*, May–August 2003.

Jesus Ventanas, ed., *Tecnología del Jamón Ibérico: De los sistemas tradicionales en la explotación del sabor y el aroma*, Ediciones Mundi-Prensa, 2001.

James Villas, "Cry, the Beloved Country Ham," *Esquire*, May 1974.

Jeanne Voltz and Elaine J. Harvell, *The Country Ham Book*, University of North Carolina Press, 1999.

Taste and Diet

Leslie Aiello and Peter Wheeler, "The Expensive-Tissue Hypothesis: The Brain and the Digestive System in Human and Primate Evolution," *Current Anthropology*, vol. 36, no. 5, 1995.

John S. Allen and Susan M. Cheer, "The Non Thrifty Genotype," Wenner-Gren Foundation for Anthropological Research, published in *Current Anthropology*, vol. 37, no. 5, 1996.

Jose F. Aquilera and Rosso Nieto, "The Growing Fattening Iberian Pig: Metabolic Profile and Nutrition," 54th Annual Meeting EAAP, Rome, 2003.

Juan Luis Arsuaga, Andy Klatt, and Juan Carlos Sastre, *The Neanderthal's Necklace: In Search of the First Thinkers*, Four Walls Eight Windows, 2002.

Juan Luis Arsuaga, "Requiem for a Heavyweight," *Natural History*, vol. 111, December 2002 no. 10, January 2003.

H. M. Barnes and C. W. Kaufman, "Industrial Aspects of Browning Reactions," *Industrial and Engineering Chemistry*, vol. 39, 1947.

B. Bower, "Spanish Fossils Enter Human Ancestry Fray," *Science News* 151, no. 22, 1997.

S. Boyd Eaton, Stanley B. Eaton III, and M. J. Konner, "Paleolithic Nutrition Revisited: a Twelve-Year Retrospective," *European Journal of Clinical Nutrition*, vol. 51, 1997.

Peter Forbes, "Recipe for Success: Food Just Wouldn't Taste as Good with the Maillard Reaction," *The Guardian*, January 23, 2003.

Alan R. Hirsch and Jason J. Gruss, "Human Male Sexual Response to Olfactory Stimuli," *Journal of Neurological and Orthopaedic Medicine and Surgery*, vol. 19, no. 1, Spring 1999.

Timothy Johns, "The Chemical Ecology of Human Ingestive Behaviors," *Annual Review of Anthropology*, vol. 28, 1999.

Danuta Klosowska and Ilse Fiedler, "Muscle Fiber Type in Pigs of Different Genotypes in Relation to Meat Quality," paper presented at conference Effect of Genetic and Non-Genetic Factors on Carcass and Meat Quality of Pigs, April 24, 2003.

William R. Leonard, "Human Nutritional Evolution" in *Human Biology: An Evolutionary and Biocultural Perspective*, ed. Sara Stinson, et al., Wiley, 2000.

William R. Leonard, "Food for Thought: Dietary Change Was a Driving Force in Human Evolution," *Scientific American*, December 2002.

Harold McGee, *On Food and Cooking*, Scribners, 1984.

Harold McGee, *The Curious Cook*, Wiley, 1992.

Christian Parra, *Mon Cochon de la Tête aux Pieds*, Payot and Rivages, 1998.

James Randerson, "Early Chefs Left Indelible Mark on Human Evolution," *New Scientist*, vol. 177, no. 2387, March 22, 2003.

J. Ventanas et al., "Hydrolysis and Maillard Reactions During Ripening of Iberian Cured Ham," *Journal of Food Science*, vol. 57, no. 4, 1992.

A. C. Wilson and R. L. Cann, "The Recent African Genesis of Humans," *Scientific American*, vol. 266, no. 4, April 1992.

Richard W. Wrangham et al., "The Raw and the Stolen: Cooking and the Ecology of Human Origins," *Current Anthropology*, vol. 40, no. 5, December 1999.

History

Thomas G. Andrews, "The Colorado Coal Strike of 1913–1914 and Its Context in the History of Work, Environment, and Industrialization in Southern Colorado," *Research Reports from Rockefeller Archive Center*, Fall/Winter 2001.

Julia Clutton Brock, *On Agriculture*, chapter 7, Cambridge University Press, 1999.

Alvar Nuñez Cabeza de Vaca, *The Journey of Alvar Nuñez Cabeza de Vaca*, trans. Fanny Bandelier, Allerton Book Co., 1922.

Daniel W. Gade, "The Iberian Pig in the Central Andes," *Journal of Cultural Geography*, vol. 7, no. 2, 1987.

Temple Grandin, ed., *Genetics and the Behavior of Domestic Animals*, Academic Press, 1998.

Conrad Lorenz, Foreword in *The Wild Canids: Their Systematics, Behavioral Ecology and Evolution*, ed. M. W. Fox, Van Nostrand-Reinhold, 1975.

Antonio Gázquez Ortiz, *Porcus, Puerco, Cerdo: El Cerdo en la Gastronomia Española*, Alianza Editorial, 2000.

Antonio Gázquez Ortiz, *La Cocina en Tiempos del Arcipreste de Hita*, Alianza Editorial, 2002.

Luis M. de Diego Pareja and Jose C. Canalda Camara, *Alcala de Henares, Cronica General*, Brocar Alacala de Henares, 2001.

James J. Parsons, "The Acorn-Hog Economy of the Oak Woodlands of Southwestern Spain," *Geographical Review*, vol. 52, no. 2, 1962.

Richard W. Redding, *Breaking the Mold: A Consideration of Variation in the Evolution of Animal Domestication* (in press).

A. Rodero, J. V. Delgado, E. Roder, "Primitive Andalusian Livestock and Their Implications in the Discovery of America," *Archivos de Zootécnia* vol. 41, no. 154, 1992.

Michael Rosenberg and Richard W. Redding, "Early Pig Husbandry in Southwestern Asia and Its Implications for Modeling the Origins of Food Production," University of Michigan MACSA Research Papers in Science and Archaeology, vol. 15, 1998. Also "Ancestral Pigs: A New Guinea Model for Pig Domestication in the Middle East," MACSA Research Papers in Science and Archeology, vol. 15, 1998.

Juan Ruiz, *The Book of Good Love*, ed. and trans. E. Drayson MacDonald, Everyman, 1999.

Steven Stoll, *Larding the Lean Earth: Soil and Society in Nineteenth-Century America*, Hill and Wang, 2002.

David E. Vassberg, "Concerning Pigs, the Pizarros, and the Agro-Pastoral

Background of the Conquerors of Peru," *Latin American Research Review*, vol. 13, no. 3, 1978.

James Vincens Vives and Jorge Nadal Oller, *An Economic History of Spain*, Princeton University Press, 1969.

Greg Wadley and Angus Martin, "The Origins of Agriculture—A Biological Perspective and a New Hypothesis," *Journal of the Australasian College of Nutritional and Environmental Medicine*, vol. 19, no. 1, April 2000.

John Noble Wilford, "First Settlers Domesticated Pigs Before Crops," *New York Times*, May 31, 1994.

Gideon Wurdz, *The Foolish Dictionary*, John W. Luce and Company, 1904.

Ecology History

Lawrence Barden, "Historic Prairies in the Piedmont of North and South Carolina," *Natural Areas Journal*, vol. 17, no. 2, 1997.

Connie Barlow, *The Ghosts of Evolution: Nonsensical Fruit, Missing Partners, and Other Ecological Anachronisms*, Basic Books, 2000.

Connie Barlow, "Anachronistic Fruits and the Ghosts Who Haunt Them," *Arnoldia*, vol. 61, no. 2, 2001.

Hazel R. Delcourt, *Forests in Peril, Tracking Deciduous Trees from Ice Age Refuges into the Greenhouse World*, MacDonald and Woodward, 2002.

James E. Horne, *Rural Communities and CAFOs: New Ideas for Resolving Conflict*, Kerr Center for Sustainable Agriculture, 2000.

Daniel H. Janzen and Paul S. Martin, "Neotropical Anachronisms: The Fruit the Gomphotheres Ate," *Science*, vol. 215, January 1982.

Han Olff and Mark E. Ritchie, "Effects of Herbivores on Grassland Plant Diversity," *Trends in Ecology and Evolution*, vol. 13, no. 7, July 1998.

Deborah Popper and Frank Popper, "The Great Plains: From Dust to Dust," *Planning*, vol. 53, no. 12, December 1987.

Deborah Popper and Frank Popper, "The Buffalo Commons as Regional Metaphor and Geographic Method," draft, accepted by *Geographical Review*. www.gprc.org/buffalo_commons_popper.html.

R. García Trujillo and C. Mata, "The Dehesa: An Extensive Livestock System in the Iberian Peninsula," Network for Animal Health and Welfare in Organic Agriculture, 2001.

F. W. M. Vera, *Grazing Ecology and Forest History*, Biddles Ltd., 2000.

Gail Vines, "Gladeruners," *New Scientist*, vol. 175, no. 2359, 2002.

Sustainable Agriculture

Helen Armstrong and David Bullock, "Stock Grazing in Woodland, Part 1," *Biotype*, no. 24, April 2003.

Edward Behr, "The Lost Taste of Pork," *The Art of Eating*, vol. 51, September 1999.

Wendell Berry, *Citizenship Papers*, Shoemaker and Hoard, 2003.

Lavado Contador, J. F. Schnabel, Trenado Ordoñez, *La Dehesa. Estado Actual De La Cuestión*, Universidad de Extremadura. www//clio.redris.as/geografia.htm.

John Ikerd, "Small Farms: Their Role in Our Farming Future," *Agro-Ecology*, vol. 8, no. 3, 2004.

Aldo Leopold, "Engineering and Conservation," lecture delivered April 11, 1938, to the University of Wisconsin College of Engineering.

Aldo Leopold, *A Sand County Almanac*, Ballantine Books, 1990.

Gene Logsdon, *Living at Nature's Pace: Farming and the American Dream*, Chelsea Green Publishing Company, 2000.

F. B. Morrison, *Feeds and Feeding, a Handbook for the Student and Stockman*, Morrison Publishing Co., 1936.

Begoña Peco, Juan J. Oñate, and Susana Requena, "Dehesa Grasslands: Natural Values," Proceedings of the Seventh European Forum on Nature Conservation and Pasturalism, June 2000, Universidad Autónima de Madrid.

Jo Robinson, *Why Grassfed Is Best*, Vashon Island Press, 2000.

Pat Stith, Joby Warrick, and Melanie Sill, "Boss Hog: North Carolina's Pork Revolution," *Raleigh News & Observer*, February 19, 21, 22, 24, and 26, 1995.

The Sustainable Agriculture Network, *Profitable Pork: Alternative Strategies for Hog Producers*, Sustainable Agriculture Research and Education, 2001.

C. Talbott et al., "Potential for Small Scale Farmers to Produce Niche Market Pork Using Alternative Diets, Breeds, and Rearing Environments," unpublished.

Hog Factories

Greg Barnes, "Hog Country, the Legacy of Smithfield," nine-part series, *Fayetteville Observer*, December 2003.

Wendell Berry, "The Whole Horse," in *The Fatal Harvest Reader*, ed. Andrew Kimbrell, Island Press, 2002.

Diane Halverson, "AWI Helps Consumers Reject the Products of Pig Factories," Environmental Protection Agency from Waterkeeper Alliance, July 30, *AWI Quarterly*, vol. 50, no. 2, 2001.

Marlene Halverson, "The Price We Pay for Corporate Hogs," Institute for Agriculture and Trade Policy, July 2000.

Charlie LeDuff, "At a Slaughterhouse, Some Things Never Die: Who Kills, Who Cuts, Who Bosses Can Depend on Race," *New York Times*, June 16, 2000.

Richard Manning, "The Oil We Eat," *Harper's*, February 2004.

Melva Okun, "What's That Smell in the Air?," Environmental Resource Program School of Public Health, University of North Carolina at Chapel Hill, 1997.

Robbin Marks, "Cesspools of Shame," Natural Resources Defense Council, July 2001.

Matthew Scully, *Dominion: The Power of Man, the Suffering of Animals, and the Call to Mercy*, St. Martin's Press, 2002.

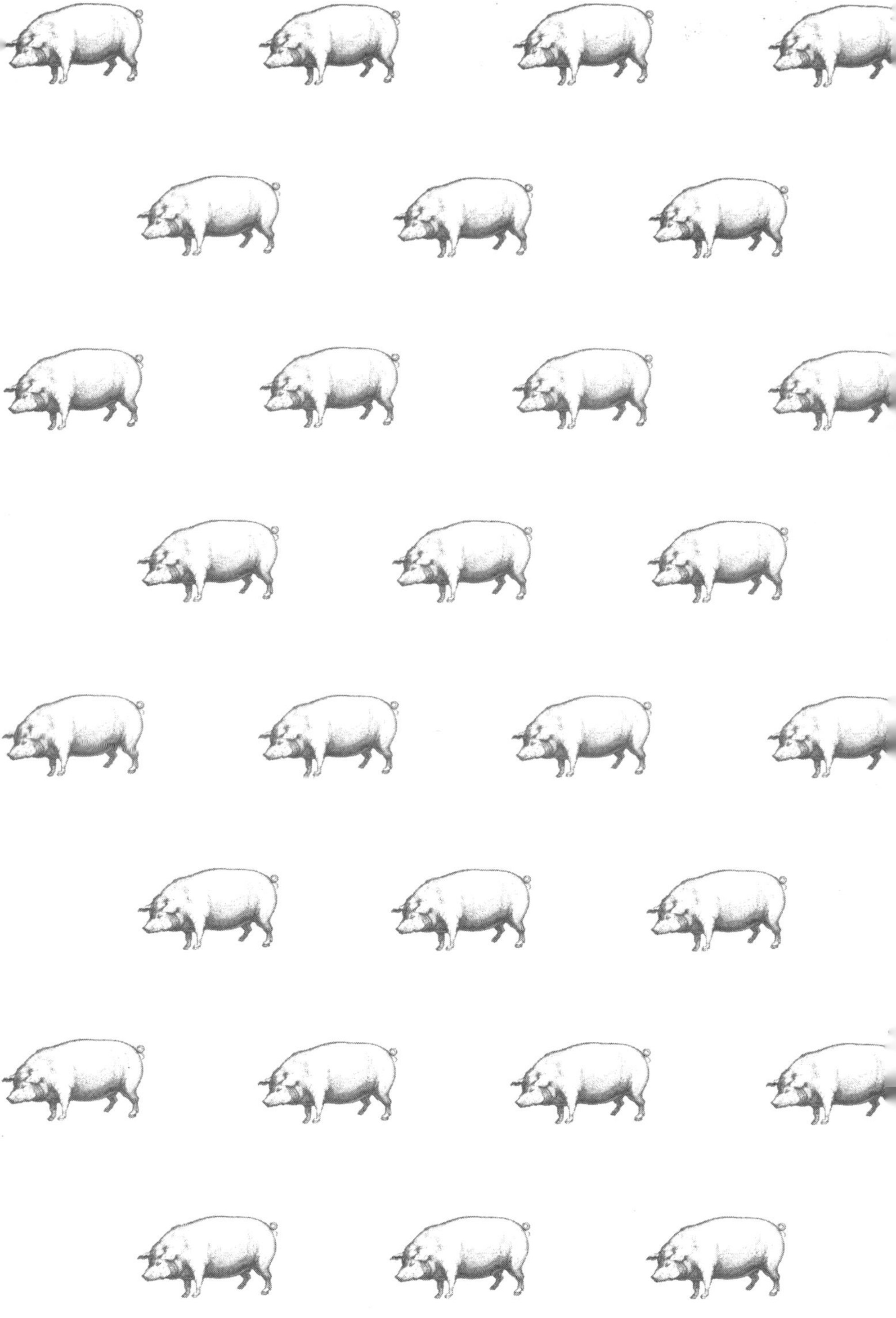